FAR HORIZONS

Unusual Journeys and Strange Encounters from a Travelling Life

FRANK GARDNER

With a Foreword by Michael Palin

BANTAM BOOKS

LONDON • TORONTO • SYDNEY • AUCKLAND • JOHANNESBURG

TRANSWORLD PUBLISHERS
61–63 Uxbridge Road, London W5 5SA
A Random House Group Company
www.rbooks.co.uk

FAR HORIZONS
A BANTAM BOOK: 9780553819311

First published in Great Britain
in 2009 by Bantam Press
an imprint of Transworld Publishers
Bantam edition published 2010

This book is a work of non-fiction based on the experiences and recollections
of the author. In some limited cases names of people have been changed to
protect the privacy of others. The author has stated to the publishers that,
except in such minor respects not affecting the substantial accuracy of the
work, the contents of this book are true.

A CIP catalogue record for this book
is available from the British Library.

Addresses for Random House Group Ltd companies outside the UK
can be found at: www.randomhouse.co.uk
The Random House Group Ltd Reg. No. 954009

The Random House Group Limited supports The Forest Stewardship Council
(FSC), the leading international forest certification organisation. All our titles
that are printed on Greenpeace approved FSC certified paper carry the FSC
logo. Our paper procurement policy can be found at
www.rbooks.co.uk/environment

Typeset in 11/14pt Sabon by Falcon Oast Graphic Art Ltd.
Printed in the UK by CPI Cox & Wyman, Reading, RG1 8EX.

2 4 6 8 10 9 7 5 3 1

Born in 1961, Frank Gardner is the BBC's full-time Security Correspondent, reporting for television, radio and online on issues of domestic and international security.

A fluent Arabist, with a degree in Arabic and Islamic Studies, he was previously the BBC's Middle East Correspondent based in Cairo, and before that in Dubai. He has written for the *Economist*, *Daily Telegraph* and *The Best of Sunday Times Travel Writing*. His first book was his best-selling memoir, *Blood and Sand*. Awarded an OBE in 2005 for services to journalism, and the prestigious El Mundo Prize for International Journalism, Frank Gardner is married with two children and lives in London.

www.rbooks.co.uk

'Gardner tells his remarkable tale well and bravely, with an astonishing lack of anger and enduring love and respect for the Islamic world'
Sunday Times

'The book stands on its own merits . . . as a fine account of journalistic life and a brave account of Gardner's continuing struggle'
Evening Standard

'*Blood and Sand* is a remarkable book from a remarkable man'
Yorkshire Evening Post

'Frank's honest account of his life-changing experiences offers a message of hope in a dangerous and divided world'
The Good Book Guide

'What makes Gardner's moving, often humorous, deeply personal story so important is the fact that he has woven into it a brilliantly dispassionate, clear-eyed account of the Islamic world which offers a unique insight into al-Qaeda'
The Scotsman Magazine

'His story, mixing the personal and the political, is both moving and insightful – a testament to one individual's will to overcome a terrible experience, and a powerful piece of reportage'
Books Quarterly

'Written with honesty, integrity and humour, this is a powerful, haunting account of survival, of overcoming adversity and a determination to carry on – a moving and inspiring personal story'
In Dublin

'A compelling autobiography'
Woman's Weekly

For Melissa and Sasha

Contents

Foreword

Frank Gardner doesn't really need an introduction. Anyone with the remotest interest in world affairs knows him as the BBC's Security Correspondent, who is lucky to be alive after six bullets were fired into his body from close range as he was filming in Saudi Arabia five years ago.

In the twenty-five chapters of *Far Horizons* only a couple of pages are spent on the events in that Riyadh suburb in 2004 which left his cameraman dead and Gardner himself fighting for his life, but the repercussions of that day are stamped indelibly on the last part of this absorbing book.

In many ways I feel an affinity with Frank Gardner. Both of us are addicted to travel. We've been to roughly the same number of countries – over ninety, but less than a hundred – and often enough to many of the same places, though I greatly envy him Oman and Jordan and the Islands of Sumatra and Socotra. He, like me, relishes the promise of a new journey to a new destination, preferably somewhere a little difficult to get to. We both love travelling in the back of pick-up trucks at the end of a hard day's work, and on trains in which you can sit at the open door and watch the world go by. We have both eaten nasty things in nasty places and though, unlike him, I've never been attacked by a wolf or shared a swimming pool with a snake, I understand Gardner's healthy suspicion of the natural world. Both of us appreciate the importance of having a sense of humour, and not having a sense of self-importance. But there are significant differences between us. Frank, a naturally active, sports-mad son of parents in the diplomatic service, began travelling much earlier than I did. By his early twenties he'd already been to Transylvania, the Yemen, Lapland, Hungary, Greece, the Philippines and Sumatra, when all I could manage was one measly skiing holiday in Austria. *And* he'd learnt Arabic.

Most of my intrepid travelling has been with a BBC film crew in tow, but as you will learn from the first chapters of this book, Frank Gardner's early adventures were often on his own or with one other companion. And without spoiling the pleasures of the book, I can tell you that these adventures make mine look tame. He eats 'glistening purple entrails', has to kill a rabid dog because none of the locals will, and survives a nightmarish stay in a Greek hospital where he's wrongly diagnosed with typhoid. All of this is recounted with the infectious enthusiasm of a man for whom pain and pleasure are as inseparable from real travel as leeches are from a walk in the jungle.

His fondness for the Middle East, and particularly for the people of the Gulf, is well described and it's an irony that the terrible attack that changed his life should have happened in lands he understood so well. And here his experience and mine part company quite conclusively. I can't begin to imagine what it must be like to be transformed in an instant from being a man with the world almost literally at his feet, to someone unable to walk unaided. The way that

Frank Gardner comes to terms with this awful predicament is for me the heart and soul of this book. Refusing to waste time laying blame, or seeking vengeance or retaliation for what was done to him, he concentrates all his efforts and energies on getting back as much of his old life as he possibly can. This involves some hair-raisingly brave or seriously foolhardy (whichever way you look at it) forays into scuba-diving in the Red Sea and quad-bike riding in the desert, and an outward-bound weekend on Exmoor, as well as the less spectacular but poignantly described discomforts of flying on planes ill-equipped for any disability. His attitude is occasionally testy and sometimes desperate, but he never loses sight of his ultimate goal – to travel the world again, to be a good journalist and to engage fully in any area where his expertise may be useful.

Frank Gardner doesn't see himself as any kind of hero, but he does see himself as someone who was blessed with physical skills and an insatiable curiosity about the world out there, and nearly being gunned to death is not for him the beginning of the end, but the end of the beginning. The fact that his reassuring presence and balanced, well-informed reports are still on our screens in these difficult times is a sign of an unquenchable spirit. It's the spirit that courses through the pages of this book and the spirit that, whether he might like to think so or not, is a huge inspiration to many like him. And like me.

Michael Palin, London, 2009

Portrait of the author by his mother

Introduction

Changed Horizons

I AM LYING ON A BED IN A HOSPITAL IN LONDON'S EAST END and someone is talking animatedly to me. I know him because we have filmed together in Afghanistan and now he is reminiscing about that trip. Was it really only six months ago? He makes a joke about us both going back there to do a story, but I don't get it because I am too tired and weak to concentrate. I can't stop thinking about the two bullets still lodged inside me. We are very different now, me and this BBC producer at the end of my bed. When this conversation is over he will rise from his plastic chair and walk out of here, while I can't even move my legs. I am certain that the world he talks of – a place of normality, of laughs, of drinks with friends, of getting on aeroplanes and travelling independently – is a world now beyond my reach. It is late 2004 and I am still recovering from being shot six times by fanatical gunmen in Saudi Arabia, my upper body a tangle of tubes and pipes, my legs a pair of wasted, lifeless limbs because the shockwaves from the bullets have blasted the crucial spinal nerves that allowed me to walk.

A nurse enters the room and silently prepares a needle, my friend leaves, and I start to daydream about travelling, wondering if I will ever do it again. Slowly I write down all the countries I have been to: ninety-four if you count Puerto Rico. As I try to recall the best trips, fragments of memories come drifting back: the smell of a wooden spoon blackened by a campfire in the highlands of the Philippines; the intoxicating feel of the Sumatran jungle just before it rains; the absurdity of being chased out of a dodgy Tokyo nightclub by a gangster missing a finger.

An only child raised by diplomats, I developed an early fascination with being 'abroad'. When the time came for my gap year between school and university I was bursting to explore the world. I had little money but I knew how to eke it out, sleeping on platforms with other travellers in railway stations, living off discarded, overripe tomatoes in Greece, or buying a slab of cheese to last all day. I took my cross-country skis up to Finland and glided silently across the Arctic Circle in a forest full of reindeer, I got a cheap train ticket down to Morocco, then all the way across to Istanbul. I bought a one-way ticket to Manila simply because it sounded like an ice-cream flavour, and went trekking amongst thonged tribesmen in the remote highlands, keeping diaries all the way that have provided the basis for many of these chapters. This kind of travel was utterly liberating, but there was a price to pay: when I returned to Britain I was a fish out of water. Just before going up to university that autumn friends invited me to

Cornwall and after the tropics I shivered every day; capsizing a dinghy several times into the English Channel probably didn't help. But most of all, I could not relate to the conversations around me. There we would sit, perched on the wall outside The Mariners at Rock, nursing our cider and stout, while girls with pink puffa jackets and unblemished complexions begged Nigel or Sebastian to tell the story about what happened on uncle's farm in South Africa. Almost no one else, I realized, had spent their gap year with anyone who didn't speak English; in fact, apart from grape-picking in France, they did not seem to have ventured outside the Commonwealth.

This only redoubled my quest to tread the path less travelled. While my more sensible university friends spent their savings on a Mini or a hi-fi, I spent mine hitching round Algeria in the holidays with the vague excuse of improving the Arabic I was now studying. There was something indescribably sensual about sitting on a Saharan dune at dusk with six French lycée girls and our Berber guides, listening to the warm wind whisper through the sand as it slowly buried our bare feet. Then came the summer holidays, nine glorious weeks of them, which was an opportunity for my friend George and me to buy £280 return tickets to Bangkok and explore South-east Asia. We had no fixed plan but ended up spending a month in Sumatra, where we yo-yoed between the highs and lows of travelling: one day we went tiger-tracking with an Indonesian soldier, the next we found ourselves having to batter a dangerously rabid dog to death. It was all very far from The Mariners at Rock.

Growing up and getting a salaried job did not need to

constitute a barrier to travel, I decided, as I persuaded my long-suffering girlfriend to come with me to obscure places like Yemen and Transylvania. Banking jobs in my twenties and thirties allowed me to tack some travelling on to business trips, enabling me to explore parts of the Arabian Peninsula off-limits to normal tourists. Switching careers to news journalism and the BBC opened up even more avenues for exploration and I can remember feeling blissfully content, after a morning's filming in the bazaars of south Tehran, to go hiking alone in the foothills of the Elburz Mountains above the capital. To stroll along in the clear mountain air, high above the fug and fumes of Tehran, drawing ever closer to the snowline, with the only sound coming from the sheep that grazed amongst the sun-baked rocks, was perfect peace.

And then one day, without warning, my travelling came to an abrupt halt. At the age of forty-two I was left in a wheelchair by those gunmen's bullets. Life seemed to be on pause. Yet now, thanks to all the encouragement from my wife Amanda and our two children, to hard hours down in the gym and to a stubborn determination to make the most of what I still have, I have managed to claw back much of the enjoyment of life before paralysis. Hidden beneath the skin there has been microscopic improvement in my nerves, so that I can now feel and move my upper legs, though I will probably never be able to walk on them without wearing metal callipers beneath my trousers and holding on to a Zimmer frame. I have since been skiing, strapping myself into a device called a bobski and rashly taking part in the BBC's 2008 Ski Sunday Grand Slalom contest in Courmayeur (I came last, by a considerable margin). I have been scuba-diving in the Red Sea, descending to 22 metres below the surface to explore the wreck of a Merchant Navy freighter, propelling myself with specially designed webbed gloves between submerged motorbikes and boxes of rifles. But let's get this in perspective. I am not some gung-ho nutter, addicted to dangerous sports, nor am I bent on trying to prove a point to the world; these just happen to be activities I enjoyed before my injuries and so I have decided to carry on doing them now.

When it comes to exploring other countries, I am slowly rediscovering the thrill of travelling for travelling's sake. Out of the twenty-five chapters in this book, only five relate to trips undertaken for BBC work; the rest were for the simple pleasure of travel and discovery, both before and after my injuries. This book is all about sharing some of the weirder and more unusual trips I have undertaken, illustrated with my own photos and sketches made at the time. As a university student I tended to have more time than money, so I often had the leisure to sit down in some café in Budapest or beneath some betel-nut tree in Sumatra and spend an afternoon sketching whatever caught my eye. Later on, when student holidays gave way to paid leave, counted in days, I sketched less and photographed more, so some chapters are conspicuously devoid of appropriate drawings.

That aside, this book does, I hope, carry some message of inspiration to all those who have taken a terrific knock backwards that despite a catastrophic blow like being shot and paralysed, life does go on and you can still take an active part in it. Since I emerged chrysalis-like from hospital, the horizons that I had feared had become so limited have now stretched out far into the distance. In 2008 I was able to report from Afghanistan and Colombia, then travel with a friend around Cambodia, achievements which I would never have thought possible as I lay inert and demoralized in a spinal-injuries unit. Travelling with a wheelchair can be awkward, at times even comical – frequently I am loaded into an aircraft through the catering door by forklift truck like hot lunch. Yet I have found that old thrill returning, the deep-down instinctive quickening of the pulse as you arrive in a new country and breathe its air for the first time. For me, this is everything. It's like emerging from a long tunnel and finding on the other side that despite the bad forecast, the sun, after all, is still shining.

1

Finland

A Teenager in the Arctic

CHRISTMAS DAY, AND A VISION OF HELL WAS PURSUING ME up an Austrian mountain in the rain. Sergeant Terry Palliser was all Royal Marine: muscled, moustached and superfit. 'Get up there, you bastards!' he roared to his unhappy bunch of trainees. 'I'm going to make you regret every drop of beer you drank last night!' Christmas Eve was already a distant memory, with its warm, candlelit *Gasthaus* atmosphere, a choir outside singing 'Silent Night' in German, steaming plates of dumplings and sauerkraut, and that faint smell of human excrement that used to linger in certain Alpine hotels because their plumbing worked rather differently from ours.

Along with half a dozen other teenage schoolboys from around Britain I was on a week-long biathlon ski course with the Army. It was a plot dreamed up by Bruce Tulloh, my hugely inspirational athletics coach at Marlborough College who had set the record for running across

America. Since running and rifle shooting were two of the few things I excelled in, then why not combine them, he reasoned, and send me off in the holidays to try biathlon skiing? I had never even heard of this sport and had never been near a ski slope, but it sounded like a free holiday in the Alps to me. How little I knew.

Biathlon skiing was about as different from downhill skiing as it was possible to get. First off, it involved very little contribution from gravity: this was a sport where you had to power yourself over a twenty-kilometre course with around a third of it on the level, a third downhill and a third uphill. And then there was the added joy of having to carry a rifle on your back, since after every five kilometres you had to stop, unsling the rifle and shoot out the bull's-eyes from five targets. Miss one and you had to ski a penalty lap of four hundred metres. Instead of using broad downhill skis, this sport used thin, flexible Nordic cross-country skis and a lightweight boot where only the toe was attached. You moved by kicking off with one leg, raising your heel free from the ski as you moved the other leg forward over the snow. In each hand you gripped a long, powerful ski pole to help propel you forward. Getting this whole leg–arm–ski-pole thing in sync was called the 'Swedish Step'. And there were rules. 'Keep your front knee bent and ahead of your foot,' shouted the trainers, 'and do not, I repeat, *do not* bring the ski poles across your chest. Why? Because if they hit an obstacle in the snow they'll drive straight into your chest and you'll be skewered like a kebab.'

Britain's national biathlon ski team had no commercial sponsorship so it was run by the Army Physical Training

Corps in Aldershot under a middle-aged fitness fanatic called Colonel Moore. Every team member had to join the Army as a private, then live, breathe and dream biathlon skiing for the next few years. The A squad was busy training for the next Winter Olympics at Lake Placid in Vermont, but Colonel Moore had his eye on the future and was already scouting for talent for the 1988 Winter Olympics in Calgary. Since I was only sixteen and still at school I did not have to commit to anything yet, which suited me just fine, but it was agreed that a schoolmate, James Montefiore, and I would be taken on trial for a couple of years of training in the school holidays to see if we had what it took. We would have to apply ourselves completely and solemnly undertake never to go near a downhill ski slope, because the Army trainers knew that after just one taste of proper skiing we would be tempted to dismiss all this biathlon stuff as a lot of needless hard work.

There was, however, one key ingredient to biathlon skiing and that was snow. The problem with cross-country skiing is that because it is mainly done on the flat it takes place in the valleys, where, not surprisingly, the air is milder than higher up the mountains. On our first foray into the Alps in that winter of 1977, a warm wind suddenly descended on our village of Mandling in Austria's Steiermark province. On the afternoon of Christmas Eve we had been sliding smoothly across trails that cut like railway lines through crisp, fresh snow, but the next day we woke up to driving wind and rain; all skiing was cancelled until further notice. But Sergeant Palliser was not the sort of instructor to give anyone

Christmas Day off. At twenty-nine he knew he was already past his peak when it came to the Winter Olympics; we couldn't tell if he was driving us hard out of personal career frustration or whether, buoyed up on a wave of altruism, he was determined to give us the best chance of getting to the Olympics. Either way, here he was at seven thirty in the morning on Christmas Day, looming in our bedroom doorway like a bad dream and barking instructions. 'Right, lads, get yer running kit on. Downstairs. Five minutes.'

At an hour when all sensible people should have been either asleep or unwrapping presents round a tree, our Marine nemesis had us running *Fartleks* uphill. These were hundred-metre bursts of sprinting followed by hundred-metre stretches of jogging, and I use the term 'jogging' in the loosest possible sense. Palliser was not even breaking a sweat while we were all close to throwing up. 'Try sucking in air,' Mont advised me. 'That's it, breathe in deeply.' A veteran of plenty of illicit pub crawls round the backstreets of Marlborough by the time he was fifteen, Mont knew all the tricks. 'What are you two lesbians gossiping about?' roared Palliser from somewhere behind us. 'Right! If you've got the energy to swap stories you can both give me twenty press-ups . . . Proper ones! Not like that! Get your arse down flat, Gardner! What are you? A bloody camel? Right. Start again.'

And so it went on. The snow returned, the skis went back on, but the training was relentless. Whenever we got back to our hotel for meals we learned to snatch a few precious minutes' rest on our bunks, zoning out completely and letting our aching muscles relax before we trooped out for more punishment. It is a technique I have often found useful in later life, grabbing a few moments' respite in the midst of something quite demanding. We must have been burning up the carbs because I remember being permanently hungry, at one point blowing the last of my precious Austrian schillings on a block of truffle chocolate which I ate in one go. There were occasional interludes of light relief but they were few and far between. One night we got ourselves invited to an Austrian party and as we all piled into someone's chalet a girl came up and gave me a long, lingering French kiss. I stood there stunned as she asked me something coyly in German, but my language skills failed me just when I needed them most. 'OK,' she said, giving me a parting peck on the cheek, 'I go back to my boyfriend now.' I looked over and there was a strapping blond Austrian watching us with a bored expression. This was all a bit weird.

'So what d'you think, Mont?' I asked my schoolfriend at the end of that first week. 'Are we going to keep this biathlon ski thing up?' Mont had both stamina and a fiercely competitive streak (he was later commissioned into the Royal Marines); in one timed race he lost his temper when one of the other trainees overtook him, and hurled his ski pole after him like a javelin. It was quite a good shot, hitting his opponent on the calf from some distance, and I think the instructors secretly admired his spirit, but Mont still had to be reprimanded because they really couldn't have half the team impaling each other every time they were overtaken. We agreed to give it another year, then promptly forgot all about biathlon skiing as soon as term began. But in the holidays we were summoned back to Aldershot for short, sharp training sessions where they would clamp cold, wet heart-rate sensors on to our bare chests as we pedalled like crazy on stationary bicycles called VO2 machines. 'It's all about hearts 'n' lungs,' said the instructors. 'You need a strong engine for this sport.' At the blast of a whistle we would have to jump on and off a bench until we were well and truly out of breath, then fire off ten rounds from a rifle at a target, to simulate the breathing control needed to shoot straight during a race. In the summer we pounded round an artificial ski track made out of wooden grooves built on a Hampshire hill; the following winter we were back in Austria, and in the spring we were competing with other juniors in Scotland. I had mixed feelings about all this. On the one hand, I really enjoyed cross-country skiing – I loved the freedom and independence of being able to go anywhere across a silent, snowbound landscape, powered by my own muscles, without being dependent on the noisy machinery of ski lifts or cable cars. On the other hand, these races were really very hard work and with the constant mention of the 1988 Winter Olympics I was becoming increasingly wary of committing the next nine years of my life to a sport in which, to put it bluntly, Britain did not excel. The East Europeans and the Scandinavians had proper winters and trained for months in real snow, often by floodlight, and in retrospect I suspect that artificial chemicals probably played a significant part in some of the Eastern Bloc successes back then. Despite all the effort the British squad put in, it was extremely rare for them to get anywhere near the top ten finishers in a race. In short, I was having my doubts. But so was Colonel Moore, the man in charge, who ever so nicely agreed that neither Mont nor I were what he was after for the Seoul Winter Olympics of 1988. After all that pressure, we felt like birds released from a cage.

By now I had bought my own set of cross-country skis, boots and poles, which stood propped up against the wall in my parents' garage, a constant reminder that I should take them away and use them somewhere interesting. In my final year at school I had started to get the travel bug: at the age of seventeen I announced I was spending half-term at a friend's place in London, then secretly bought a return boat fare to Holland. My parents were none the wiser until I got back and confessed I had hitch-hiked from Amsterdam to Antwerp and back. As road trips go, standing thumb-out beside a featureless motorway in the Lowlands on a mild afternoon in October is about as tame as it gets. But for me at the time it was pretty exciting. I had fond memories of living in Holland before I was ten and was delighted to be back on the Continent at last, savouring the freedom to roam wherever I wanted. As I got dropped off from one lift beside a field on the outskirts of Antwerp, the enormity of what I was doing suddenly hit me: I had very little money, I was several miles short of a town where I knew no one, I had no idea where I would spend the night and it was getting dark. And my parents thought I was in Bayswater. To this day, the smell of certain pungent vegetable crops like kale and cabbage reminds me of that liberating moment in the Belgian countryside. I wasn't in the least bit worried, I was exhilarated. Hours later, having failed to find anywhere cheap to stay, I flagged down a police car and the Belgian gendarmes obligingly dropped me off at a backpackers' hostel, or 'YMCA' as it was known. I don't recall seeing any handlebar moustaches, Californian biking leathers or Red Indian outfits as we queued to wash our dishes in the dreary communal kitchen – but when a new song of the same name came on the radio we all sang along, completely unaware of the enduring cult hit it was to become.

Now eighteen, with a place at Exeter University to study Arabic miraculously secured, the glory of the fabled gap year stretched ahead of me and in February 1980 I announced that I was going to take my skis up to Arctic Finland. My parents took it quite well, offering sensible advice and practical help: my father lent me his fleece-lined RAF flying boots that he had bought off a pilot after the War. Having skied quite a bit in Norway, he made little secret of the fact that he was very envious.

Back in those days before EasyJet and Ryanair it was almost inconceivable that a hard-up student like me would fly to Scandinavia; instead the trip would be a long slog by boat, train, boat again, then more train – but that, of course, was half the fun of it. I bought a ticket at Victoria station, crossed the Channel, watched Holland turn into Germany from the train window, then raced a fellow backpacker, a spiky Yorkshire punk called Muzz, up some medieval tower in Copenhagen. In Stockholm I killed time before the Finland ferry by exploring the cobbled backstreets of the historic Gamla Stan quarter and stuffing myself with hot waffles dripping in whipped cream and molten strawberries. But it was disturbingly mild for

February. I had expected the place to be in the grips of a bitter Scandinavian winter; instead, by the time I crossed the Baltic to Helsinki it was raining. The Finns were wearing light raincoats and going for strolls in the park while I was clumping around in my wool-lined boots lugging a pair of skis. I must have looked ridiculous. But I did have a plan of sorts: a crumpled address in my pocket and an open invitation to stay with a Finnish girl halfway up the country in a place called Seinäjoki. I had met Elona a couple of summers earlier in a sweaty disco in Majorca. Glitter ball on the ceiling, coloured patterns on the dance floor, Bony M's 'Brown Girl In The Ring' playing on the turntable. After I'd had several glasses of sangria the three blonde Finnish girls sitting in the corner had looked irresistible. 'Why you not ask them to dance?' asked Olivier, my French-exchange host, his arms already entwined, octopus-like, round a freckly girl from Liverpool. I was supposed to be spending my pre-A-level summer learning French with his family, but they had transplanted themselves to their summer apartment in the Spanish resort of Magaluf, which rather defeated the object. Still, this was fun, I had never been clubbing before. 'OK,' I said and stumbled over to the girls. Two got up immediately but one stayed and patted the couch next to her, and when we parted that night addresses were exchanged, then later Christmas cards, although I really had no clear recollection what she looked like. That should have been the end of it, but on my skinflint backpacker's budget I liked the idea of a free pad on this trip; I would see Finland the proper way, I told myself, staying with a Finn, meeting her friends, learning a bit of the language.

In the fading late-afternoon light the train from Helsinki slowed to a halt at Seinäjoki station, where Elona had agreed to meet me. Here the snow lay thick on the ground and my skis no longer looked out of place, in fact quite a few other people on the platform were carrying them too. But who was I looking for? What did Elona look like? She was blonde, I knew that much, but in Finland that was hardly a distinguishing feature. The crowd on the platform began to thin out, train doors were being slammed, whistles blown. A tall, svelte girl with shimmering blonde hair and piercing blue eyes stood by herself, looking around for someone. Wahay, I thought, here we go! And then she ran into the arms of a man with a briefcase. There was now only one other person left on the platform and she was staring right at me, her unkempt hair falling across her face, which was slightly smudged with mascara. 'You are Frank?' she asked tentatively. I have always been rubbish at disguising my emotions and in that moment I'm ashamed to say that my disappointment must have shown. Elona was perfectly nice – after all, she was putting me up in her flat – but I did not find her attractive, and the feeling may well have been mutual. Her English was very limited and my Finnish was almost non-existent, so we rode in the cab in awkward silence broken only by brief, pointless exchanges like: 'Lot's of snow, I see' (me), 'Excuse please?' (her), 'Snow – plenty of snow here', 'Slow?', 'No, snow – you know, white stuff', 'Ah yes. Snow. We have snow.' This was going to be a long week.

The taxi pulled up at a low block of flats and Elona shrugged almost apologetically, saying, 'Is home.' She pushed open the door to reveal a wonderfully clean and functional Scandinavian apartment, all pine surfaces and frosted glass. I smiled in appreciation, then froze – Elona was showing me the bedroom, where the covers on the double bed were pointedly turned down on both sides. It was one of those intensely embarrassing moments when you want the earth to swallow you up. 'D'you know what?' I muttered. 'I've got this bad cold, I think I'd better stay on the couch.' Elona did have enough English to tell me that she found her job as a secretary very boring, she had no boyfriend, and at the age of twenty-four she worried she was getting old. Despite all my verbal attempts to cheer her up she seemed to be terminally morose. I made a rapid reappraisal of the wild week of booze-filled Finnish partying that my eighteen-year-old mind had allowed to ferment.

In the morning Elona went off to work and I uncurled myself from the couch and got up to inspect the view. Outside the window a cross-country ski trail snaked away through the snow beneath the larch trees and every few minutes a fit-looking Finn would stride past on skis, doing that Swedish Step thing with the ski poles that the Army had taught us. This was prime Nordic ski country and I could hardly wait to get out there, so I downed a glass of fruit juice then burst out into the cold glare of the winter sun. This was exhilarating! With my breath clouding in the sub-zero air I flung my skis down on to the snow, clipped the toes of my soft Nordic ski boots into the bindings, gripped the ski poles then launched myself off into the winter landscape, kicking out with my back leg, sliding forward with the front. The fresh snow made that wonderful crisp scraping noise as my skis passed over it, like two strips of Velcro being ripped apart, and within minutes I was gliding through a forest of white larches, passing other skiers and being passed in turn; it seemed as if the whole country was on skis. Wooden signs in Finnish pointed to exotic and unpronounceable destinations, but when I followed one on a whim to somewhere called 'Keskussairaläa' it turned out to be the Central Municipal Hospital.

Back in Elona's flat that evening I enthused about what a brilliant day I had had, which was quite tactless given that I was on holiday and she was working, in a job she disliked. But Elona didn't ski, and her indifference became the catalyst for me to move on to where I really wanted to be: in the far north of Finland, hard up on the Arctic Circle. After two days I said goodbye – in Finnish, which raised almost the only smile of my whole ill-conceived stay – and headed for the railway station, to catch the night train to Lapland.

In Seinäjoki the snow had covered the ground but the trees had been bare and dark. Now, as the train forged ever northward, I awoke to a magical winter wonderland where every pine tree was weighed down by what looked like wheelbarrow loads of fresh snow. There were few larch trees this far north, but those that grew were frosted white while the low sun sparkled across a landscape straight out of C. S. Lewis's Narnia. The train passed snowbound station platforms in towns with names like Kokkola, Oulu and Kemi; I was now far up this country of frozen lakes and forests, the land that inspired Sibelius to write all those mournful but moving symphonies, but I was about to be snapped out of my reverie. 'Rovaniemi!

Rovaniemi!' called out the guard, announcing the name of my destination. This was the 'capital' of Finnish Lapland and at 67 degrees north it was teeth-chatteringly cold – so cold, in fact, that when the door opened on to the platform I thought seriously about staying inside the nice warm train. Then I had a fleeting image of Marine Sergeant Terry Palliser, who would not have been impressed: I had come to ski in Arctic Finland so now it was time to brace myself and step out into the minus-25-degrees air. Everyone seemed to know exactly where they were going except me.

Right, concentrate, I told myself, there must be a tourist-information office somewhere. There was, and when I found it they soon directed me to a warm and cheap hostel where I immediately treated myself to the local speciality: fillet of venison with arctic cloudberry sauce. Peering out of the steamed-up window at the bleak and frozen world outside, I tried to take stock of my situation. All right, so I had made it this far, but temperatures like these were not to be taken lightly. After all, the Finnish winter had seen off both the invading Soviet troops who died in their thousands in these forests in the 1940s, and the Germans, who had burnt Rovaniemi to the ground in revenge for being driven out by Finnish ski troops. When I ventured out it had better be with a purpose and a clear idea of how I was going to get back. I unfolded the local map the tourist office had given me and traced my finger along the Arctic Circle. To my surprise, this was actually a long way south of the North Pole and quite a substantial part of mainland Norway, Sweden and Finland lay above it on the map. More importantly, it lay just a short bus ride north of Rovaniemi. Back then, in 1980, this place had yet to become the renowned 'visit-Santa' package destination it was by 2008, with 800,000 tourists flying in each year, 120,000 of them from Britain. Leaving my skis in the hostel I went out to buy supplies for the next day, loading up my rucksack with all the things I reckoned would sustain me for a day's cross-country skiing in these glacial temperatures, then went back inside and ate some more. 'Remember,' Sergeant Palliser had lectured, 'you ski tomorrow on what you eat today.'

The morning dawned pink and blue, if that is possible. The low, slanting rays of the northern sun lit up the snow-bound trees with a curious, almost supernatural light, but in the shadows everything was blue and purple. I had never seen a light like this before. Stamping my feet and clutching my thin cross-country skis, I boarded a bus bound for the town of Kemijärvi on the other side of the Arctic Circle. But almost immediately the doors hissed open, depositing me at a wooden cabin on the edge of the forest. A colourful sign at the side of the road announced in several languages that this spot lay right on the Arctic Circle. 'You can get a certificate inside,' said a voice behind me in English. I turned to see a man clothed from head to toe in what I took to be fancy dress. On his feet were reindeer-hide slippers with pointed, upturned toes like shoes worn by an elf, and above them he wore embroidered trousers, a quilted red and blue jacket and a woollen cap that covered his ears. 'This is not fancy dress,' he said defensively, as if reading my mind. 'This is our Lapp national costume. You can buy it inside.'

Ten minutes later I emerged from the 'Arctic Gift Shop'

with my souvenir certificate and a nifty pair of Lapp reindeer slippers which I could envisage my father wearing in front of the fire at home. Now for what I had really come for. I squinted up at the morning sun then walked away from it in the opposite direction, crossing the road to the north and entering a silent, frozen world. I snapped on my skis, shouldered my rucksack and glided off into the wilderness.

At first I was concentrating hard on carving a path through the deep snow as there were no trails, no tracks, in fact nothing to distinguish one patch of forest from another; this was Hansel and Gretel country and it would be easy to get lost. When I finally looked up, something was moving between the trees, something large and slow. I began to wonder if you could out-ski a bear. But this turned out to be a far more benign and familiar creature: it was a reindeer, one of nearly 200,000 that roamed this part of northern Scandinavia, crossing at leisure the heavily armed border with the Soviet Union to the east. The animal looked up from foraging in the trees and held my gaze for a long time before vanishing into the forest. It gave me a glimpse of a natural, nomadic world and in that moment I longed to go after it, skiing on recklessly into the wilderness as the snow became ever deeper and harder to negotiate. I glanced at my watch: it was only early afternoon but I had been skiing for several hours and with the short Arctic winter days it was already growing dark. It was time to head back to the road, the bus and my warm hostel before the temperature plummeted with nightfall. To have spent the day skiing alone in the frozen forests of Arctic Finland had been a liberation. Now, I thought, let's see the rest of the world.

2

Greece

The Hospital for Infectious Diseases

'YES, MR GARDNER, THE TEST SHOWS POSITIVE. I'M afraid you have typhoid fever.' These were not words I wanted to hear. I had woken that morning in a fleapit hotel in the northern Greek city of Thessalonica with my head pounding and my guts churning like a combine harvester; I had spent much of the night commuting between the sagging mattress and the foetid loo. I suspected I knew the culprit: for the last week I had been in Istanbul, hanging out with Dutch backpackers, and on our last day we had pooled our resources and eaten at a particularly suspect kebab stall. From then on, the train journey westwards across Thrace had been tough going, sandwiched as I was between large, belching, sweating men and their interminable cigarettes, feeling ever more nauseous as I tried not to vomit, standing up to clear my head, swaying in the aisle, then immediately having to sit down with a bump.

In the 35-degree heat I had wandered alone and bewildered around Thessalonica, hunting for a hospital. My rucksack was cutting into my shoulders and my forehead felt as if it was on fire. I clutched a note, written in Greek by someone on the train from Istanbul, which said I might have typhoid and could the reader please direct me to a hospital, but it was hours before I finally found one. A nurse read my note, looked at me gravely, then told me to wait in line with the old women queueing for their physiotherapy. After an hour of moving no closer to the front of the queue I could bear it no longer; I felt like death warmed up. I got up, tottered over to some men in white coats, clutched my stomach and groaned. They ignored me. But then I uttered the magic word 'Constantinoplou' (Greek for Istanbul) and they turned and grinned. Why of course, if I had come from *that* place then surely I must have a genuine medical complaint, so I was taken straight into the surgery. The Greek doctors spoke some English but were unsure what to make of me, so they gave me an injection in the backside for good measure then took a blood sample. They told me to come back in an hour to hear the result, but when I did they confessed that they had lost the sample and asked if I would mind giving another. This time they analysed it on the spot and there followed a sudden flurry of form-filling. They told me I had caught typhoid and needed to be transferred to another hospital that specialized in highly infectious diseases. I did not like the sound of this one bit, but by now I was so exhausted that the prospect of a ride in an air-conditioned ambulance was quite appealing. It was not to be. 'So now you must find taxi,' I was told. 'Here is address.' With that, the nurses hoisted my rucksack back on to my shoulders, turned me around to face the door and all but shoved me through it.

The Limodon Hospital was a substantial building on a small hill, surrounded by a wrought-iron fence; I could not be sure if this was to keep the public out or the patients in. From reception a doctor led me to a basement where I was cross-examined. The medical staff were very concerned about where I had spent the previous night in case I had set off an epidemic of typhoid in the city. I told them I could not remember the hotel's name but could show them if they drove me. At that, the matter was dropped. I was then told to strip off and put on a pair of hospital-issue pyjamas, and was escorted to my ward. This turned out to be in a separate outhouse, set in a dusty courtyard; a woman with a handbag was sitting sobbing quietly outside. There might as well have been a sign above the door reading 'Abandon hope, all ye who enter here.' The hut contained only about a dozen patients but it was already full so I was given a bed in the corridor, between the peeling wallpaper and the open door on to the courtyard. From behind me I could hear the Greek patients whispering, 'Typhus! Typhus!' I did not know what illnesses had brought them in here, but they all gave me a wide berth on that first day.

I slumped on my bed and took stock of my surroundings. Every few minutes a squall of hot wind blew dust and dirt into the 'ward' from outside, though it did not seem to bother anyone. Cats pawed around in the rubbish heaps, which seemed to consist mainly of rotting bread. Inside the hut, the much-in-demand lavatory was one of those colourful footprint jobs where you squat double behind a door with no lock and whatever you produce has a habit of bouncing back up at you. The stone floor, I noticed, frequently flooded with urine and faeces, yet I never saw anyone wash their hands. It occurred to me that if I was not careful, I would end up considerably sicker than when I came into this place. I was just wondering how long I would be stuck here when a young man with terrible acne came up and introduced himself in English. Johann was from Belgium and his spots turned out to be chickenpox. He was very excited to find someone he could communicate with as the Greek patients, he said, were a surly lot. 'They will talk to you in Greek but they will never sit on the same bench as you. Really, it is most comical.' This wasn't turning out too badly, I thought, but then at midnight a nurse came round and insisted on extracting another blood sample, this time a whole test-tubeful of the stuff. She then motioned for me to roll over on to my stomach for an injection in the backside. It was, without doubt, the most painful injection I had ever experienced to date, administered like a public execution with the whole ward watching. That night I wrote in my diary: 'as the drug was forced into the muscle it felt like I imagine it must feel to be shot'. At eighteen I still had a lot to learn.

Somewhere in the small print of the rules and regulations of Limodon Hospital, I decided, there must be a clause that read, 'Do not on any account allow the patient a whole night's sleep.' Midnight injections were mandatory and the nurses came again at five thirty a.m. for more injections and blood samples. Just when I was drifting off to sleep again there would be a stampede for the loo by the more elderly inmates. One old man seemed to be groaning in there at regular intervals, but when I eventually went to investigate it turned out to be a sheep. This did not seem to strike anyone as strange, in fact the animal came and went as it pleased, wandering into the ward from the courtyard, nuzzling the odd patient, then leaving, although often not before dumping a load of droppings on the floor. One nurse made the mistake of trying to pat it and the beast turned nasty, charging at her and knocking her over.

Meanwhile, apart from the mosquito bites, nobody here actually seemed to have anything wrong with them. Far from being confined to our beds, we were left to wander around the yard in the sun, which is where Johann and I would sit and chew our breakfast. In fact, I was feeling pretty good for someone supposed to have typhoid. 'You must drink milk!' said the doctors. 'And eat bread!' But the bread was dry and hard to swallow, while the milk tasted like sugary water, so I resolved to pour it away when no one was looking. But this was Greece and there was always someone looking, particularly since the other patients had developed a touching concern for my welfare. If I was to have any hope of disposing of this sticky liquid I had to tiptoe round to the back of the hut, which was always buzzing with flies. When lunch arrived it was rice, vine leaves, meat and peaches – in fact a veritable Mediterranean buffet – for the other patients, but a bowl of foul-tasting baby food for me. I obtained permission from a doctor to eat biscuits since he was confident I didn't have any, but I soon discovered there was a highly developed system for smuggling forbidden food in from outside. First you had to go round to the front gates of the hospital and make friends with the guards. You then had to bribe them with a few drachma notes, and they would then send for a grocer who would happily pass food through the fence at extortionate prices. Fortunately no one had checked the contents of my rucksack when I first came in and I managed to eke out a packet of chocolate-chip cookies for some days.

In the sultry hours of the afternoon I chatted to a police-man who was a patient in the main block. He had caught viral hepatitis in an Athens jail, only noticing something was wrong when his urine turned the colour of cognac. That evening a new set of doctors came to peer at me. 'You must not drink milk!' they announced. They also admitted that they did not know what, if anything, was wrong with me. With some persuading they began to come round to the theory I had been working on in the blessed hours between injections: that my blood was only showing positive for typhoid because of the inoculation I had been given before I set off from Britain, and that this had in fact been a simple case of food poisoning. Doh! I decided to press home my advantage, winning a reprieve from their beloved buttock injections, but that night the men in white coats padded over to my bed with worried expressions. 'We feel very sorry for you,' they began. Oh God, what is it now, I thought. Salmonella? Cholera? Gastro-enteritis? The doctors glanced at each other and cleared their throats to deliver the bad news. 'England nil, Italia one. You lose bad in the football, yes?'

The next day no fewer than eleven doctors and nurses

were gathered around my bed, the cream of Thessalonica's medical profession, listening while I argued my case for early release. 'Look,' I reasoned, 'I've felt fine for three days now, I have no temperature, and anyway this couldn't be typhoid because I've learnt it has an incubation period of two weeks and I wasn't in Turkey then.' At the mention of Turkey their faces darkened; the two countries may have been NATO allies but they really didn't like each other one bit.

The doctors countered with a suggestion of their own. 'Maybe you caught an amoeba?' said a man with a luxuriantly bushy moustache. This was clearly medical diagnosis by group negotiation. I requested a three-day trial without any drugs but was refused; every few hours I was to be given a small pharmacy of foul-smelling pills. I had no idea what they were supposed to do, but they smelt so bad I decided I would be better off without them: I pocketed them dutifully then went round the back of the hut at the first chance I got and dumped them on the garbage pile. I was not surprised to see a growing heap of other patients' pills there too. I returned to sit in the sun with the other patients and listen to my tiny radio. As luck would have it the local station was playing all the hits of The Police, so I treated the ward to the finest lyrics Sting had to offer and was finally rewarded with a place on the treasured bench.

At dawn the routine resumed. A nurse woke me at five a.m., quite unnecessarily, to tell me to take some pills at eight. Breakfast was stale bread and crumbly goat's cheese. I read my well-thumbed copy of *Midnight Express* until the doctors came round. They were palpably tense – I suspected that their professional pride had been hurt by first misdiagnosing what was wrong with me, and then being unable to diagnose it at all. As if suddenly wanting to play a new game, they now sent me off for a stomach X-ray.

Back in the yard with no one about, I stripped to the waist to bask in the June sunshine, only to be confronted by a frantically gesticulating doctor who sent me inside and banned me from the sun. As soon as he was gone I sneaked up on to the roof, but was soon discovered and ordered back downstairs. It can only be a matter of time, I thought, before I get sentenced to solitary. I wondered what my Dutch friends in Istanbul were doing, and realized that by now they would probably have crossed into Iran, well on their way overland to Katmandu. And here was I, rotting away in this stagnant dustbowl of a hospital with a bunch of cranks for doctors. I had not been ill for a decade and I wasn't ill now – all I had had was a twenty-four-hour bout of food poisoning. I was kicking myself for having panicked into thinking it was anything more serious. I began to think of escape.

The next day a nurse brought me my X-rays and said I was 'more than normal'. 'However,' she cautioned, raising an elegantly shaped eyebrow at me, 'they found a *strakulomunos* in your blood.' A what? I had visions of a heavily moustachioed Greek amoeba trundling around in my veins. Whatever it was, though, was apparently not serious. 'This hospital is not good,' she confided. 'It was built by the Italians, but our government is still paying back the money.' A group of doctors drew up and the nurse fell silent. 'We have good news!' they announced.

'You are free to go after two days.' I celebrated at lunchtime with the Greek patients, tucking into roast chicken, rice and tomatoes, then that afternoon we all climbed over the fence of our yard into the adjacent orchard and the Greeks showed me where to pick the best apricots. Then it was back to the bench in the sun, where they told dirty jokes about the nurses and the elderly patients laughed the loudest. That night there was the mother of all thunderstorms, so some of us ran around outside in the rain, in our pyjamas.

Dawn again and I woke to my name being called very slowly. 'Fra-a-a-a-nk . . . Fra-a-a-a-nk.' Was this some new roll call being delivered by a very old man? No, it was that sheep, back again and now doing the rounds of the ward. Its bleat sounded so like my name I couldn't help but whirl round each time it opened its mouth. As daylight seeped into the ward the thermometer man shuffled in, but he was in no mood to take anyone's temperature. Instead, grumbling quietly to himself, he just scribbled down any old figure on each person's chart and shuffled out again. In the afternoon we all had a game of football in the yard, with bedroom slippers flying everywhere in the dust. The atmosphere felt more like a holiday camp than a hospital for infectious diseases. Then we rounded off the day with a twilight raid over the fence into the apricot orchard.

At last, my release day came. A nurse had noticed me writing my diary and there was a sudden frisson of concern about what I was going to say about this place. Was I a journalist, asked the doctors? In fifteen years' time I would be, but not yet. 'Please excuse us,' they said, 'but the war in Cyprus stopped hospital building all over

Greece.' As if to make amends for all the well-meaning failings of the past ten days, they gave instructions that I be given extra helpings of moussaka for lunch. One hour later I walked out of the Limodon Hospital into the blazing afternoon sun and bought myself the biggest ice cream I had ever seen. I was free, and fit, and healthy. I was ecstatic to be out of there and yet, perversely, I look back on that time as a happy interlude in my life, un-encumbered by the responsibilities and demands of adult life that were to come.

3

The Philippines

The House of the Dead

'IT'S TEMPTING, ISN'T IT?' SAID A VOICE BESIDE ME. WE were staring at a sign in an Athens travel agent's window one afternoon, two British backpackers preparing to clock on for our evening shifts as casual waiters in a rip-off tourist restaurant. 'MANILA. £100 ONE-WAY. ONE SEAT REMAINING,' read the sign. The traffic growled and hooted behind me and I could taste the fumes in the back of my throat; perhaps it was time to kiss goodbye to Europe and grab that last seat before it went.

Newly liberated from the ramshackle confines of Thessalonica's Limodon Hospital, I had taken a month to make my way gently down through Greece, hitchhiking and hopping on slow trains that swam through the summer heat, which shimmered and wobbled, bearing aloft the heady scent of pines. The Greek villagers I met were invariably kind and hospitable. But if I thought I was seeing this country at a leisurely pace, my schedule was downright frenetic compared to two backpackers from London I met. Tom and Chris had traded their wrist-watches for a donkey and were walking the length of the country with Costas, the donkey, in tow. At Delphi's famous temple we camped out in a hillside olive grove, got drunk and silly on foul-tasting retsina, raced each other up flagpoles and sang Pink Floyd songs under the moon.

Reaching Athens, I realized I would run out of money unless I found some work, so I took a job as a waiter in a restaurant in the Plaka, the tourist area beneath the Acropolis. The owner disapproved of my jeans and T-shirt. 'Wear these,' he commanded, brandishing a pair of crotch-huggingly tight terylene slacks and a baggy white shirt with all the upper buttons missing. 'Now you look like a proper Greek!' he exclaimed. This was not strictly true since I still lacked a medallion nestling in a thick mat of curly chest hair, but I was soon deployed outside in the street to hustle the northern European punters in. 'Hello madam, hello sir, you like souvlaki? You like bouzouki music? It's all inside. Tonight special menu.' Sadly it was not to last. When I asked for my wages at the end of my first week, the patron tried to fob me off with food instead. 'Give him something from the bread box,' he called out. A fellow waiter lifted the lid to reveal a large chestnut-brown cock-roach racing round in panicked circles. Greek cockroaches were huge – in fact I had never seen an insect that big until then. Somehow I managed to resist the bread box, but it was obvious I was not going to get paid. My outrage at having been royally ripped off was only mitigated by staging a secret rendezvous with the boss's daughter in an olive grove the next afternoon. 'He would kill us both if he found out,' she whispered as she slid her hand down my chest. It was probably time to leave Athens.

The next day I spotted that sign in the travel agent's window advertising a one-way flight to the Philippines. A hundred pounds? What a snip, I thought. And it was. All right, so it was on Egyptair, with its curious abhorrence of in-flight entertainment, and there were four legs to the journey, including an overnight stop in Cairo's airport hotel, where I unwisely drank the tap water and then regretted it for days. But how cool was this, to cross the world on some of my last remaining savings and land in a city that sounded like an ice cream?

Manila airport was everything I had always imagined the tropics to be. Lush coconut palms lolled in the sticky air, their fronds lifting briefly with the breeze then drooping back limply as if exhausted by the effort. Droplets of sweat formed on my arms and within minutes of stepping off the plane my T-shirt was clinging to my back. Customs formalities were non-existent. Outside the terminal, in the rude glare of the overhead sun, I saw people without shadows for the first time. This close to the Equator the midday sun shone directly overhead, so the Filipinos' glossy black hair reflected back the sunlight while their faces remained in shadow.

Warding off the persistent cab-drivers I boarded a crowded yellow bus and headed into town, entering a world of manic drivers, blaring horns, dashing pedestrians and gaudy, decorated jeep taxis known as jeepneys. On the back of a lorry a sign read, 'Distancia, amigo'. I found a budget hostel, sharing a room with a snoring salesman, but it was an interrupted night. The walls were crawling with ipis, big fat Filipino cockroaches that would scuttle right up to my face, their antennae twitching. Was there no getting away from these creatures on my gap year? Several times we got up to splat them, their innards making a terrible mess on the wall and spraying yellow goo on to our clothes.

Outside in the street the next morning, Manila did not seem quite as attractive as its name had suggested. The river leading down to the harbour was choked with garbage. Beneath a poster of smiling first lady Imelda Marcos a small bloated dead pig floated downstream, its hide black with dirt, past a sign that read 'IT'S A CLEAN, CLEAN WORLD WITH KLEENEX'. Some laughing children called out to me, 'Joe! Joe! Hey Joe!', thinking I was from the nearby US Naval Base at Subic Bay. They came up and pinched the hairs on my forearms, which were clearly a novelty to them, then ran off giggling.

Some off-duty policemen appeared and invited me to join them for a drink, so there we sat in the sun in Manila's South Harbour, squatting on upended crates and popping open bottles of San Miguel while someone produced a guitar and started singing a local favourite, the 'Magellan Song', about the Portuguese explorer who 'discovered' this archipelago several centuries ago. We were joined by a couple of Philippine Navy sailors who invited us to look

round their ship, just back from anti-rebel operations in the troubled south.

Security around the Navy harbour was as lax as Customs had been at the airport: a man in a baseball cap swung open a big gate and waved us through with a nod and a shrug. The ship was a landing-craft carrier for both tanks and marines and it had just steamed north after dropping off troops and supplies at the port of Zamboanga. Yet now the ship was crammed full, not of hardware but sailors and their families. Large women wrapped in blankets swung in hammocks, children with streaming noses stared up at porn pin-ups, and girlfriends were bedded down with naval ratings. Litter was strewn across the floor, the toilets were overflowing and everything was damp with humidity. It wasn't at all what I had expected. Mario, our host, grew quite animated as he described how last month he had been up on deck manning a heavy machine gun to give covering fire as marines had assaulted some rebel stronghold. Back on the dock, he tried to give me a farewell present of his helmet, but I explained that I couldn't really see myself lugging it round the highlands and islands of the Philippines on top of my already overstuffed rucksack.

As I strolled back to the hostel through the darkened streets of Manila in the small hours, past stall-holders and street-vendors sleeping in the gutter or on their wooden carts, it struck me what a friendly, hospitable country I had come to. But this big, dirty city was not for me and I resolved to catch the first bus the next morning out to the mountains.

* * *

The journey from Manila to Baguio took five hours, the bus winding its way northwards from the coast through the bulbous Luzon peninsula. Although the driver was hell-bent on breaking the speed limit, it was a pleasure to watch the flat, watery padi fields give way to sheer mountain gorges cloaked in rainforest. In the quiet intervals when we stopped to pick up villagers from tiny bus stops I could just make out the trill and whoop of tropical birds, calling from dense forests that glistened with freshly fallen rainwater. As we continued to climb, the coconut palms were replaced by pine trees, which I had not expected to see in the Far East, and a sign proclaimed: 'WELCOME TO BAGUIO CITY, HIGHEST TOWN IN THE PHILIPPINES'.

Back then, before the earthquake that so shattered this community in 1990, killing hundreds, Baguio seemed to me to be a happy, enchanted place. There were cool pine forests interspersed with rushing waterfalls and lush banana groves where butterflies flitted in the sunlight. But Baguio and the surrounding hill country were also home to the ancient Igorot tribespeople. I had read that they believed in a hierarchy of spirits, revering Nature in the form of a deity they called Lumawig, and that they also believed fervently in the spirits of the deceased, known as *anitos*, who had to be continually appeased with offerings of food. Surely not still, I thought, wrongly assuming that such animist traditions could not have survived into the 1980s. But I was soon to discover that despite the partial introduction of Christianity up here in the highlands, to many Igorot people those spirits had far more significance than the teachings of Jesus.

To try to get a feel for this culture I walked from the bus

station to Baguio's dusty museum, where a collection of seven-hundred-year-old mummies were disturbingly well preserved, with skin intact, complete with tattoos, and lifelike expressions still fixed on their faces. Outside I found two Igorot boys playing the nose flute, a curious instrument made of slender bamboo and decorated by hand with minute, geometric patterns. Smiling self-consciously, they would block one nostril while blowing through the other, creating a haunting, eerie tune, all from one breath. I declined their invitation to have a go.

Travelling on my own meant that the Igorot were far more forward than they would have otherwise been in coming up and approaching me, and the invitations flowed thick and fast: to dinner, to tea, and then, on my third day, to a *mang-mang* ceremony, a cleansing ritual to ward off evil spirits from a newly built house. It was to be my introduction to the secretive world of Igorot sorcery and superstition. As afternoon turned to dusk I strolled down a dirt track to a low, wooden-slatted shack surrounded by a banana grove. Teresa, the host's wife, greeted me at the gate and led me round the muddy garden. 'We are Christians,' she explained in slow, halting English, 'but we also fear the spirits. If we do not carry out the rituals we are afraid of what will happen.' Her brow was furrowed in thought; obviously something had happened to this family. 'What do you mean?' I asked.

'When my husband first started to cultivate this garden, one morning he forgot to ask the spirits to move aside. By lunchtime his left foot was starting to throb with pain so he went to the doctor in the village. The doctor could find no physical signs of anything wrong, yet by evening the pain was unbearable.' Teresa had stopped walking now and was leaning against a wall, remembering. 'The family all feared that the spirits were to blame so we went to the oldest woman in the village, who knows about the supernatural. She told us she would have to sleep on it, and we would have to wait until morning to hear the result of her dream. My husband spent a sleepless night and we all feared for him, but in the morning the old woman had the answer. When he had begun to till the ground the spirit children had been playing there and his tools had struck them. To punish him, the mother of the spirit children had begun whipping the soles of my husband's feet, causing this invisible pain.'

Teresa must have caught my look of scepticism. 'I know what you are thinking,' she smiled. 'But listen. On the old woman's advice we sacrificed a chicken to the spirits and within an hour the pain was gone. It is true, you know. Every time we do anything to defy the spirits we always suffer in some way or another.'

By now it was nearly dark, but as Teresa pointed towards the mountains I could just make out a purple shadowed valley where the spirit mother was said to live. There were storm clouds gathering overhead, giving off a low menacing rumble, and at that moment I could see how persuasive this local superstition would be if one grew up and lived here.

It was time for the *mang-mang* ritual. Teresa led me into the house, where I blinked in the flickering candlelight. A dozen men were sitting cross-legged on the floor, their smooth, waxy faces illuminated by the candles as they nodded for me to join them. Teresa's father made room for me beside him, his rough farmer's hands patting the bare floorboards. This ceremony was only for family members, he said, but since I was to eat under their roof I was considered an honorary member of the family. A chicken had been butchered that afternoon and then burnt, not cooked, over a fire. Because the spirits liked to drink as well as eat, a few drops of gin were now spilt on the floorboards. Next, the men took the half-burnt chicken carcass and broke it into pieces, mixing it with 'salted meat', which was really just white chunks of pig fat attached to a thin layer of meat. (I never really took to Filipino food.) This was now shared out amongst everyone and we ate in silence with our fingers. Actually I only pretended to eat the pig fat, which smelt foul, but I was loath to offend anyone. The ritual over, we rose and left the house to go for rice coffee, leaving the leftovers and scattered drops of gin behind in the flickering candlelight. The spirits had been fed; there would be no sole-whipping tonight.

I was keen to see more of the Igorot culture but Baguio was a little too developed for me; I felt an urge to head on up into the mountains, to visit the remote villages where men still wore boars' tusks behind their ears and where cannibalism had only just died out. And so at dawn I boarded a low-roofed bus for the eight-hour journey to Bontoc; I say low-roofed because every time we went over a pothole I hit my head, to the great amusement of my fellow travellers. As the bus wound its way along 'Guerrilla Saddle', the highest road in the Philippines at 2,260 metres, the route became perilously steep. As we twisted above gorges there was little to prevent our bus from slewing off the track into the valley below.

Headsore and weary, I peered out of the grimy window as we clanked into Bontoc, capital of Mountain Province and centre of the Igorot culture. Its low, tin-roofed huts lay huddled together in a fertile plain, hemmed in by mountains where storm clouds were again building. As the first fat raindrops began to fall I set out to find somewhere to sleep, teaming up with Claude, a hardy French traveller who had just come from hiking the highlands of Papua New Guinea. The local men, I noticed, were all carrying heavy steel machetes that swung from their waists in wooden sheaths, but no one was hostile and a heavily tattooed woman soon led us to a place calling itself the Happy Home Hotel. It was, essentially, little more than a hut, but it was shelter and that was all that mattered to us.

On local advice we set out the next morning for Guinaang, a three-hour hike up a muddy track in an area that had until recently been famed for its head-hunting. I thought about this each time we passed men working on the rice terraces or chopping bamboo with their murderous-looking machetes. They gave us noncommittal looks. As the heavens opened once more we arrived at the scattered collection of wooden and grass-thatched huts that made up the village of Guinaang. It was one of the most squalid places I have ever been to. Each hut had its own little stone-walled compound at the back where the family kept a number of black pigs, really just domesticated wild boars, that snuffled around trotter-deep in excrement. Large rats ran around everywhere, sometimes swarming inside the pig pens. It was soon apparent that the villagers used the pig pens as their latrines, and as I discovered to my cost when I put my hand out to cross a wall, they also used the dry stones in place of toilet paper. Wrinkled men in filthy loincloths splashed past in the mud, bent double under giant sacks of rice, their muscled backs straining with the load.

A Filipino Episcopal priest approached us, his dazzling Hawaiian shirt and dog collar looking oddly out of place amidst the rain-soaked greens and browns of this highland landscape. 'Welcome! Welcome, friends!' he called out in an American twang. 'Come have some coffee with me.' The Bishop of Baguio had sent him up here, he told us, 'to try and civilize these pagan people', and a small church had been built for the purpose. In a tiny room off the church, humming with flies, we sat round a table while a nun prepared coffee and rice and a scrawny dog tugged at our trouser legs. Through the open window I noticed the rain had stopped and an enormous blue butterfly as big as my hand was fluttering past. 'These people are so primitive,' the priest was saying. 'They have so many superstitions, I feel it is my duty to help them. Sugar?' Then, as if remembering a piece of good news, his face suddenly brightened. 'Hey! Did you know that the oldest man in the village died this morning? Would you like to come to the House of the Dead?'

Together we climbed up through clumps of banana and avocado trees until we came to a hut where people looked suitably dejected. A group of elders sat round a smouldering fire in a circle, naked except for their scanty loincloths. On their heads they wore tiny rattan hats shaped like baskets, into which they tucked flimsy leather pipes, and behind their ears they each wore a vicious-looking pair of boar's tusks. Some of the men wore heavy metal trinkets in their right ears, which over the years had stretched their earlobes right down to their shoulders. Their crumpled, ageless faces contorted as they chanted a dirge in a low monotone. Just inside the doorway someone was butchering a large pig and the blood ran everywhere, staining the parchment-like skin of the village elders. One man proudly showed us a basket bulging with glistening purple entrails and I felt like throwing up.

This was heady stuff for me. This time last year, I had been cloistered in a Wiltshire classroom revising eighteenth-century English history for my A-levels. Now I found myself in surroundings that were about as alien as it was possible to be. Seeing the dead body left me feeling strangely undisturbed, perhaps because of the peaceful atmosphere. Somehow, up here amidst the smoke-filled thatched huts, boars' tusks and loincloths, death seemed the most natural thing in the world. Claude, however, was annoyingly blasé. He had, he assured me, seen all this and more in Papua New Guinea. Yet I noticed he declined the invitation to come and inspect the corpse, and had turned quite pale.

Judging by the large number of great- and great-great-grandchildren the old man had had over the years, the priest estimated that he must have been at least a hundred years old. The veins on his head were squashed between his stretched skin and his skull, and flies crawled in and out of his open mouth. That morning he had been alive, but now he already resembled the centuries-old mummies I had seen in the museum in Baguio. The people who mourned this man were old enough to remember a time when they had been active head-hunters in these hills and forests, decapitating their enemies for trophies with little interference from anyone down in Manila. On the advice of the priest, we paid our respects, gave the men some matches for their pipes, shuffled out of the hut and hitched a lift on a jeep going back to Bontoc. I exhaled a long, slow breath and made a mental note to try and politely refuse any further offers to examine a corpse.

That night the radio announced that a 'Signal One' storm warning had been issued for the whole of the Luzon peninsula; children were to skip school and everyone was advised to stay indoors. The Philippine Met Office was not exaggerating. As I huddled into my sleeping bag in the Happy Home Hotel, there were tremendous winds and lashing rain. Windows slammed shut, glass shattered, palm trees bent double, and two pigs outside my window squealed in alarm.

In the morning, I learnt that an overnight landslide had blocked the road to my next destination – the fabled rice terraces of Banauwe, which Filipinos assured me were the eighth wonder of the world – but a jeep was just leaving, which could take me and the other Europeans halfway there if we hurried.

It was one of those dry, deep-blue mornings that follow a storm, and having no wish to be cooped up inside the covered jeep I rode on the tailplate, lurching with the vehicle each time it bounced over rocks. The driver took each bend at frightening speed but I felt curiously safe, knowing that if we did go over the edge to join the other wrecks in the ravine below I should be able to jump clear in time.

At the first landslide we stopped, shouldered our ruck-sacks and scrambled over the muddy scree and crushed bamboos to continue on foot. A local explained cheerfully about the snakes here as we walked. 'You must not be afraid,' he said, 'they will only bite at night, and then only when the moon is in the third quarter and waning.' The tribal group up here, the Ifugao, he told us, still held a six-day ritual whenever a rich man was sick. On the sixth day the *haw-aw* appeared without fail – a large purple snake which was lethally poisonous but never bit anyone. Why the snake only turned up for rich sick people, he could not explain. 'Ah, look!' he exclaimed, pointing at the road, and as if on cue there was a dead snake, about four foot long. 'Poisonous?' we chorused. 'Yes, certainly.' We hiked on in silence, our boots making sucking noises in the wet mud, each of us wrapped up in our own thoughts. Personally, I was in the middle of ordering a large pizza margherita somewhere warm and cosy when there was a commotion at the front of our group. 'It's the rice terraces!' someone shouted. Stretched out below us was a lush landscape of green sliced hillside, a sort of giant version of something a celebrity chef might do with a cucumber and a very sharp knife. The rice terraces were cut horizontally into the mountain and they extended far into the distance. If we strained our eyes we could just make out hill villagers struggling up them with impossibly large loads on their shoulders. It was perhaps a slight exaggeration to call them the eighth wonder of the world, but they were certainly impressive.

That night something very strange happened, something which I have never been able to explain since. We slid and slithered our way down the hillside that afternoon to stay in a basic hostel in the village, we ate supper and we went to bed. Let me be very clear about this: when I went to bed that night, tucked up in that wooden hut high up on the mist-shrouded rice terraces of Luzon, I had not been drinking alcohol or even smoking. (A school friend once did me the huge favour of offering me a cigarette when I was twelve and it managed to put me off for life.) When I came up to my empty room I locked the door behind me, washed my face, brushed my teeth and crawled into my sleeping bag. I was exhausted after trekking all day and I soon drifted off to sleep, lulled by the sighing of the wind outside.

I am not sure whether it was a sound or a movement that woke me a few hours later, but when I opened my eyes the wind had dropped and there was not a sound in the room. But something was there and it terrified me. Dimly perceptible in the dark was a figure, no more than ten feet away. Standing at the end of my bed was an Ifugao tribesman in full regalia: embroidered headband, feathers, boar's tusks, tattoos and machete. I was completely dumbfounded. How could he have got in? There had been no one else in that tiny room when I came in, and I had bolted the door from the inside. Now there was a knife-wielding tribesman in the room and he was staring straight at me, holding himself motionless. I stared back, not out of bravery but because quite simply I did not know what else to do. My brain began to follow a logical path: whatever this creature was it could not have walked through a wall, so it must surely be an apparition. I suddenly recalled how a school friend had been convinced that he had seen the ghost of a Victorian woman down in the basement changing rooms, but it had turned out to be one of the staff on her way to a party. Yet I could find no such explanation for what was in my room. Fine, said my brain, if it's a ghost then why not just duck back beneath the cover and in the morning it will be gone? Slowly, like someone avoiding sudden movements when dealing with a dangerous reptile, I pulled my sleeping bag up over my head. My eyes were wide open in the dark yet I felt curiously safe in that enclosed space, as if whatever was at the end of my bed would not follow me inside there. It was a ludicrous, child-like response to a situation that I was quite unprepared for. But it worked. Nothing happened.

In the morning, the sun came filtering through the paper-thin cracks in the wooden walls, illuminating the dust motes that hung in the air. I shuffled out of my sleeping bag and went over to the door to check the lock. Just as I thought: it was still locked and showed no sign of being forced. This was frankly a little too much to take in. 'Um . . . did everyone sleep OK?' I asked at breakfast. The other travellers grunted, as backpackers do at that time of the morning. I studied their faces but found no clues, only straggly beards and sunburn. I was on my own for this one.

4

Sumatra

Tiger-Tracking and Volcano-Trekking

AFTER SPENDING MOST OF MY GAP YEAR BACKPACKING with no fixed itinerary, it was something of a shock to find myself in the cosy confines of Exeter University for the start of my four-year degree course in Arabic. The campus was perched on rolling Devon hills, and quickly became all too familiar. When I passed a vague acquaintance for the third or fourth time in a day we wouldn't really know what to say to each other. 'Forgot my books,' I would grunt, or 'Just going back to the library,' or something similarly anodyne. Hell, I thought, two weeks ago I was on a coral island in the Philippines living in a thatched hut with people who couldn't speak a word of English, and frankly I felt more at ease there. But Exeter was nothing if not friendly, and before long the weeks were flying past in a blur of smoky pubs and cidery picnics; it felt like no time at all before nine glorious weeks of summer holidays beckoned. But where to go and who to go with?

To earn some extra money at the weekend, I had joined the University Officers Training Corps or OTC, where I eventually made some lifelong friends. The OTC was supposed to be a way of luring hard-up students into considering a career in the Army, but at first it was hard to take it seriously. For a start, there was a man with a head like a football bellowing across a parade ground: 'You blithering idiot!' *Blithering?* Did anyone really still use words like that? We quickly nicknamed him the Elephant Man. There was even someone on the staff whose name was Captain Carruthers, who seemed to spend every military exercise dozing in the back of the camouflaged ambulance. Then there was a large and fierce man with a shiny wooden stick and a swirly embroidered design on his sleeve, which apparently identified him as the Regimental Sergeant-Major, a man to be feared. RSM Pete Gove had spent his career frightening the local county regiment, the Devon & Dorsets (known affectionately as the Devon & Doughnuts), and he had a face like an angry rhino which he used to good effect. I once accidentally trod on his foot while queueing at the bar in some rainswept camp. I quickly apologized, but he threw his arm around my shoulders in a paternal fashion, saying, 'That's all right, me old buddy.' He paused for effect as I instinctively relaxed, then roared into my ear, 'DO IT AGAIN AND I'LL BREAK YOUR LEG!' Gove appeared to dislike everyone, especially a cadet from Plymouth who unwisely turned up on parade wearing an earring. But he had a soft spot for anyone who could shoot straight.

The training consisted initially of sitting in a classroom learning how to strip and reassemble weapons so fresh from the factory they were still covered in grease and poly-thene wrapping. Half the cadets were girls and many of them were noticeably better than the boys at taking apart a machine gun. Then there was Signals – or, as the Elephant Man called it, 'Wireless Training' – and study periods on imaginary battlefields out in the Devon countryside known as TEWTs (Tactical Exercises Without Troops). There were also infantry tactics, which meant piling into 'four-tonners', the Army's deeply uncomfort-able slat-benched trucks, and chugging down to Woodbury Common outside Exeter. Here, to the despair of the training NCOs, all of them professional career soldiers on secondment from the Regular Army, the Elephant Man would insist on taking charge, standing on a grassy tussock, striking a pose in his fantastically baggy green fatigues, and demonstrating a bayonet charge with his walking stick. 'When you get to the enemy lines,' he proclaimed, 'simply blunder through like this – and this,' jabbing the air while we looked on in amazement. To us students this all reeked of Dad's Army, but hey, it was a great way to meet girls and we were getting paid for it.

The training only began to remotely resemble the modern military when we went down to Dartmoor or Lympstone to visit the Commando Training Centre. I loved Dartmoor for its bleak, treeless landscape that blended into the horizon and for its wild, craggy outcrops, known as tors, that in winter were often wreathed in snow. At Lympstone we all had a go at the Tarzan course, which involved climbing up a tower then sliding down a hundred-foot diagonal rope, followed by an aerial assault course. Watched by the Physical Training Instructors

(PTIs), muscled supermen in white-and-red gym vests, we were told to leap from one platform to another thirty feet above the ground. One test involved a literal leap of faith: from high up we had to launch ourselves across a gap and grab hold of a rope-mesh safety net. If we missed our grip we would slide and fall a long way down, but there was a further challenge. 'Resist the temptation to grab the rope with your open hands,' commanded the PT busters, 'because you will break your fingers and fall. You have to punch your way through a gap in the rope mesh and lock your arm round it like this—'. This turned out to be every bit as difficult as it sounded, and several of us missed the gaps and punched the rope knots instead, only to slide down to earth in shame. Those of us who made it had to then inch our way along a stretched horizontal rope. 'Bloody 'ell,' remarked one of the PTIs as a petite cadet pulled her body along its length, 'I wouldn't mind being the rope.' On subsequent visits the courses grew more demanding as some of us were selected to go on endurance runs with full kit and rifle, or wade up to our necks through a swamp called Peter's Pool. But what we all dreaded were the tunnels on Woodbury Common: the idea of having to make your way through a completely sub-merged tunnel terrified everyone. What if you got stuck and drowned? In fact the water tunnel turned out to be just eight feet long and there was a hulking marine NCO at each end to sling you through. Far more alarming were the dry tunnels: great snaking underground tubes of corrugated iron that twisted and turned in the dark for what seemed like a hundred yards beneath the gorse-covered heath. The local village boys thought it was the best fun ever to throw pebbles and sticks down there overnight so we would cut our knees the next day, but that was nothing compared to the claustrophobia we felt as we crawled along, nose to boot, in a line of a dozen cadets at a time, suddenly and inexplicably stopping, unable to move forwards or backwards, blind in the dark, just feeling our way along the narrow pipe walls. Then someone would fart and the tension would snap like a twig as laughter echoed up the line.

Alongside the few officer cadets marked out for future stardom – like Julian, who went on to serve several tours with the SAS – were students like Andy, whose demeanour was so bovine that each time he wore uniform it inspired a chorus of that Bob Marley reggae song, 'Buffalo Soldier'. There was Tim Johns, who after unwisely claiming that you could eat grasshoppers was then persuaded to prove it, and Tony Campanale, who I first met propped up outside a Nissen hut, regurgitating the contents of the introductory cheese-and-wine party. And then there was Henry, who fell foul of a devilish plot thanks to the RAF. Hovering in a Puma helicopter thirty feet above Salisbury Plain, we all took turns to abseil down to the ground below, where the excess rope lay coiled in a pile. When it came to Henry's turn, someone discreetly coaxed the pilot into ascending ever so slowly without Henry realizing, so that however far he abseiled down the rope, he remained the same distance above the ground; the poor man got through over a hundred feet of rope before he worked out what was going on.

One highly improbable officer cadet at Exeter was George Seel. A pensive, intelligent history undergraduate with a passion for literature, his large frame meant he always got lumbered with carrying something heavy on exercises, like a machine gun, an anti-tank rocket-launcher or, more often, a more mundane cargo like a bunch of batteries for the radio. George had picked up the squaddy's habit of sneaking puffs from a roll-up cigarette held between thumb and forefinger, which he then quickly concealed behind his back whenever anyone was approaching. George and I became good friends, and I would have to try very hard not to catch his eye whenever I got harangued by Elephant Man, who more than once hauled me aside on some parade ground to tell me, 'Now look here, Gardner, there are some people here, myself included, who think you're a waste of rations.' I was unable to stop myself stealing a glance at his own capacious girth as it strained to break out from the confines of his 1940s-vintage stable belt; the Major, we all knew, was fond of queueing twice for breakfast, but by sitting somewhere different each time he hoped to get away with it unnoticed.

By the end of our first summer term George and I had struck up enough of a rapport to resolve to spend our summer holidays travelling together around South-east Asia. I had already backpacked alone around an absurd number of countries the previous year and had been well and truly bitten by the travel bug: I was desperate to get out there and see new places. So, in a bucket shop in Oxford Street I booked us a pair of rock-bottom tickets – £280 return to Bangkok on Bangladesh Biman Airways – and off we set. To this day I still get a slight tingle when I pitch up at Heathrow's longhaul Terminal 3 as it always makes me think of that summer afternoon in 1981 when we arrived at check-in, not really knowing what we were going to do with nine weeks backpacking around the Far East, but just happy to embrace whatever adventure came our way. The flight was colourful, with four stopovers: after a brief refuelling stop in Dhaka the plane took off with a live bat onboard. No one had noticed it sneak in, but now it was flying up and down the aisle above our heads. As soon as we levelled out the flight attendants tried desperately and unsuccessfully to swat it with pillows, until eventually it got snagged in a passenger's hair and was confined to a cupboard for the rest of the flight.

Nurul Huda Mosque, Pintu Padang, West Sumatra, 1981

Our days in Thailand passed in an exotic blur. There was our first, memorable meal after we arrived at

Bangkok airport in the small hours of the morning. 'Hey, this spicy prawn soup looks really good,' I said. Two hours later I was crouched over a footprint loo in the airport terminal as the formidable Thai chillis showed they were not to be messed with. At first glance, Bangkok did not impress: it was all roaring traffic, clouds of exhaust fumes, broken pavements full of festering puddles, streets lined with greying coconut palms and dilapidated stalls selling cheap clothes and bizarre fruit. But that afternoon we got drawn into an impromptu game of Thai football in the street, where several young men stood round in a circle and tried to keep a hollow, rattan ball continually in the air, using their knees, feet, heads and shoulderblades. George, who demonstrated a lot more skill than I did, unfortunately managed to knock the ball into the path of an oncoming truck which squashed it flat. We were mortified and began reaching into our pockets to pay for another one when the rattan ball sprang neatly back into shape, undamaged.

We felt we could not come to Bangkok without having a drink in the famous red-light district, Patpong Road, where right above a go-go bar there hung a large sign advertising 'Dr Choong's VD clinic'. It was indeed an eye-popping display of pulsating, gyrating flesh, and we were amazed to see girls leaving the bars arm-in-arm with tourists, then stopping to bow and pray to a Buddhist shrine before climbing into a tuk-tuk taxi to go off and have sex in a nearby hotel. The Vietnam War had ended just six years previously and the place still screamed 'R&R', even though the American GIs were long gone.

* * *

The following day we boarded the slow train south from Bangkok to Surathani. And it really was slow, allowing us to sit on the foot ramps with the doors open as we glided past villages, canals and lush, tropical scenery with the warm night air in our faces. These are the moments I love most when travelling: the gentle, rhythmic jolt of train wheels on rails; the long, mournful blast on the loco-motive's whistle way up ahead; the feeling of being taken inexorably on a journey, heading somewhere new, yet moving slowly enough to have time to take in the changes along the way. Tiny village stations went past with names like Bang Bang Man, where smartly dressed station managers would hold out a flag to signal the passing of the overnight train.

At dawn we stopped abruptly. 'Something's up,' said George, who was never one to be rattled by the un-expected. I tried to look out of the window, but it had fogged up with condensation on the outside so I made my way to the open doorway at the end of the carriage. Dimly visible in the undergrowth were Thai soldiers in full combat gear, cradling M16s. 'They are looking for rebels,' said the conductor rather wearily, as if to say, 'Well, they're not going to find any on *my* train, are they?' George joined me in the doorway, rolled up a cigarette and watched the patrol move off into the jungle.

At Surathani we boarded a boat for Koh Samui (these were the days before this now world-famous island resort even had an airport), crossing the sea by day as the pirates made it too dangerous after dark. Lamai beach was pretty basic back in 1981, just a few bamboo-and-straw huts on stilts beneath tall, swaying coconut palms, and a trio of large Australian nurses who invited us to join them sun-bathing naked behind a smooth rock shaped suggestively like a pair of buttocks. The local fishermen sat around in their doorways, squinting into the sun and watching the world go by, and the owner of almost the only restaurant pulled in the punters by getting his daughter to parade topless outside.

After a few days of life on the beach we continued south, hitching a lift with a Chinese businessman from the mainland down to Butterworth in Malaysia, Penang Island, a short flight across the Malacca Strait to Medan in Sumatra, then a five-hour, non-stop, standing-room-only bus journey to one of the most beautiful places on earth. Towards late afternoon the bus rounded a bend to reveal, hundreds of feet below us, the shimmering expanse of Lake Toba, at fifty miles long the largest lake in South-east Asia and one of the deepest, surrounded by misty mountains and tiny fishing villages. Here, at three thousand feet above sea level, the air was clear and dry and the sky a deep cloudless blue. In the market at Parapat, women were selling baskets of spices and dried fish, their heads bound with colourful lengths of cloth, on which they balanced their baskets. Lake Toba, we learnt, is something of a geological phenomenon known as a caldera, the result of a cataclysmic eruption millions of years ago. The lake fills the crater where the volcano blew its top off and in the middle of the lake is an island, Pulau Samosir, to which we were now heading by ferry.

As soon as we docked at the jetty, people approached us to promote their guest houses. We opted for one of the many traditional wooden longhouses with great sweeping

Indonesian Batak House, Sumatra, 1981

roofs and intricate painted carvings to ward off evil spirits. The people who lived here were the Batak tribe, who according to *The Indonesia Handbook* were descendants of wandering clans of Neolithic mountain-dwellers from northern Thailand and Burma who were driven out to sea around 1,500 years ago. Once famed for their martial traditions, their villages were often at war with each other, and during a siege Bataks were said to be able to live on a potato a day for months on end. They also used to be Sumatra's only cannibals and in the nineteenth century Raffles reported that: 'For certain crimes, four in number, a criminal would be eaten alive. The flesh was sometimes eaten raw, or grilled and eaten with lime, salt, pepper and a little rice. Blood was drunk out of bamboo containers. Palms of the hands and soles of the feet were delicacies of the epicures. Parents were eaten when they were too old to work.' It came as some relief to know that cannibalism was no longer in fashion here.

The next morning, George and I set out to explore Samosir Island, following the shores of the lake past grazing caribao buffalo and laughing children, along a precipitous track that wound up to the five-thousand-foot mountain ridge. Here was a world of green ravines and secondary jungle, where the silence was broken only by the electric hum of cicadas. Someone was waving to us, a Batak girl beckoning us to come and have coffee with her family. Here they prepared it very strong, in tall glasses which they refilled with hot water that swirled around the thick oily sludge at the bottom. We gathered cross-legged on a rush mat in the family's clean-swept longhouse, coils of woodsmoke drifting between us, as the daughters in their patterned shawls moved among us with the coffee, occasionally looking up with a coy expression. Already we were finding the language barrier evaporating since Bahasa, the language of Indonesia and Malaysia, is one of the easiest to learn. Written in the Roman alphabet, unlike Thai or Chinese, its words are pronounced exactly as they are spelt and plurals seemed to consist of just saying the same word twice. Being able to hold basic conversations in Bahasa came to make all the difference to our time in Sumatra. After we had made our thanks that afternoon we headed back down through the forest, shadowed by a noisy troupe of black apes.

That night, back in our hammocks, we were woken by the sound of rhythmic drumming near by. We pulled on our sandals and raced out to investigate, discovering it was a Batak tribal celebration called Manulangi. It seemed to be entirely for the benefit of the village elders, who were flinging themselves around a longhouse like teenagers while a five-piece orchestra kept up a cacophonous rhythm with a row of drums, gongs and a long black wooden pipe that produced a sound like a bagpipe. Every so often the young drummer would grimace and let out a long, piercing wail; this, we were told, was to show everyone that he was happy, although he didn't look it. The festival continued into the following day, with the music becoming increasingly wild and pulsating and the dancers throwing their arms around each other's necks or wrapping dance scarves around their relatives as a sign of unity. In the dusty courtyard between the longhouses slender women in dazzling sarongs danced beneath the sun, balancing tall rush sacks of rice on their heads. In the afternoon there was a scene reminiscent of the Vietnam War film *Apocalypse Now*, when a young tribesman with bulging muscles calmly hacked the head off a buffalo with a machete then scooped out the brains. We were the only non-Bataks there, and after sharing a family's meal on a rush mat George and I were persuaded to join in the dancing, trying our best to keep time with the rhythm. But we both danced like a block of flats, so things soon descended into farce as we kicked off our sandals and pretended to kick each other in the chest to huge and undeserved applause. Dripping in sweat, we were invited to drink glasses of 'stoddy', a milky alcoholic brew made from coconut palms. 'You are now our brothers in the great Sidabutar family,' said the Bataks, and a number of mothers came up to suggest we might be interested in marrying their daughters. We declined, but not before rewarding them with a crumpled gift from London: a Prince Charles and Lady Diana commemorative engagement plastic bag, which induced big smiles all round. Back then, it never occurred to us that this was the last thing their unpolluted environment needed.

Our week on Lake Toba had been idyllic but it was time to move on. After buying our tickets for the ferry the next morning, I must have said something to upset the tough-looking young ticket-collector. Once he had collected all the stubs he came over to where we were sitting and prodded me in the chest. 'You like to take me on?' he asked. 'Yes? I take you on and I kill your banana.' I didn't like the sound of this one bit and apologized for whatever had upset him. Immediately he relaxed, sat down and shared his meal with us. It turned out that he, like us, was nineteen, and had just completed a year's training in the Indonesian martial art of Pencak Silat in Bandung on Java. 'For our final test,' he announced proudly, 'we must fight baby tiger in a pit. No problem. Now I looking for someone to practise on.' Discretion had certainly been the better part of valour here; we wished him luck in finding someone who might be itching to have their banana killed, but it was not us.

We were heading south for the lush central highlands of Sumatra and a volcano we had read about that sounded like a good climb. From the town of Padang Sidempuan we took a ten-hour night bus to Bukitinggi; there were no seats and the bus was thick with acrid cigarette smoke. There was also precious little to hold on to as the vehicle lurched from side to side on the pitted roads with only a sliver of room to pass if anything came in the opposite direction. To help the driver concentrate an in-built stereo system kept up a continual blast of Indonesian disco hits like 'You For Me, Baby!' George and I made ourselves as comfortable as we could by squatting on our rucksacks, but however I arranged myself a child kept kicking me softly in the kidneys in his sleep while an old woman coughed, dribbled and retched into a plastic bag just behind my ear. As we passed some dimly lit village in the small hours a toddler threw up spectacularly over his mother and the seat in front; the stench was appalling but the windows were jammed shut. On the stereo, 'You For Me, Baby!' was making a second pass. 'Gotta love travelling,' quipped George, who was more of a natural stoic than me.

When the bus finally ground to a halt shortly after dawn, in a terminal full of muddy puddles, we tracked down a fleapit and slept. Unfortunately, when we awoke we found it had lived up to its name, as a small yellow spider had dug itself into the flesh next to my hip. The few backpackers we had encountered in Sumatra had all heard the same no doubt apocryphal story about spiders: a woman goes on holiday to Java and returns with a painful red lump on her forehead which grows larger and larger. Eventually it erupts and hundreds of baby spiders spray all over her face. Right, I thought, let's not take any chances here, and I attacked the burrowing creature with a pair of tweezers, doing exactly what you are not supposed to do by leaving half of it buried in my skin. However, I seemed to suffer no ill effects and a few days later, now in a remote Sumatran village, we set out on what was to be one of the most intense days of my life and one which very nearly ended in disaster.

At six a.m. we rose to the smell of woodsmoke drifting across the hillside. Skeins of mist clung to the coffee groves beneath a sky of pure eggshell blue, and there was a freshness to the air that we knew would soon be gone. A knock on the door of our hut revealed a girl in a crisp white school uniform. She had padded silently up on sandalled feet and now she smiled shyly as she placed two glasses of steaming coffee on the earth, the thick sediment filling up nearly half the glass. She also brought a single toffee biscuit, which George and I fought briefly over before deciding to keep it for later. This turned out to be a blessing.

For a week now we had been living in the shadow of Gunung Merapi, a towering three-thousand-metre jungle-clad volcano – not the one in Java, but an obscure mountain in central Sumatra. It was usually swathed in cloud, its upper slopes remote and mysterious, appearing for a fleeting minute through a break in the clouds before vanishing again. Our Sumatran hosts in the village of Pariangan spoke of it with awe; when we announced we wanted to climb it they thought we were insane. But our youthful enthusiasm overrode any sense of caution. Our grasp of Bahasa was not as good as we thought. We understood that no European had ever climbed Gunung Merapi, but what were all these arm gestures about? Why were the villagers puffing out their cheeks, throwing up their arms and holding up three fingers? It did not make sense.

By eight o'clock that morning we were slogging up the mud track that led to Guguk, the last village before the jungle, striding through thick groves of bamboo. We were wearing long trousers for we had been warned about leeches, and we each carried a small rucksack containing water, a camera and insect repellent. We passed a woman bent double with a sack on her back. 'Do you realize,' remarked George philosophically, 'that you will never see that woman again, ever, in your entire life? Think about that.' George had a habit of saying things like that. A rustling in the bushes revealed a young villager who offered to be our guide. When he smiled it looked as if his whole mouth was bleeding, but it was just the crimson juice of the betel nut that everyone chewed here. With athletic leaps and bounds he skipped across streams and scrambled up grassy banks, leaving us gasping to keep up, so before long we told him we preferred to do this climb alone.

By now we had entered primary jungle, where the canopy was so high above us that it had never been cut down. Beneath our feet the path wound up steeply through dark, rotting, dripping vegetation. At times we had to duck beneath bunches of brown decaying ferns which hung from fallen logs, and once we saw a thirty-centimetre-long poisonous jungle millipede feeling its way over one of these dead logs. The jungle, we soon discovered, was crawling with life. Up in the canopy birds with gorgeous plumage swooped from bough to bough, and monkeys swung from the branches calling out to announce our presence. We had been warned there were savage wild pigs deep in the forest, with sharp tusks and a bad temperament.

It was not long before the leeches homed in on us. I had

always imagined jungle leeches to be fat and juicy, but in fact they are thin and unobtrusive. On sensing our foot-steps they would swiftly rear their thin black bodies, which were about three centimetres long, and with alarming speed they would slide over our boots in search of a way to access our skin. We had tucked the bottoms of our trousers into our socks, but the leeches soon found their way inside our boots and although they died in their quest – crushed between foot and boot – they left nasty-looking dark-red puncture marks.

After two hours of hiking up through the jungle we emerged into a strange world of blackened, motionless trees. So now it was clear. Twisted and scorched, these were the stark reminders that we were standing on an active volcano and the last eruption looked disturbingly recent. By now George's previously mild cough had developed into a bad cold and with the air being thinner up here he was having to breathe in short, constricted gasps. As we stumbled through this ravaged, burnt landscape, the going became so steep that we could only move forwards in dreamlike slow-motion. We wondered absently why nothing had grown up here since the last major eruption two years previously; we later learnt that in fact there had been another minor eruption just three months ago. We were walking on a tinderbox.

We now entered yet another landscape, a world of dead, broken trees covered in a powdery yellow sulphurous dust. Everything we touched was either covered in sulphur or grey volcanic ash; it was clear we were getting closer to the crater. To complete this eerie picture, we were now in the midst of the near permanent cloud bank that ringed the upper slopes, so visibility had dropped to just two hundred metres. As we moved through this silent world, twisted tree stumps loomed out of the grey void like creatures from a horror film, brushing their gnarled boughs through our hair and dropping dust on our boots. Nearing the summit, we felt as if we were approaching the end of a hunt for some fictional beast. A jabberwock, waiting crouching on a rock, would not have been out of place up here, watching us calmly as we blundered unwittingly into its lair.

The path had long since petered out, obscured by the litter of sulphurous debris that covered the steep sides of this final slope. The scree was so treacherous that we could only negotiate it by traversing slowly in zigzags. We were now breathless, as much from anticipation as exertion. Then at last, high up in the equatorial clouds, we reached the volcano's rim to see . . . nothing. Cloud and steam filled the crater and all we could hear was a subdued hiss coming from somewhere far below us. But then the cloud cleared and the full extent of the terrifying abyss was revealed. Hundreds of metres down below, in the pit of the crater, clefts in the rock spewed out clouds of hissing yellow gas at high pressure, making a strange muffled roar. The floor of the crater was flat, smooth and purple, streaked with leaf-vein patterns of rapidly cooled sulphur.

We had just begun to circle the volcano's rim when George cried out, 'Hold your breath! Don't breathe!' As he spoke, great billowing clouds of sulphurous gas rose up without warning and engulfed us for nearly a minute. It had us coughing, choking and on the point of vomiting. As we stumbled to get clear of the fumes, our eyes streaming, we had to be incredibly careful where we trod. In some places there were fissures in the ground releasing heat from the earth's mantle, so there were thirty-metre-long streaks in the rock where the boulders were glowing red hot. It dawned on us then that there was more than one crater up here. For two hours we moved around like automatons, exploring this extraordinary lunar plateau. It was hard to believe we were even on the same planet as Medan, Penang, Bangkok and all those other places we had travelled through that summer. There you could sit in a café, hear noises all around you, talk to people, eat food. Up here, we might as well have been on the surface of the moon.

That afternoon and evening were to be nothing short of an ordeal but we didn't know that yet and, oblivious to what was to come, we marvelled at the beauty of the craters. Some were wide and flat, cool enough to walk across and peer into the smouldering fissures, while others were dark caverns so deep you could not see the bottom, only stare at the surreal shapes made by the molten rock and scalded sulphur etched on the walls. In a moment of quiet contemplation we sat down on a rock and shared our only food, neatly breaking that toffee biscuit in half and savouring every crumb.

Enough, we decided finally. It was two p.m. – time to start moving down the mountainside if we were to get back to the village by nightfall. So, where exactly was the path? We could see the yellow scree where we had accessed the plateau but between us and that slope lay a precipitous ravine, too steep to cross. It began to rain. We may have been on the Equator but the temperature was a brisk 6°C and cold, biting rain began to fall from an upper layer of cloud thousands of metres above us. Within minutes we were soaked through. We shivered as a light wind picked up. In the mist that now swirled around us we had only a vague idea of our direction from George's compass, which was starting to fog up. George himself was in a bad way too, complaining that his cold was now turning into a fever.

For two hours we waded through thick, sodden bracken that concealed tree stumps and fallen branches, which tripped us up continually. With no path to follow we had to slide down one ridge then claw our way up the next, never able to see more than fifty metres in front of us, concentrating always on moving downhill. By four p.m. the undergrowth had become green and fertile once again. Great, we thought, we must be over the worst now. But after ninety minutes of forcing our way through dense tangled bamboo and prickly tree ferns, all at head height, we had covered only a few hundred metres. It was demoralizing work since everything we trod on was rotting and mushy, giving way with a crash whenever we put our weight on it but refusing to yield when it blocked our path.

'Oh my God!' shouted George. 'We've disturbed some kind of nest! They're all over me!' It was a hornets' nest and in blind terror we crashed headlong through the undergrowth to escape. Breathless, we reached a rocky stream. We seemed to have shaken off the enraged insects, although we could still hear them droning menacingly somewhere back up the slope. Incredibly, we had escaped without being stung. The steeply flowing stream would be our saviour, we reckoned, because we could now follow its course downhill. As we inched our way along it, our boots filling up with water, I joked, 'We're stuffed if there's a waterfall!' At this point the stream plunged down a picturesque twenty-metre sheer drop with absolutely no footholds on either side. We had no choice but to retrace our steps back up the slimy rocks of the stream, a task made only slightly more bearable by a fleeting glimpse of the distant orange sunset. Dusk was approaching. It had been hard enough to make headway through the dense, tropical undergrowth when we were going downhill, but trying to haul ourselves uphill when every bamboo spike, every prickly fern, every pointed branch seemed to be poking in our faces, was enough to sap what energy we had left. It was as if Nature was throwing as many obstacles in our way as possible to see how we would cope. Not very well, was the answer. George and I had both been fit and healthy when we set out on this Far East trip at the start of the summer holidays, but successive bouts of food poisoning in remote Sumatran villages had made us lose a lot of weight. George was now close to physical exhaustion and seeing double. His legs buckled under him as we crossed a treacherous rocky scree made slippery by the freezing rain, and he promptly skidded thirty metres down a rocky ravine on his back. That's it, I thought, we are now truly stuffed. How on earth do I carry my injured friend down this mountain, through pathless jungle, in the gathering gloom? But George still had some reserves, and his sense of humour. When he finally came to a stop he calmly got back up, did a little bow, and stumbled on. There were few other friends, I thought, whom I would rather be with on this madcap adventure than him.

Still struggling through tortuous undergrowth, we came to a crest from which we silently watched a strange ape bound away up the opposite slope. This, we were told days later, was a primate found nowhere else in the world: it had an orange, hairy coat and its nostrils were turned upwards instead of downwards. When chased – not something we were in any condition to do – it does not jump from tree to tree like most apes, but runs to the base of a tree and tries to hide itself amongst the bushes. But for us, that ape had a greater significance: it showed us the only way up the steep, charred slope of the final ridge we had to cross before we re-entered the jungle we had come through on our way up, hours earlier. Just before we latched on to the path the clouds parted below us, giving us a glimpse of distant Lake Singkarak, miles away in the fading purple light of the equatorial dusk.

We took the path down through the jungle at breakneck speed. The villagers had told us to beware of the jungle at night here, and they were afraid to enter it alone, perhaps because of the aggressive wild pigs. As we crashed through the forest a noisy group of bats began to flutter and whirr above our heads, as if determined to distract us. George was in pain and clearly suffering, but I had to force the pace. I was only just able to steer us through the undergrowth in the half-light, but once it was fully dark I feared we would quickly get lost again and the torch would be unlikely to help. When at last we emerged at the base of the jungle we thought we could relax, but now, in pitch darkness, we found ourselves marooned in a coffee grove surrounded by a dense, almost impenetrable thicket. In the tangle of indistinguishable foliage, the torch threw up such strong contrasts of light and dark that it only confused us more.

There was nothing for it but to charge bull-headed through the thicket in the dark; to lift our spirits briefly, we remembered the Elephant Man's instructions on Woodbury Common about 'blundering through the enemy lines'. It began to rain again and we were cold, drenched, tired and hungry; apart from half a toffee biscuit we had eaten nothing all day. It seemed to go on for ever, thicket after coffee grove after thicket. Even in the less dense coffee groves the low level of the branches made us bend double, only able to concentrate on the next tree in front. The one bit of useful kit we had remembered to bring was a pair of vacuum-packed thermal space blankets, and the prospect of wrapping ourselves in these and spending the night in the long, soaking grass began to seem a distinct probability. But then, oh joy, we stumbled back on to the track we had taken that morning and an aeon ago from the village of Guguk. It was another mile or more down the muddy path to the village, but it went past in a flash; it could have been ten times that and we would not have cared, we were so relieved at no longer being lost.

How strange it seemed suddenly to see human beings again, moving like ghosts behind lamplit windows set in smoky, fire-blackened thatched huts. We were back in Indonesia after our trip to the moon. The family at the first hut we came to was preparing to go to bed, but they offered us cold tea, then showed us the way down to our village of Pariangan. The people there had been staying up waiting for our return, and now they plied us with hot noodles, bananas and coffee. We were exhausted but happy, having climbed the volcano as we had set out to, stupidly ignoring all advice to take a guide. We could tell by the looks on the Indonesians' faces that we must have been a dreadful sight: our hands were lacerated and bleeding from grasping at so much bamboo, our fingers were numb with cold, our clothes were torn and covered in volcanic ash, and we reeked of sulphur. The villagers helped us pick out the crushed bodies of the leeches one by one from the soggy, foul-smelling mush inside our boots. And then, almost as if it were a final test of our patience or our sense of humour, an old man leant over, his black felt hat tilted towards us in the firelight, and, confusing his words, remarked in English, 'I think you are lazy. Yes, you are very lazy now.' We had been lucky to survive and we knew it. When we blew out the candle in our hut and sank into exhausted sleep we were probably both thinking the same thing: glad I did that, but never again.

George and I felt we could have stayed for ever in Pariangan village. Living amongst the kind, generous Minangkabau people in their curiously shaped houses with roofs that swept up into peaks like buffalo horns, we were under no pressure to move on. But we had heard of a distant, remote place called the Harau Valley, where a few Sumatran tigers still hunted in the jungle, so on a whim we decided to go there.

After allowing a day to recover from the volcano adventure and to let our hands heal, we set off down the mountain and hitched a lift south on the back of a grain truck. It took us several days to reach Harau; we stopped at a town called Batusangkar, where the sky was filled with giant fruit bats, and eventually rode into the valley on a truck piled high with quarry stones, savouring the sun and the wind on our faces. 'Do you realize,' shouted George into the wind, 'that we have just crossed the Equator?' So we had. We were now in the southern hemisphere for the first time in our lives.

The quarry truck dropped us at a *warung*, a roadside stall, leaving us suddenly in silence amidst the padi fields that sparkled and glittered in the afternoon sun. Peaceful-looking men came in from the fields to drink glasses of rich, grainy Sumatran coffee, enquiring politely where we had come from. Overhead the sheer five-hundred-foot walls of the canyon rose up from the valley floor, the tops of the cliffs wreathed in jungle. George and I looked at each other, nodded, then drank up our coffee, shouldered our rucksacks and set off on foot down the track through the valley.

At first we were surrounded by vivid-green paddy fields, where snow-white egrets stalked in the sun, but as we grew closer to Harau village the skies darkened. We made it to an open-sided thatched hut seconds before the heavens opened. I have always found something deeply comforting about being outdoors yet under shelter during a rainstorm. When I was ten, a friend and I built a tiny stone hut in the Hampshire woods and found a sheet of corrugated iron to lay across for a roof, which we covered with branches. Our hut had a window and we lined the floor with abandoned fence posts (we called it parquet flooring) so it was dry and cosy. When it started to rain we were ecstatically happy, peering out of the window at the raindrops flattening the bracken all around and watching a squirrel searching for shelter.

I felt the same way now, standing in the open doorway of a thatched hut on the other side of the world. This was a tropical downpour par excellence: thunder crashed overhead, lightning turned the valley pink, and the rain was so intense that it was impossible to see further than fifty yards. But our elation was short-lived. In a perfect world the rain would have stopped as abruptly as it began, the sun would have come out and birdsong would have filled the air. Did it hell. The rain continued for six hours solid, forcing us to splash the last mile into the village and hunt around for somewhere to sleep with water trickling down our backs.

Once again, the local Sumatrans were kind and hospitable, offering us a small, stone-floored room that belonged to the headman as they told us we were the first Europeans they had seen in years. That night we were invited to dine with the village elders, sitting cross-legged in a longhouse and dipping our right hands into bowls of steaming hot rice. The chilli dishes were volcanically hot and as tears sprang from my eyes I made the mistake of wiping my face with my hand, so, you've guessed it, I ended up with chilli in my eyes. Which I don't recommend.

In the morning we were introduced to Samsuar and Muhibbal, expert local trackers who had heard about our interest in seeing the jungle tigers. 'We must trek for about two miles over the hills,' they told us in a mixture of Bahasa and sign language. 'You must be silent, you must be fit and alert. You must be able to climb trees and, most important . . .' they paused for effect, 'you must not wear anything with an artificial scent, like hair oil.' George and I were about the least likely two people on the planet to wear hair oil, but we did have clumping great heavy boots which Samsuar eyed with disapproval. 'You must follow my instructions,' he continued. 'Listen, I will tell you why. Three years ago a man-eater – yes, a man-eater – killed a villager near here. We do not think he is still around these parts, but the tiger we hope to see is a mother with two male cubs and she can be unpredictable. Can you shoot straight?' George, who despite nearly two months in the tropics had managed to retain an English winter pallor, now went even paler. 'Do not fear,' said Muhibbal. 'It is only a precaution. We will most likely be up in the trees and there will be no danger, but to be safe we will carry an M16 for protection. Besides, the tiger is always asleep at three o'clock in the afternoon when we will be there.'

Samsuar then showed us around his village, starting with the *mandi*, the washing place, where cool mountain spring water splashed out from a bamboo pipe in the ground and where a large spider was hard at work paralysing a captured dragonfly. A lithe forty-eight-year-old, Samsuar was proud of having fathered eleven healthy children; by local standards he was a wealthy man, with a well-fed white cow, numerous chickens, a chilli patch, coconut palms, banana and orange groves and a small coffee plantation. He gave us an impromptu demonstration of coconut culling, kicking off his flip-flops and fearlessly shinning up a seventy-foot coconut palm by pressing the soles of his feet flat against the trunk and reaching around it with his arms. He then lopped off two huge ripe coconuts with his machete, sending them crashing to the ground.

Two hours later, sated on rice and coconut flesh and led by Samsuar, we set off for the tiger caves, winding our way up the forested side of the canyon to emerge on to a forested plateau hundreds of feet above the fertile valley. George was having a terrible time trying to suppress his cough, but we both rather liked the idea of creeping through the jungle with an M16 assault rifle. We felt sure that Elephant Man would be proud of us.

Suddenly Samsuar froze up ahead and held up his hand, then his shoulders slumped in despair. The mission was off. Deep in this remote forest we had run into a pair of loin-clothed Sumatrans sawing down trees and cutting them into planks. A manual task without machinery or chainsaws, it was nevertheless noisy enough to kill off any hope of seeing the tigers. By incredible bad luck, the men had only just decided to start work here this morning, just five hundred yards from the tigers' lair. To rub salt in our wounds, they told our guide Muhibbal in great detail how they had peered over the ledge into one of the forest caves just two hours ago and the tiger had reared up and snarled at them. 'She is over nine feet long!' they exclaimed. Great. But Samsuar saw our despondent expressions and suggested we press on to the caves anyway.

Huge, dark and foreboding, these were formed by several giant boulders measuring about thirty feet in diameter, piled naturally around the jungle floor. Some protruded singly from the leaf mould underfoot, while others were jumbled one on top of each other, as if dropped there by a playful giant, giving rise to natural passageways leading many feet below ground level. The atmosphere was hauntingly eerie and dank, with twisting creepers drooping down over the cave entrances; the walls were covered in slime, and bats whizzed noiselessly around our heads in the semi gloom.

Now Samsuar was showing us an earthy scrape beneath an overhanging ledge where the tiger cubs had been playing that morning. Scuffs of fur lay scattered around and there were spoor marks clearly visible. 'Look here,' he gestured, indicating a small patch of rock that had been scraped white by persistent rubbing, marked with shallow grooves. This, he explained, was where the mother had been sharpening her fangs over the last few months.

'OK,' said Muhibbal quietly, 'I have an idea. I know where her second lair is, but we must go quietly.' Samsuar, I noticed, had unsheathed his long machete, a sight I found far from comforting; this was the tigers' territory and perhaps we had no business encroaching on it.

'Bad news,' said Samsuar, shining his torch on the damp earth, where we could clearly see the fresh imprints of a tiger's paw. 'These are only one hour old at most, but she is running – see the spacing.' Our tiger had clearly been spooked by those two woodcutters and had taken her cubs even deeper into the jungle.

For the next hour we moved gingerly around more caves, probing the silent, dripping darkness with a torch, but there were over a thousand of these potential lairs hidden away in this part of the forest and we searched in vain. Samuar sat down on a damp, moss-covered rock, fished into his breast pocket and lit up a Gudang Garam, an Indonesian clove-flavoured cigarette. 'We have only one more chance to show you the tiger,' he said, blowing smoke rings up at the roof of the empty cave. 'She will return tonight after those men finish work, so we must come early tomorrow, before dawn, before she runs.'

Years later and with the benefit of hindsight, I can see that this smacked of harassment. Sumatra's vanishing tigers were already on the retreat from encroaching villages and timber merchants, so the last thing this little family needed was a pair of Europeans and their guides blundering around their lair. But of course at nineteen we didn't see things like that. We desperately wanted to see a Sumatran tiger in the wild, and if that meant getting up in the middle of the night that was fine by us.

In the grey light of a mountain dawn, Samsuar, George and I slipped from the sleeping village along the path that led across the valley. We had not gone far when Samsuar stopped abruptly by a thicket and began making *pssht* noises, as if to scare something away. Neither George nor I had seen or heard anything, yet, incredibly to us, Samsuar had detected by scent that there was a wild boar in there, a menace to the village crops. As we climbed up through the jungle, we were already sweating. When we paused to rest on a boulder halfway up the seven-hundred-foot slope, peering down through the foliage at the silent valley draped in mist, we felt as if we were the only three people awake in the world.

We moved on and now Samsuar called for absolute silence, gesturing for us to stick close behind him and for me to have my camera at the ready. Just ten yards from a ledge overlooking the she-tiger's lair Samsuar stopped suddenly and we all heard it: the just audible sound of a large, heavy creature padding swiftly through the under-growth. We had absolute trust in Samsuar, who the villagers had told us was the most experienced tiger tracker in West Sumatra, so now we followed him step by step, inch by inch, into the murky gloom of the tiger's lair. I glanced at George, who looked as if he was about to give birth with all the contortions he was going through to stifle his cough with a snot-soaked handkerchief. But the mother tiger was cunning: she had chosen a lair with an escape tunnel leading out the back into the jungle, and Samsuar told us just what we did not want to hear: 'We have missed her by less than five minutes.' There were tantalizing signs everywhere: fresh spoors and claw marks, vicious scrapings and scratchings in the soil that revealed where her cubs had been playing that morning, and that pervasive, unforgettable smell of a really heavy animal.

By now the sun was well up and the jungle was alive with noise. Black monkeys had latched onto our presence and were squawking in the treetops, while brilliantly plumaged jungle birds flitted among the branches. We had come close to our goal, but it was time to admit defeat: we had failed in our quest to see a Sumatran tiger in the wild. Samsuar was more despondent than we were – he had so wanted to show us this giant of the forest that he had spent a lifetime tracking – but we were sanguine about our defeat: the tiger had outwitted us through her superior sense of hearing, smell, cunning, and ability to blend then vanish into the jungle. Although she had evaded us, it felt like a privilege to have even entered her world, thanks to the skills of our Sumatran host.

* * *

Back in Harau village there was a scene developing. Samsuar's wife and daughters were making that *pssht!* noise that people make to shoo away unwanted animals, but they had no idea how dangerous this one was. Samsuar had three identical dogs of a breed similar to a jackal, but this one, they said, was ill and they were trying to scare it away from the house. 'Ill' was an understatement. Neither George nor I had ever seen an animal die of rabies before, and the experience shook us to the core. The dog was standing perfectly still when first saliva began to pour from its jaws, then vomit. A villager chuckled and pointed to her stomach, as if we were dealing with a mild stomach upset here. The animal suddenly dropped to a crouch and began to shudder uncontrollably, yelping and moaning. The most terrifying thing about it were its eyes. They were neither fierce nor insane but consumed by sadness and pain. Past caring, it ignored the village women who were poking brooms at it and

Half-thatched 'Romah Batak' in hill village, Sumatra, 1981

laughing; instead, this dying animal's eyes seemed to be fixed on the middle distance. The dog then rolled over on to its side in the dirt, howling, clawing and biting the ground in agony while its body was seized with convulsions and blood and saliva dribbled from its mouth.

I was suddenly furious with the Indonesians for doing nothing. I'm not sure what incensed me more, their indifference to this dog's agony or their nonchalant attitude to the proximity of an extremely dangerous, infectious animal that could lunge forward and bite anyone at any moment. 'For Christ's sake, do something!' I yelled. 'It's ill,' they replied, grinning. 'Go and get a policeman!' we implored them. 'Tell him to bring his pistol and put this animal out of its pain.' 'Not possible,' came the reply. 'He has drunk too much whisky this morning.' 'Well, can we borrow his pistol and do the job for him?' 'Not allowed.' George and I were left with little choice: we rushed over to a pile of large rocks and hurled them down at the rabid dog's head – I don't believe I have ever put so much force into throwing anything – then we finished it off with a long-handled hoe. Afterwards we stood around panting in silence. We took no pride in this horrible task, in fact we both felt nauseous, it was just something we knew we had to do. There was contagious blood, vomit and faeces everywhere; we later learnt from the police that in the last month over eighty animals had died of rabies in this part of Sumatra, yet no one seemed to care. 'It's very dangerous,' we told them, and they would just smile and nod. We tried to explain that rabies does not simply appear from nowhere and there had to be another rabid animal at large that had bitten Samsuar's dog; only the day before we had seen the animal that now lay dead at our feet fighting with his other two pets. It was most definitely time to move on, since neither of us fancied being licked, bitten, scratched or mauled by any of Samsuar's rabid livestock, but it was sad to be parting on such a note. This village had been good to us, we had seen a wild and untouched part of Sumatra that was vanishing fast and I had come within a hair's breadth of realizing my dream of seeing a jungle tiger in the wild. But our parting image of Harau village will regrettably always be the one from that morning: of a policeman too drunk to take charge, while a dog turned mad with rabies lay dead beneath a cairn of blood-stained boulders, hurled by George and me.

5

Eastern Europe

Behind the Curtain

P RAGUE, IN THE WINTER OF 1983, WAS BITINGLY COLD. Muffled against the wind that blew down from the distant Tatra Mountains, I stood on the Charles Bridge that spanned the River Vltava and peered up at the baroque spires of the old city, wondering why there were no tourists here. A giant red Communist five-pointed star stood embedded on the opposite riverbank, looking deceptively festive. But when I brought out my camera I noticed nearby pedestrians discreetly crossing to the other side of the bridge; some even covered their faces surreptitiously by pretending to scratch their foreheads. Five years earlier a Bulgarian dissident, Georgi Markov, had been assassinated on London's Waterloo Bridge by having a poison pellet fired into his leg by a KGB-designed umbrella. This was the age of the Cold War and in 1980s Czechoslovakia nobody wanted to be on the files of the Secret Police, and they certainly did not want their photograph taken by a stranger. I realized I must have stood out when a man grabbed my arm in the doorway of a house in the old quarter, grinned wolfishly, then shook his head and hissed in German, '*Communist – nein!*', spitting theatrically on to the cobbles.

I had a few days' stopover on my bargain-basement Czechoslovak Airlines flight back to Cairo, where I was living, and I was exploring the winding baroque back-streets in the shadow of Hradčany Castle, where the pale winter sun lit up the creamy yellow- and pink-painted walls. Pigeons fluttered about the roofs and sparrows chattered from the old black wrought-iron lamps that protruded from the flaking walls. Many of the houses bore faded murals above their doorways. It was as if I had stumbled into another century, a world of medieval Central Europe. The rev of an engine brought me back to reality. A convoy of sleek black limousines was winding its way out of the castle gates, the red flags of the USSR fluttering from their bonnets and some rather well-fed Russians staring blankly out of the back windows.

In the 1980s the Cold War – between America and Western Europe on the one hand and the Soviet Union and Eastern Europe on the other – was very cold indeed. The two blocs loathed each other and the arms race was in full spate. In 1981 there had been a real fear in Whitehall that Moscow was about to launch a full-scale invasion of Poland to crush Lech Walensa's 'Solidarity' movement of Gdansk shipworkers. After all, the Soviets had brought in tanks to crush Hungary's uprising in 1956 and Czechoslovakia's in 1968. The 'Iron Curtain', the phrase used by Winston Churchill to describe the new frontier that divided capitalist, democratic Western Europe from the Communist East, was an actual physical barrier guarded by watchtowers, minefields, barbed wire, attack dogs on long leashes and electrified fences. Hundreds of East Germans had died trying to escape across into the West.

To visit an Iron Curtain country you needed a visa, which meant applying in advance from the relevant embassy in London, where your details were sent back to the Interior Ministry in Moscow, Budapest, or whatever the capital was, to be checked to see if there was a file on you. But for me, in my late teens and twenties, it was worth the effort. To cross into Eastern Europe was to enter a different world, a strange and sometimes sinister place of crimson Communist Party slogans on hoardings, of uniformed guards in fur caps, of muffled figures silhouetted in the gloom of a winter's afternoon. Compared to the West, which had raced into the technological age, Eastern Europe seemed, in some places, to have changed little since the end of the Second World War. East Berlin often smelt of cheap brown coal, neon street signs were rare, and some cities were so incredibly dark and drab that it felt as if daylight was fading hours earlier than it did in the West. Yet the Iron Curtain countries ignited my curiosity far more than our more familiar neighbours closer to home, so much so that during the 1980s I crossed into Eastern Europe ten times, mostly by train, which for some reason held a special thrill.

On that February afternoon in 1983, I glanced up at the leaden sky to see that it had suddenly darkened. A second later the air filled with swirling snow, visibility dropped and the baroque spires of Hradčany Castle on the opposite bank were obliterated by snowflakes, while the wind whipped up into icy blasts and the good citizens of Prague scurried along the pavements in search of shelter. At intervals a pair of Czech soldiers would loom out of the sudden snowstorm in their winter-issue fur caps and leather boots, their trenchcoats belted at the waist, gritting their teeth and grimacing at the wind, before vanishing silently into the gathering gloom. What better conditions could you ask for, I thought, in which to visit one of Prague's hidden attractions – the floating sauna of Slovanskí Ostrov, a traditional wood-fired sauna on an island in the River Vltava, which flowed through the heart of the Czech capital.

Outside the hut there were snow-covered logs stacked up against the walls, where burly men were stamping their boots to shake off the snow. I was disappointed to discover that the sauna was men-only, but I joined the queue inside for towels and flip-flops, stripped off and pushed my way into the stifling furnace room to take a seat on a pine-wood rack alongside twenty sweating Czechs. All around me were the strange trills of this Slavic language; I had never before heard so many consonants jammed together like a motorway pile-up. I mean, how on earth

was one supposed to pronounce '*Vrchlického*'? Or the local bohemian beer, '*Przdroj*'?

Inside the sauna every inch of the walls was covered in metal foil to reflect the heat, and in the middle of the room sat an antiquated stove, silently emanating a colossal heat. When I looked at the temperature gauge I did a double-take. In Britain it had only to reach 29°C for the tabloids to shout 'Phew! What a scorcher!' An uncomfortably hot day in Cairo might nudge 40 degrees. The world record, I recalled, was something like 59°C in India. But here in this snow-bound sauna in Prague I was sitting in a closed room in a staggering 90-degree heat. That was close to boiling point! At what stage, I wondered, did your blood start bubbling in your veins? With every intake of breath I felt the scalding air burn the inside of my nostrils, while the skin between my eyes stung continually. The Czechs seemed to be taking it all in their stride, calmly sitting around, joking and showing no sign of discomfort, but I was out of my depth here.

When I could stand the heat no longer and felt I was going to explode I got up off the wooden slats and stepped out into the winter afternoon, wearing nothing more than a towel round my waist. This was obviously all part of the sauna's shock treatment: judging by what everyone else was doing, you were now expected to discard your towel and plunge naked into the icy river, protected by an under-water stockade to prevent you from being swept downstream into the Bohemian wilderness. I was still so overheated that when I submerged myself in the wintry current it was a relief rather than a punishment, but I did find the nibbling fish a bit disturbing. The next bit seemed very strange indeed, yet it was exhilarating to lie stretched out on a wooden bench without a stitch of clothing on, letting my body cool down after that furnace heat, while gazing up at the darkening sky and feeling snowflakes alight on my skin like confetti. It is how I will always remember Prague.

Hegyeshalom border crossing on the Austro-Hungarian frontier, Boxing Day, December 1983. It was the Christmas holidays in my final year at university and I had accepted an invitation to spend New Year's Eve with a Hungarian girl I had met the year before in Budapest. I had met Zsófia at an open-air rock concert during a summer spent backpacking around the Carpathians with George, my travelling companion in Sumatra, and we had kept in touch by letter. 'Don't do anything foolish' was my mother's advice. After spending her own late twenties working as a diplomat at the British Legation in Budapest in the Stalinist era of the 1950s, she was suspicious of any contact with anyone from behind the Iron Curtain. Part of her suspected a honey trap, part of her was deeply envious of my visiting Hungary, a country she had grown to love. I had saved a bit of money by working in the university holidays at Liberty's, the Regent Street department store in London, earning £100 a week in the cloth sales depart-ment until a mate and I got the sack when we were overheard promoting a fine Hebridean tweed to shoppers as 'Genuine Welsh Beaver fibre'. But that seemed an age ago as I made my way eastwards by train across a wintry Europe. 'Passaport! Passaport!' snapped a voice in the corridor outside and I craned my head out of the window. A posse of Hungarian frontier guards was gathered on the platform as the Vienna–Budapest express slowed to a halt. They were all fur hats, high boots, belts and holsters. While one squad boarded the carriages and checked the passengers' passports, another worked its way along the length of the train, swinging long hammers beneath the wheels to check for stowaways. Ladders were fetched to search the roofs. I wondered idly if this was all for show; wouldn't stowaways be heading in the other direction?

Outside the window a watery sun broke through the fog; the frontier guards vanished and the train rolled slowly into Hungary. The wheels clicked rhythmically beneath me as we passed villages of low, yellow-walled cottages and bare orchards where women dressed all in black cycled slowly past onion-domed churches. Past the town of Györ, a squadron of Russian tanks stood strung out in a column in the cold, still air, their engines fuming, their muffled crews standing around smoking.

I was sharing my compartment with a Hungarian family who were on a mission to see how many homemade cakes they could cram into me; I had recently run a marathon back in England, and perhaps they thought I needed feeding up. 'Look!' cried the daughter, pointing out of the window as we rattled across a girder bridge. 'Duna!' I turned to see the magnificent sweep of the River Danube stretching away to the north and I felt a smile spreading across my face. There was the old town, Buda, on the left and there on the right was Pest, the more urban half of the capital. A cluster of historic buildings, the Vár, stood on a low hill, catching the last rays of the afternoon sun.

* * *

In the cavernous expanse of Budapest's Keleti station I helped the Hungarian family with their bags, embraced them in farewell, then greeted Zsófia, who had been as uncertain as I was that we would both show up. A thin, freckly girl with a quiet, intelligent manner, she was typical of so many young Hungarians: proud of their country and its history, fed up with living under Communism, and eager to make as much contact with the West as their system would allow. 'Please,' she said, thrusting a crumpled wad of what looked like cardboard stubs into my hand, 'your tickets for tram and Metro.' They had cost the equivalent of about six pence, which even my student grant could stretch to, but Zsófia refused to let me pay. I was full of news, chattering away for Britain, but it was only when we were on the Metro, standing swaying between one unpronounceable stop and another, that I realized I was the only person in the packed carriage to be talking; here, apparently, it was just not done. Riding up the steep escalator at our stop, surrounded by these silent, stolid Magyars, I felt as if I was visiting a mortuary. We emerged by the domed Parliament building to find the enigmatic baroque spires of the Vár silhouetted against a sinking sun. Together we strolled past fortresses of Central European architecture, stopping to squat by the icy waters of the Danube on a flight of secluded stone steps and watch the winter sunset turn the ripples yellow. It had taken me twenty-four hours to get here by train and I felt a lot further from London than the thousand miles I had travelled.

We ate dinner in Zsófia's family's cottage in a southern suburb of Budapest, a low-roofed cosy bungalow with well-tended pot plants in the window. Her mother bustled around me with plates of mutton, oversized chips, gherkins and *csipös*, a hot, spicy salami – the name, explained Zsófia, means literally 'it bites'. Her father poured me a huge glass of the local red wine from a bottle with no label and raised it with a grin. '*Egesegeray!*' he toasted me in Hungarian. '*Egesegeray!*' I replied. Cheers. Despite Zsófia's best efforts, this was almost the sum total of my Hungarian and her father spoke no English, yet somehow, as so often happens in these intimate family settings, this really did not matter. Zsófia's teenage brother Berti showed me his Rubik's cube, an item of national pride since Rubik was Hungarian. Berti could solve it in under two and a half minutes; I know because I timed him.

The next morning I woke to find Budapest shrouded in thick fog; visibility was down to a hundred yards at most. Outside the steamed-up windows of the cottage, dark silhouettes drifted mysteriously through the swirling mist. 'We must check you,' said Zsófia with an unexpected, new-found authority. 'What?' I replied. Was this some sort of Iron Curtain citizens' procedure for monitoring foreigners that I hadn't heard of? 'Yes,' said my host, already dressed in padded coat and gloves, 'we must register you with police. Otherwise big problem.'

Sure enough, my visa stated baldly that I had to register with the police within twenty-four hours or there would be 'consequences', but in vain we trudged from one police station to another, the truncheon-toting duty officers shaking their heads and waving us away. This, I must admit, was the less appealing part of visiting Eastern

Europe: wasting countless hours on needless bureaucracy. We would approach some suburban police station, push open the door to face a human bloodhound with ice-cold eyes who would tell us we needed to buy a form from the kiosk opposite. The man at the kiosk would say he didn't have any, so back in we would go. 'So you must go to the post office,' said the policeman. The post office was shut.

'I am tired of this,' said Zsófia, and indeed so was I; imagine having to live here, I thought. 'Come,' she said, brightening up, 'let us go and make lunch.' I thought this sounded promisingly suggestive but she turned out to mean just that. Lunch in the family cottage was a huge bowl of goulash washed down with more rough, red wine, followed by plates piled high with hot pancakes, some filled with nuts, others with a fresh lemon cheesecake cream. Hungarians, explained my hosts, have two jobs: an official state one, which paid a pittance, and another more lucrative black-market one, like driving a taxi or selling home-grown vegetables. Anyone who could had an allotment. Back on the tram, heading into town, Zsófia confided that she had hardly eaten anything because she had been too busy translating her father's jokes; we laughed and I bought her some chocolate.

Somehow I had managed to get myself invited to the British Ambassador's residence that evening; perhaps British backpackers were thin on the ground in Budapest in the winter of 1983. I certainly was not craving the company of my fellow Britons, but this was something I wanted to do in honour of my mother's two years here at the Embassy in those dark days of Stalinist repression.

As a light flurry of snowflakes drifted down on to Old

Buda, I pressed the bell on the enormous iron gate and waited. A maid opened the door and let me in, then an immaculately dressed servant appeared in a starched white jacket and took my coat. Nervously, I offered up the bottle of Tokaji wine I had brought, but he gave me a withering look as if to say, 'You've obviously never been to an Ambassador's house before, have you?' Surprisingly, I hadn't. In all those years growing up in The Hague I don't ever remember being taken along to the boss's residence.

'His Excellency' the Ambassador now greeted me affably and his wife made the introductions: several teenage girls were sprawled on the floor playing a card game. I fancied all of them at once and wanted very much to kick off my shoes and join them, but felt I should really take an interest in the grown-ups. 'You're something of a rarity,' said Peter, the Ambassador. 'There are hardly any Britons here in Hungary, just a couple of university lecturers. I think we've got two families here in all. Ah, I believe we're being summoned.' A gong had sounded and we filed into an ornate dining room dominated by a portrait of the Queen and a weeping willow in a wooden bucket. Put me next to Katie, I thought, go on, put me next to Katie. She was the eldest, the prettiest and the most interesting-looking daughter, but instead I was seated between the Ambassador's wife and a friend with fluffed-up hair. 'Oxford is just soooo boring,' she said by way of an opener, 'I'm studying zoology, you know.' 'Great,' I replied. 'What are you going to do with it when you graduate?' Goodness, I sounded like my parents already. 'Oh, nothing,' said Big Hair. 'I'm going to get into life and drugs and things.' I glanced up instinctively at the

Ambassador but his head was turned away diplomatically. 'I'm a Communist, you know,' she continued. 'Yup, that's me. You should really visit the Socialist Workers' Museum while you're here.' What a load of bollocks, I thought. There I was, staying in the suburbs of Budapest with an actual Hungarian family and they hadn't got a good word to say about Communism, yet here was this girl from Oxford who was out here staying in the lap of luxury, and she'd probably go home and tell everyone how wonderful life was for Hungarians under Communism.

A squeal from the Ambassador's cloakroom. 'Ooh, Mummy, you've *got* to leave this in here, she's bound to see it!' 'Darling, you know I can't. What would they think?' I looked up to see the Ambassador's youngest daughter brandishing a collection of *Private Eye*'s 'Dear Bill' stories. The Prime Minister, Margaret Thatcher, was coming to stay in three months' time, accompanied by her husband Dennis, so leaving a bumper issue of imaginary letters poking fun at their lives lying around would probably not have been the fastest track to promotion.

A clink of silver cutlery against bone china brought everyone's eyes back to the candlelit table, now piled with plates of roast duck and purple cabbage. Had I been to the sauna at the Gellöt baths beneath the Citadel, someone asked? 'Oh, Mummy, it stinks of sulphur there!' Was I learning Hungarian? It's really not so hard, you know. Yes and no, I replied; after three years of Arabic I found it a pretty impossible language with all those indistinguishable vowels.

Dinner over, we withdrew, Victorian-style, to a large but cosy drawing room and settled down on sofas around the crackling log fire. It seemed the right moment to ask if there were still wolves in this country. 'Oh, I should think so,' said the Ambassador. At which point, on cue, an eerie, blood-curdling howl erupted outside in the snowy night. 'Caspar! . . . Sorry, that's the dog.' He got up and opened a bottle from his special reserve, a Tokaji five-star (the more stars on the label, the finer the vintage is thought to be). 'There exists a vintage here,' he said, 'that I have yet to taste. It's called Tokaji Essenz, and is said to be so rare they only give it to dying emperors. Legend has it that they then jump up off their deathbed and rule Hungary for another twenty years. Drop, anyone?'

It was time to bow out of the Ambassador's dinner. With the snow still falling I left that tiny British outpost and staggered off to the bus station at Moskva Ter. For a student like me, public transport in Budapest was a boon: it cost just 1 forint (less than 2p) to go anywhere by Metro, 1 forint for the tram and 1½ for the bus. But which ticket to use? I tried to remember what Zsófia had told me: blue for bus – or was it tram? Hard to know, my head was swimming after all that Tokaji. But no one came to collect the tickets and I slumped contentedly into my seat as I headed for the darkened suburbs, happy to be staying not with other Britons but with my incomprehensible but ever-hospitable Hungarian family.

New Year's Eve in Budapest and you could feel it in the air. The city's usual drab grey uniform was now broken up by bright-pink hats and masks on sale at street corners, while down in the Metro stations even the gypsies were smiling, hawking their plastic kitsch with renewed fervour. But

Zsófia was troubled. 'We must act now,' she said, as if plotting a revolution. 'If we do not register you with the police it will be bad.' Ah yes, the police. I had conveniently forgotten about this registration business, but now it had returned to bother us like an old and unwelcome ailment. But Zsófia had a plan. She led me miles away to some tiny suburban police station, where the officer on duty at first refused outright to register me. Eventually a 'fine' of a hundred forints was agreed upon, which was of course a bribe in all but name. My documents were stamped with a flourish, then we were waved away; I was no longer an illegal immigrant trying to enter the Socialist People's Paradise. Zsófia lightened visibly and glanced at her watch. 'Quick!' she said. 'We just have time.' OK, I thought, I'm well up for this: a heavy-metal Hungarian rock concert. At midday.

Stamping our feet with cold, Zsófia, her friend Piros and I joined hundreds of other students in the queue to see Pandora's Box, who were apparently a household name in Hungary. Eastern Europe, I learnt later, has a deep affection for heavy-metal groups and Pandora's Box did not disappoint: the bearded lead singer, complete with denim jacket and boots, spent most of the concert with his back to us, banging his fist against his thigh as if deeply troubled by something he wasn't prepared to share with us. In one of his brief face-to-face encounters with the audience, he pointed out the tambourine he had just bought in neighbouring Czechoslovakia. The Czech who had sold it to him, he said (Zsófia translated for me between swigs from a shared beer bottle), had asked him if he wanted some of their new Russian missiles as well. 'No,' said

Bearded Thigh-Banger, 'and Hungary doesn't want them either!' A cheer erupted, then the band broke into a hugely popular song about Hungary's eleventh-century King Stephen, who was a national hero. We were all on our feet, clapping and cheering; somewhere up in the sweaty front row the red, white and green flag of Hungary waved frantically, devoid of the obligatory Communist red star. 'It was smuggled in under a coat!' shouted Zsófia into my ear above the music. Incapable of understanding one word of the lyrics, I could still feel the emotion of the moment. A girl next to me broke through the crowd to touch the flag, tears streaming down her face. I felt suddenly privileged to be there.

We headed back to the family's cottage in Soroksár for a traditional New Year's Eve lunch of sauerkraut, hot cheese straws and apple cakes, followed by an afternoon siesta, then we set out once more for the city centre. At the tram stop I caught sight of a vision of Old Hungary: an elderly man dressed all in black with a broad hat, a thick, florid moustache and trousers too long for him that were piled up around his calves. In his gnarled hands he gripped a faded old cello. He was no doubt off to some wild evening in the suburbs, I thought, and a big part of me wanted to go with him.

Zsófia and I surfaced from the Metro into a world gone mad. The whole centre of Budapest resounded to the deafening sound of party hooters, whistles and squeals. It seemed as if half the city was out on the streets, singing and blowing cardboard horns at each other, dressed in costumes and masks. I had experienced something similar as a teenager in Trafalgar Square one New Year's Eve when a friend and I had challenged each other to see how many policewomen we could kiss, but I had never expected a public party like this in an Iron Curtain capital. Covered in confetti, Zsófia and I bought witches' hats and paper whippersnappers to flick at everyone we passed. Few people took any notice of a corpse stretched out on the pavement, a drunken tramp who must have collapsed and hit his head, since a pool of blood was running into the gutter. A boy danced past and said, 'That's life.'

Trying not to think about the dead tramp, we moved on to a student party in a flat, where someone was playing the piano with their feet and we all broke off from dancing to drink Bull's Blood wine from our cupped hands. I found myself besieged by people wanting to know about life in the West, but I was much more interested in hearing their Hungarian jokes. 'Three men,' began a young student in a waistcoat, 'are travelling together in a railway carriage – a Hungarian, a Russian and an American. The American takes out a cigar, lights it, takes a few puffs then throws it out of the window. "What did you do that for?" demands the Russian in amazement. "Ah, don't worry, buddy," replies the American, "we've got masses of those in our country." The Russian then opens a bottle of vodka, takes a few swigs and throws the rest out of the window. "What the heck?" snorts the American. "Do not worry, comrade," replies the Russian, "we have plenty of that in our country." The train then passes through a long, dark tunnel and when they come out on the other side the Russian has vanished. "Where did he go?" asks the American. "Oh, do not worry," says the Hungarian, "we have plenty of those in our country!"'

I was starting to get the impression that the Hungarians did not much care for their Soviet allies. It had been twenty-seven years since Russian tanks rolled into Budapest and crushed the Hungarian Uprising – none of us had even been born then, yet even half-drunk, these students seemed to be more aware of world politics than most of us back home at university in Devon. 'We do not like Bush,' said one. 'Bush?' I asked. I had heard the name but could not quite place him; this was, after all, 1983. 'Yes. American Vice-President George Bush. We put out – how you say? – the red carpet for him when he came here this year. He spent twenty-eight hours in our country, then crossed into Austria and made a big speech against us. I think this is bad manners.'

Suddenly it was midnight and there were toasts with Georgian champagne, a rousing rendition of the

Hungarian national anthem and embracing all round. Amidst a chorus of '*Boldog Uj Évet!*' ('Happy New Year'), the politics were mercifully forgotten.

The next day, I summoned my best Hungarian to say my farewells. Zsófia's father, who had not uttered a word of English during my stay, advanced towards me, then abruptly came out with, 'Kiss me sport.' 'What?' I replied. 'Is OK. I translate,' interrupted Zsófia. 'My father is saying "*Kérsz még bort.*" It means "Would you like more wine?"' I presented the family with a pottery jug I had bought them and they gave me a packed lunch for the thousand-mile train journey back across Europe, then Zsófia and I rode on the tram into the centre of Budapest for the last time, squashed between army conscripts all returning to duty in their bristly greatcoats and fur-lined caps. It felt like the eve of the 1914 war.

I glanced at this girl who had invited me into her home and her life on the basis of a fleeting meeting at an open-air concert two summers before. Zsófia looked pale, delicate and even thinner than I remembered her – in fact she claimed that she had somehow lost 3 kg during my visit. As we walked through the streets to the station, past the sombre, bullet-pocked walls blasted by the uprising of '56, I wondered how long she would stay put in this country she loved yet whose regime she loathed.

I was still thinking about this as we kissed goodbye on the platform of that great, echoing railway terminal, with the slow train leaving for Ukraine and an express rattling in from Krakov. Within five years Zsófia was to meet a Swedish man who offered to take her away from that world and live with him in Sweden. Years later, she wrote to me from a frozen Scandinavian village, married now, a mother, and achingly homesick for Hungary. Did I ever think of those times, she asked, of drinking Bull's Blood wine with our hands? Of shouting our heads off at that heavy-metal concert? Of misty mornings in Old Buda? I did.

6

Transylvania

With Club 18–30

A MORE UNLIKELY COCKTAIL WOULD BE HARD TO FIND. Take a recent graduate in Arabic (me), a girl with a psychology degree from Plymouth Polytechnic (Carrie, my girlfriend at the time) and Tim, an officer cadet at the Royal Military Academy at Sandhurst who thought he was the modern incarnation of a nineteenth-century explorer, and send them to the Carpathian Mountains. In winter. On a Club 18–30 ski holiday.

It wasn't meant to be this way. I didn't suddenly wake up one morning, look in the mirror and decide my life would be incomplete unless I went on a Club 18–30 holiday to Romania. But in the winter of 1984 we were all fresh out of college and we fancied a ski holiday somewhere a little different, somewhere with a bit of character. Transylvania offered it in spades. Club 18–30, which even back then had acquired a reputation for booze-fuelled shagathons, was the only British tour company offering ski trips to Romania, so we went with them. Carrie and I both had our doubts about the wisdom of introducing Officer Cadet Tim to the delights of Club 18–30. Tim was a mature student of Arabic at Exeter University and despite being only in his late twenties he dressed like someone twice his age from a bygone era: tweedy green suits, polished brogues and a pipe. He was quite unique on campus – apart from anything, he was the only student I had ever met who wore a tie each day – and we nicknamed him Batterby after an imaginary explorer.

Romania was a new venture for both Batterby and Carrie, but not for me. Two years earlier I had spent a summer backpacking round the Carpathians with my friend George, drinking fantastically cheap, foamy beer at hillside restaurants, living off tiny grilled sausages probably made from some unspeakable entrail, and buying punnets of wild raspberries from the gypsies. I liked Romania, its friendly people, its cream-painted cottages, its cobbled backstreets and its countryside, where instead of combine harvesters we had seen farmers tossing hay into stooks, a practice that had died out in England over fifty years earlier. In fact, some villages appeared to have changed little since medieval times. So I had convinced Carrie and Batterby that this was a country worth visiting, even in winter. But now we were at Heathrow and already Batterby was complaining about the lack of single girls on the trip. 'If this is it,' he harrumphed, 'then I shall keep to my room and write dispatches.' The Tarom Romanian Airlines in-flight lunch was as dismal as expected, but Batterby quickly raised morale by firing a champagne cork at the roof of the plane during take-off, no doubt an imprisonable offence had this been post 9/11. He then wasted a small amount of cash and a large amount of time buying drinks for a girl who turned out to be the girlfriend of the rep at the resort. 'Down in flames, old chap' was his comment on returning to his seat.

We had left a grey, rainswept Britain behind for the depths of a Carpathian winter: Bucharest's Otopeni airport looked every bit the part. We touched down after dark on a runway covered in sheet ice, skidded slightly and recovered. Huge fir trees went past the window, laden with barrowloads of snow, and security guards crunched across the frozen ground with high boots and short sub-machine guns. I felt a tingle of excitement; this was not cosy Western Europe with its familiar institutions such as parliaments, democracy and a free press, this was the other side of the Iron Curtain. We were also far from the conventional ski resorts of the Alps; here in Eastern Europe the forests still harboured serious wildlife like bears and wolves.

Inside the airport terminal soldiers snapped to attention as a Soviet general swept past us with his entourage, all crimson insignia and hammer and sickles, then we were through Customs and into a coach. Out of Bucharest and up through the frozen Prahova Valley we drove, past dark, sinister pine forests that crowded right up to the roadside; unpronounceable names of villages were illuminated briefly in the headlights and vanished in the night. The lads started a singsong in the back.

Shortly before midnight we reached Sinaia, Romania's premier winter resort, once favoured by its ex-king Carol and his family, where a 'welcome meal' awaited us of coleslaw and stale, unleavened bread. 'Hell's teeth,' muttered Batterby, stuffing his pipe with tobacco, 'this promises to be a gastronomic tundra.' Matters were only relieved by several glasses of Hunters' Tea, a hot spicy clear punch.

'Excuse please,' said a voice behind us and we all turned. 'I am Igor, your driver.' Surely not. *Igor?* Was he serious? He was. Igor was a character, his dark, haunted face capped by a huge black woollen hat. 'It is better we go now,' he said, as if an unmentionable fate awaited anyone who didn't immediately hop aboard his ageing minibus. Igor revved the engine, drove us about a hundred yards, then deposited us outside a wooden chalet, its low roof jagged with icicles and with a log fire burning inside. The chalets had names that slipped easily off the tongue like Florilor, Carpiliş and Dubrava. 'My God, man,' announced Batterby rather obviously, 'we're in Transylvania.'

The morning dawned bright and blue, but Batterby was not happy. 'Confound it,' he spluttered, 'I've been moved out of my room and now I'm stranded with Chas and Kevin.' Chas and Kevin, who had come dressed for a disco, wore earrings, which the Romanians found quite curious. Batterby was dressed in plus-fours, which the Romanians also found quite curious. 'Remind me why we've come here,' he snorted. 'Because,' I replied half-truthfully, 'we were inspired by the snow-chalet video in Wham!'s "Last Christmas".' 'Never heard of them,' he retorted.

It was time for the ski assessment. Kitted out with boots and skis, we piled into a swaying cable car to ascend La

Furnica, at eight thousand feet the highest point around, where we were split into groups and allotted our ski instructors. Despite having just one week under my belt I was alarmed to be placed in the 'advanced' class under a man called Sorin, who liked to shout 'Tally Ho!' at the top of his voice. He bonded with Batterby immediately.

Back at the chalet, a ripple of excitement was coursing through the assembled punters; it was New Year's Eve and a poster had gone up showing some drunken lads above the caption 'CLUB 18–30. THE FUN GOES ON AND ON'. But outside in the snow the Romanians had their own traditional way of celebrating. Responding to a knock on the door, we opened it to reveal a dead fox's head on a stick, then a man struck up on an accordion while his friends began a song. 'No! No! No!' interrupted the rep. 'We don't want that bollocks here. Piss off!' I was mortified – this was the one bit of real Transylvanian culture we had seen and we had rudely shooed them away. What must they think of us? Batterby and I chased after them to try and make amends, but this only made matters worse. They took one look at him, crossed themselves and fled. It was the first time I had taken in his costume. 'Whoa, Tim!' I cried. 'What are you wearing?' Batterby had come prepared; he had kitted himself out in the full regalia: black silk-lined cape, white tie, monocle and fangs. A small rivulet of joke blood was even now dripping from his teeth. It didn't matter that Count Dracula had never worn a monocle, because Batterby looked the part and the Romanian villagers seemed genuinely afraid of him, hurriedly crossing to the other side of the street to avoid his path. Strangely, Batterby as Dracula looked very much at home out there in the darkened, snowbound village. He looked rather less so an hour later as we sat through a risqué Romanian floorshow beneath neon lights in some soulless Warsaw Pact hotel, having already drained the bottles of cheap Georgian champagne left out on the tables and moved on to the distinctly dodgy vodka. 'I've had enough of watching Magda and her G-string,' he announced. 'I think I might take a stroll outside.' He was back within seconds, complaining to anyone within earshot of the impossibly low temperature. 'Good God, man, it's thirty below out there. You'll never make it back alive.' Batterby seemed to live his entire life in a 1930s comic action book and we loved him for it.

Sinaia village on New Year's Day was quite magical. There was no sound except for the church bells and the soft plop of snow falling from branches outside the window. Then a curse from Batterby's room and shouts of 'Shut up, ya git!' from Kevin and Chas, who were clearly nursing monumental hangovers from the suspect vodka.

With the ski lifts closing early we packed in a few hours on the slopes, skiing above both the tree line and the clouds, then descended to a village café to drink camomile tea and cakes. The waiter came over to apologize. 'I am sorry for this,' he said with an awkward smile. 'Sorry for what?' we asked. 'For the cakes,' he continued. 'These no good. These Romanian cakes, made with bad ingredients. It is hard to find good cakes here. Not like in your country,' he added wistfully. We assured him that his cakes were just fine.

That evening Batterby, Carrie and I set out in the rep's

car for the neighbouring village of Predeal to experience 'the real Romania'. Dropped off in the dark, we crunched through the snow in minus 18 degrees and began to go down some steps, but when Carrie turned to ask me a question she faced not my head but my boots. I was wearing my father's wartime flying boots, which he had bought off an RAF pilot, and although they were lined with sheepskin to keep out the cold, the soles were completely grip-free. I had slipped so spectacularly on the icy step that I had flipped completely upside-down, and to this day I don't know how I didn't break my neck or crack my skull.

In Predeal I managed to track down a restaurant that I had visited two summers previously, a place of wild gypsy music and dancing on tables. We were not disappointed. Musicians with short-cropped beards and embroidered waistcoats played fiddles, cello and the cimbalom, a sort of percussion harpsichord much loved in the Carpathians. There were no other tourists, but lots of plum brandy and dancing and clapping. We caught the last train back at midnight as a blizzard began to envelop the valley. The other passengers wrapped themselves ever more tightly in their shawls as the wind howled through windows that would not shut, sending small flurries of snow into the compartment. 'We'll never make it,' croaked Batterby as a muffled woman hobbled past us, her headscarf stiff with frozen snow, and vanished into the gloom of the jolting railway carriage.

The next day it was still snowing hard, but after the luxury of a lie-in Batterby and I decided to brave the slopes. Up on the almost deserted summit there was a tearing wind driving icy blasts of snow, in fact it was a virtual white-out. Batterby was now sporting a pair of Biggles goggles as well as his plus-fours, although sadly no one else from the 18–30 group was up there to see him in his full glory. We could hardly hear each other above the roaring wind so we just gestured down the mountain and took off through the forest. It must have been about three o'clock in the afternoon when the trail passed through a particularly dark and eerie part of the woods, the sort of place that fairy tales are written about to scare children. Oh, and the light was fading too. I was concentrating on gliding down the track and not veering off into the trees, with Batterby clattering around somewhere behind me, when a large and ferocious animal leapt out at me from my right side, snarling and growling. I cried out in alarm and lashed out with my ski pole in self-defence, causing the creature to turn tail and vanish back into the forest. 'Did you see that?' I asked Batterby breathlessly as he caught up with me, both of us nearly falling over in excitement. 'Was that what I think it was?' 'No question about it, old chap,' answered Batterby, taking a swig from his hip flask as he read my thoughts. 'That was a wolf that went for you. Here, you'd better take a slug of this grog. God, man, you look like you need it.' I later discovered that there were over two thousand wolves and a thousand Carpathian bears still roaming wild in Romania. 'In harsh winters,' read one article, 'wolves have been known to come down into the villages and even attack humans.'

That night found Batterby, Carrie and me in Sinaia's town sauna, but we were not alone. A girl from the village was sitting cross-legged on the wooden slats, her slim figure still tanned from the summer, her breasts just covered by a diminutive towel. Floriana was dark, seductive and apparently flattered by Batterby's attentions – a perfect honey-trap, in fact, if he had had any NATO secrets worth betraying. Which he didn't. His spirits buoyed by finally finding a girl he could hit on, he dropped the whole Victorian-explorer persona and turned on the charm. They giggled, they flirted, there were jokes about peeking beneath the towel. 'Do you like fuck low?' she suddenly asked him, causing Batterby to do an immediate double-take. 'What? Here? Now?' he stammered. 'Yes. Folklore. Romanian folklore music,' she continued innocently. 'I send you some, you give me address in England.'

I have a very clear recollection of telling Batterby at this point that it would not be a good idea to give a girl in a Warsaw Pact country his military address at Sandhurst, but he would have none of it. He was smitten, or at least part of him was. Two weeks later he was being marched into the Commandant's office at Camberley and ordered, beneath the contemptuous gaze of the Regimental Sergeant-Major, to open a package that had arrived for him from Romania. Half a dozen harmless records of Romanian folk music led by The Timişoara Gypsy Ensemble spilled out on to the desk, but from that day on there was a permanent blot on Batterby's military career.

The next day was once again a virtual blizzard but we didn't care, we were headed for Castel Bran, otherwise known as Dracula's Castle. Dracula really did exist five centuries ago, though the vampire bit is, of course, all fantasy. His name in Romanian was 'Count Vlad the

Impaler', but he was also known by his nickname Dracula, meaning 'Son of the Devil'. Romanians say he got his reputation when he decapitated the corpses of an advance contingent of invading Turks that were lying on the battlefield, then stuck the heads on poles all around Bucharest. Even today, we were told, the expression '*Dute Dracul*' – 'Go to the Devil' – was a common insult in Romania.

Bundled into a Romania-Turist coach with steamed-up windows and intermittent wipers, we set off through the snowbound Prahova Valley, past tiny, basic villages where shepherds in tall woollen hats with drooping, walrus moustaches led their sheep through the snow. We pulled up outside the town of Braşov and peered up at a grim medieval fortress perched high up on a rock, beneath the darkening sky. A family jangled past us in a horse-drawn sleigh, muffled against the bitter cold, their faces a snapshot from a painting of a bygone era. It felt as if it could quite easily have been the year 1400.

Up in the castle we embarked on an afternoon of exploration; we had the place virtually to ourselves. Led by Batterby in bow tie and leather trenchcoat, we crept along passageways gripping a torch, occasionally stopping short as he exclaimed, 'Heavens, man, you'd better come and see this!' only to find that the shadows were playing tricks with his febrile imagination. To his great disappointment, the dungeon was locked. It was, though, a place of haunting nightmares, a twilight world of twisting spiral staircases, secret passageways, dusty icons and very old oak furniture. If ever Count Dracula was to have a lair in real life, we all felt, this was most definitely it.

* * *

It was time to go home. The bags were packed, the snow was cleared outside the chalet door and the assembled punters sat stolidly beneath the posters that resolutely proclaimed that corporate message: 'CLUB 18–30. THE FUN GOES ON AND ON'. Most of us had pulled on the first pieces of clothing we could find: jeans and pullovers or, in some people's cases, velour tracksuits. Batterby was dressed in his trademark green tweed suit, complete with pipe and bow tie. 'Standards, old chap,' he muttered. At this point his brow furrowed: his room mates Chas and Kevin were coming over to talk to him. 'You know what?' said Chas, his breath already bitter with the first beer of the day. 'We thought you was a real stuck-up pillock at first. But you know what? You're all right, you're one of us.' 'Good,' replied Batterby, lowering his crumpled, week-old copy of the *Daily Telegraph*, 'because I can assure you, dear fellow, that my opinion of you has not changed since the very first day.' Romania had been an unusual experience for everyone, but it was a wonder that a whole week had passed without anyone knocking dear Batterby to the floor.

Berliner frau tackling an ice cream, East Berlin, 1980

7

Istanbul

A Night in the Flower Passage

AFTER THAT WINTER IN TRANSYLVANIA, THE REST OF 1985 passed in a whirl. There was Bob Geldof's Band Aid, Live Aid, and getting to grips with my first proper job, which was not exactly what I had dreamt of: exporting perfumery to the Middle East from a tiny office off Regent Street. Having now finished my degree in Arabic and Islamic Studies, I was keen to use my Arabic, preferably in the Middle East, but was unsure how to go about it. Leaving it till the last minute to find a job, I had traipsed around various London offices, knocking on doors until I was offered a place by a firm that sent perfumes and chocolates to distributors in the Gulf. The company seemed to be in a perpetual state of financial crisis but it was my first taste of the business world and there was something strangely satisfying about seeing the making of a product through, from drawing board to factory production line to shop shelf – in this case, a gentlemen's aftershave in a black bottle shaped like a hand grenade. At the annual perfumery trade fair in Bologna I tried hard to look knowledgeable, but here I was in the presence of 'noses', experts who had devoted their lives to the study of fragrance. Although it provided me with the occasional chat-up line at parties back in London, there was no getting away from the fact this was an unfamiliar, effete world I had landed myself in.

Partly to compensate, I got myself commissioned into the Territorial Army, as a Platoon Commander with the Royal Green Jackets (since merged into a new regiment, the Rifles), an extremely fit infantry regiment with a reputation for fast marching and sharp shooting. Compared to the compulsory mobilization of TA soldiers to Iraq and Afghanistan in the 2000s this was tame, safe stuff, but it was still the Cold War and our battalion had a grisly NATO role known as 'the dripping woods scenario'. In the event of imminent war we were supposed to mobilize within thirty-six hours of the Queen's Order being signed and then deploy to a triangle of villages and woods close to the East German border, where we would wait to be doused with a sustained bombardment of chemical shells by the advancing forces of the Soviet Union's Third Guards Shock Army. Realistically, nobody expected us to be able to hold up the Russians for more than a few hours at best, but because we had to be ready to fight in an environment heavily contaminated by poison gas we needed to train exhaustively for nuclear, biological and chemical warfare.

On NATO exercises in Germany we would often have to dig trenches while wearing our full protective suits and respirators, with the sweat pouring off us and our masks fogging up. Once a year we would have to wait outside a small, round brick building at a training camp in Surrey, where an NCO in a gas mask or 'respirator' would beckon us in one by one, shut the door behind us, then set off a canister of CS tear gas that quickly filled the room with a grey, choking fug. It was supposed to give us confidence in our equipment, but the part I always hated was having to take off your respirator and call out your name, rank and number before putting it back on. However quickly you spoke you always caught a load of gas that burnt the back of your throat and stung your eyes. The first time I was tested I thought I had to keep my eyes open too and within seconds I was in agony; sometimes men bolted for the door and threw up violently outside.

To anyone not in the TA it must have sounded like a complete waste of time; in fact, to plenty of people in the regular Army it sounded like a complete waste of time. Back then, before TA soldiers got mobilized for live operations and started to be taken more seriously, they were often known as 'weekend warriors'. But as well as a vague patriotic notion that if the Cold War ever turned hot I wanted to be able to serve my country, I had a number of selfish motives for being in uniform. Quite apart from the money, which I badly needed, I loved the way it got me out into wild, wonderful country: great sweeping, treeless horizons in almost uninhabited uplands in Wales or Devon. The environment and the conditions we were training in were great levellers: the South London body-builder trudging along behind me may have had huge biceps and looked impressive in the drill-hall bar, I may have had a university degree to my name, someone else may have owned a flash car, but out here we were all equally cold, wet and tired. But we had a task to do, so we just got on with it as best we could. As an officer, I was expected to keep people inspired and motivated even when I was every bit as exhausted as them; it taught me a great deal about resilience, which was to come in extremely useful in later life.

By the time my first Company party or 'Smoker' came round, there was something approaching an esprit de corps in our platoon. In the Army, a Company consists of just over a hundred soldiers and every so often a Smoker would be organized, the kind of debauched social evening that would now be considered taboo, and not just because of the indoor smoking. The lads would sit in a circle round a makeshift stage in the drill hall, cradling cans of lager, while a naff comedian would tell dirty jokes into a microphone, eventually signing off with the words: 'Right, I know you 'aven't come 'ere to listen to me. 'Oo wants to see the ladies?' To huge cheers, a squaddie would press 'play' on a tinny cassette player, and to the sultry sound of Sade or Chris de Burgh a pair of strippers would totter on to the stage in glittery high heels.

Various deals would have been done on the sly before this started to stitch up certain individuals, and as a junior officer I was an obvious target. In exchange for a small bribe, members of a rival platoon had persuaded the girls to single me out for some public humiliation, and after peeling off their clothes beneath the neon lights the girls advanced, naked and suggestive, to where we were sitting. I had absolutely no intention of being dragged up on stage and at this point my platoon touchingly rallied round. Forming a protective circle around me, Boer War-style, they grabbed their unopened cans of lager, gave them a vigorous shake and hooked their fingers into the ring pulls, pointing them like aerosols at the approaching strippers. It wasn't warm in the drill hall and the girls paused to reconsider. 'It's not worth it,' the riflemen told them. 'Leave the boss alone or you'll get soaked in cold lager.' Evidently the rival platoon's bribe was too cheap because the strippers thought better of it and backed off to pick on some other victim.

By now Batterby was in the regular Army, having tired of three universities in succession, each time less than halfway through his degree course. He had finished at Sandhurst, though, and despite the black mark on his record for receiving Romanian folk songs from a girl behind the Iron Curtain, he was commissioned into the Royal Artillery. And he was bored. 'I need an adventure, old chap. I was thinking about Constantinople, what do you say?' 'You mean Istanbul?' I replied. 'Yes, quite, let's get Peregrine in on it.' We really did have a friend called Peregrine; he had studied Arabic with us at Exeter, and I had become friends with him when we shared a flat on our language year in Cairo. We had also done some travelling together in Tunisia and once hitchhiked from Cairo to Jerusalem. He jumped at the idea of a week in Istanbul.

For me, Turkey held a special attraction. At school one of the classrooms had had a poster of a giant red sun setting behind the minareted skyline of Istanbul while ferries plied the Bosphorus below. As a travel-hungry teenager it had summed up for me the romanticism and allure of the East and in my gap year I had made my way over to Istanbul by train, reading the final pages of *Midnight Express* as the slow train from Salonica pulled into Sirkeçi station. Istanbul had been everything I had hoped for – spice-laden bazaars, cobbled backstreets, sinuous belly-dancers stuffing handfuls of Turkish liras into their sequined bras – but still I had not seen nearly enough of the city.

Now I was heading back, sandwiched between two friends and scribbling in my diary as we waited for take-off: 'Turkey is beginning fifteen feet above the tarmac at Heathrow. Dimly perceived behind a curtain, a Turkish stewardess draws on her Balkan cigarette and breathes out, her eyelashes flickering to the ceiling and her lips puckering as if pronouncing some whispered intimacy.' Well, I could dream.

As we flew south-east, the crumpled folds of the Bulgarian hills slid past the window. Batterby rustled his unread newspaper, adjusted his straw hat and sank into a long and undeserved slumber. The ground paled perceptibly, turning from green to mottled brown, and suddenly we were sweeping in low over the Sea of Marmara, banking over the fishing boats and oil tankers, catching the sinking sun on the wingtips and coasting down to Atatürk airport.

Expecting pandemonium and a phalanx of jostling porters, we found only a bank of chrome carousels: the old Yesilköy airport of *Midnight Express* fame had been replaced by a squeaky new update. I had arranged a few free nights at a hotel in exchange for a write-up in a travel brochure and a chauffeur was there to meet us. As soon as he saw us he burst into laughter, pointing at Batterby and Peregrine's matching blazers and straw hats. 'Al Gaboon!' he kept giggling, which we eventually worked out to mean Al Capone. Batterby failed to see the joke.

As we inched across the Bosphorus Bridge from the European to the Asian side of the city, lights twinkled along the Asian shore and impatient hands tapped cigarette ash out of a hundred car windows. We eventually pulled up at the Khedive's Palace, perched on a hill fifteen miles from the centre, halfway between Istanbul and the shores of the Black Sea. It was built in the 1900s in an extravagant art-nouveau style, originally to house the Khedive of Egypt during the summer. The place looked like paradise to us, with its moonlit chestnut blossom and whitewashed lampstands, but we decided to eat in the only restaurant in the village, where the menu boasted of 'Roast Lamp', 'Greed Meat Rools' and, for dessert, 'Opple Compost'.

The next morning we breakfasted on the marble terrace of the Khedive's Palace, where costumed waiters scurried in and out of the dappled shade of an orchard and where the waters of the Bosphorus glittered beneath us like a rare sapphire, eclipsed at intervals by the huge form of a tanker sliding up the sound to the Black Sea. At this time of year, in May, the grassy slopes were bursting with flowers and the air carried that heady whiff of early summer. On the road outside the hotel, horse-drawn carriages were ferrying newly married couples up to a viewpoint, frequently intercepted by street pedlars who ran to block their path.

Generous bridegrooms, I noticed, paused to dispense hundred-lira notes; others ordered the horseman to speed up.

Batterby seemed oblivious to all this as he toyed with the well-thumbed pages of a Somerset Maugham novel while adjusting his bow tie; the hotel staff were giving him some dark looks since he had rung them after midnight the night before to see about getting his shirt ironed. Much to Batterby's amusement, Peregrine had spent the night in a nearby fleapit, since the deal I had struck with the travel agency did not extend to free accommodation for all three of us. We found him hot and flustered at the hotel bar; apparently as soon as his back was turned a porter had mistakenly sent his suitcase back to the airport and only a hurried phone call had spared it from being sent on to Damascus. I could not resist being annoyingly self-righteous about this. 'Well, what do you expect, bringing a suitcase to Istanbul?' I asked. 'Only my parents still use suitcases!' Batterby sprang to his defence, giving me a withering look and telling me, 'A chap's got to travel in style, dontcha know?' He left unspoken the inference that the diminutive rucksack I always travelled with was somehow letting standards slip.

Leaving Batterby to snooze off the effects of a liquid lunch, Peregrine and I wandered down to the waterfront to explore the city. As someone who shared my interest in the Middle East I found him great company, and whether it was Tunis, Alexandria or Jericho we were in, he often had me in fits of laughter with his dry, deadpan observations. He was a good Arabist, too, and although Turkey had long ago switched from the Arabic to the Roman alphabet, Peregrine was adept at spotting Arabic words concealed in Turkish sentences.

We had no idea where we were heading, which I often think, if you have more time than money, is one of the best ways to travel. We passed rows of crouching shoe-polishers with their trademark brass-plated boxes and assortment of waxes and unguents, then boarded a ferry to cross the Golden Horn, a crescent of water that curves up through the European half of the city. Bumping ashore at Eminönü, we spilled on to the dock with the crowd, weaved our way between bread-sellers, pigeons and gypsies, then cut up through the Egyptian spice bazaar to emerge, blinking, in the backstreets next to Sultanahmet Mosque. Six years earlier this had been hippy heaven, with every other doorway haunted by some cadaverous Western overlander, a roll-up pinched between his grubby fingers and an embroidered Kashmiri satchel draped over his shoulder. But now, with the mujahedin battling the Red Army in Afghanistan and Iran still digesting the Islamic Revolution, the overland hippy trail to Kathmandu had all but dried up and Istanbul's Sultanahmet was no longer the travellers' crossroads it once had been.

Sultanahmet Mosque, otherwise known as the Blue Mosque, was one of the most beautiful examples of Islamic architecture I had ever seen, but for Peregrine the experience was somewhat tarnished. Just as we were about to go in a seagull dumped its lunch on his head from some considerable height; he took it well, though.

Inside we fell into conversation with the muezzin, who spoke Arabic. Quickly, almost conspiratorially, he ushered us past the stream of tourists and into the Imam's tiny ground-floor office, embedded into the five-hundred-year-old walls of the mosque. After sipping sweet Turkish tea from tulip-shaped glasses we were invited to climb to the top of one of the mosque's six pencil-shaped minarets, which dominate the Istanbul skyline. One hundred and two steps later we emerged on to the roof of the city, our faces struck by a blast of wind that blew in off the Bosphorus. Directly below us lay the immaculate gardens of Sultanahmet, exploding into a riot of May blooms; beyond stood the Topkapi Palace and harem quarters of the former sultans, and beyond that lay the Golden Horn water-way, curving like a jewel-encrusted scimitar through the maze of backstreets and minarets that made up this historic city.

Ishakpasha
Caddesi,
Sultanahmet,
Istanbul,
May 1986

We returned to our hotel for the night – this time the Pera Palas, which featured in Agatha Christie's *Murder on the Orient Express* – to find Batterby, dressed as usual as a gentleman traveller of the 1930s, with a glass of whisky in his hand. 'Bit of a rumpus going on next door,' he said. We pushed through the double doors to find a banquet in full flow and were immediately waved to a table. A crowd of Turkish Airforce cadets and their sisters kindly shuffled up to make room for us, inviting us to join them in raising glasses of raki, the local aniseed drink, towards the chandeliers and toasting every-thing we could think of. Soon the girls were popping treacly sweets called Wazir's Fingers into our mouths and giggling at our attempts at Turkish. Suddenly a reverential hush descended as a popular female singer appeared in a shimmering sequinned dress. She tossed her dark hair back over her shoulders and raised her outstretched arms to the ceiling, as if imploring a lover, her voice trembling and ululating, captivating everyone in the room as she was showered with rose petals. This was every inch the Istanbul I had dreamt of.

The next morning we strolled down to the carpet bazaar, a wonderful warren of backstreet boutiques and hubble-bubble cafés. Beside a narrow doorway a sign said 'WELCOME TO THE 300-YEAR OLD CAĞALOĞLU TURKISH BATHS. COME AND FOLLOW IN THE FOOTSTEPS OF FLORENCE NIGHTINGALE AND THE KAISER OF GERMANY'. 'Well, when in Rome . . .' said Batterby, and in we went.

The smell as we walked in was unforgettable: a blend of sweat, soap and steam that rose up in great vaporous clouds, right up to the ancient vaulted ceiling dimly visible far above us. We swapped our clothes for diminutive white towels round our waists then awaited our turn for a massage on the slab. Our voices echoed eerily in this great chamber where men had been scrubbed down and pummelled since the time of King Charles II; this place was so steeped in history it had a hushed, almost reverential air to it.

Two large figures appeared, swaying slightly in the doorway, silhouetted against the steam, and pointed first at me then at Batterby. Escorting us, as if under guard, to the massage slab, they prepared what looked like pillows that oozed soap. This they applied roughly to our backs, necks, shoulders and legs. Then came the endurance part: the Turks ordered us to lie flat on our backs on the hard, cold slabs of marble and to cross our arms over our chests. They then seized our bent arms at the elbows and pushed down hard, causing our backbones to click in protest. 'I say, steady on, old chap,' protested Batterby, but the two masseurs grinned beneath their thick moustaches and redoubled their efforts; they did this for a living, I thought, they must manhandle dozens of lily-white tourists like us every day. A Turkish massage, I concluded later when all the bone-clicking was done, is one of those one-off experiences like bungee-jumping: everyone says you have to do it once in your life, but you never hear of anyone going back for seconds.

That afternoon I took off on my own to explore the wooden-walled backstreets of old Eminönü. Within minutes I was delightfully lost in the maze of cobbled alleyways and antique wooden houses that clung to the hillside like a flimsy house of cards. This, I told myself, was the Turkey I had come to see: brightly dressed old women in white veils sitting chatting beneath kaleidoscopic sails of washing, their patterned skirts billowing out over the doorsteps. Behind grimy windows, chocolate-smeared children beamed and waved. From round a corner charged a panting barrowman dragging toppling piles of plums and pimentos, and then, as suddenly as he had appeared, he was gone with a clatter of skewed wheels on broken cobbles. It was then that I was brought up short with a glimpse of a far less appealing Turkey. Up the street strode an itinerant gypsy with his performing bear, looking for anyone to pay it to dance; it was a miserable sight. The man, shabbily dressed in an old and crumpled suit, was tugging at the bear, which he kept chained around its neck. Muzzled, chained, humiliated, it wore an expression of almost human melancholia.

Boyaci (shoe-shiner) in Kasimpasha district, Istanbul, May 1986

Being so close to the sea was making Peregrine restless. In Tunisia he had been happiest when we were nosing around the maritime quarter of Sfax (until we blundered into a very public brothel with a queue stretching round the block and we hightailed it in horror). In Egypt he had got a tailor to run him up a pair of white naval trousers, which he wore to impress the girl on the opposite balcony. Now he proposed that we set off for the Princes Islands, a chain of tiny, forested islands strung out in the Sea of Marmara opposite the Asian shore.

We spent so long trying – in vain – to persuade Batterby

to drag himself away from the city and come with us that we only made the boat with seconds to spare, in Tintinesque fashion. Hardly had we left port than a school of dolphins appeared alongside, bucking and plunging in the foaming water, before veering out of the path of an enormous Russian liner bound for Sevastopol in the Crimea.

We resisted the temptation to get off at the first few islands, delightful as they looked, waiting instead until we reached the last, named simply Büyükada – Big Island. The wonderful thing about this place, we soon discovered, was that it had no cars, only horses, carts and donkeys. It also did the best fish kebab I have ever tasted, brought sizzling to our table on the banks of the Sea of Marmara. Strolling up through the sleepy, leafy village after lunch, we were surprised by a brass band suddenly bursting into tune from behind a corner. Then, as if overcome by the heat, the music just petered out and everyone wandered off home, leaving the village once more to the incessant chirp of the cicadas.

Back at the hotel, we found Batterby in a sour mood. A glutton for punishment, he had gone for another massage, but it had nearly ended in disaster and now he was complaining of the cold, insisting he had had an entire one of his seven layers of skin scrubbed off him in the Turkish bath. The visit had gone badly from the start. He had asked someone in the street for directions to a hammam, and they had taken one look at his unusual clothing and sent him straight off to the Galataseray baths, assuming he was looking for intimate male company. He got through the massage intact, he said, but at the end all the burly masseurs had closed in on him to demand 'chips' (tips), eyeing the flimsy towel around his waist and growing increasingly impatient – and threatening – while he fumbled for change. Each time he produced more lira banknotes, he said, they shook their heads and shuffled closer. Having finally paid his way out of trouble, he was now sitting nursing a whisky and counting his losses.

Just then a woman approached us with a disarming smile. 'Have you been to the Flower Passage?' she enquired. 'Is this some sort of joke?' snorted Batterby. 'I've only just avoided having my own passage deflowered.' 'No! No! Is good!' she insisted. 'I take you there!' She introduced herself as Naciye (pronounced Narjeeya), then took us on a magical tour of the bohemian quarter of Istanbul, where the whole city seemed to have come alive in a single backstreet known as the Flower Passage. The place was jam-packed, both inside and outside the cafés, with children playing zithers to the accompaniment of drums while blind men clapped, unshaven gypsies raised their glasses of foaming beer and the smoke of a hundred grilling shish kebabs drifted like gunsmoke across the tables. Suddenly it felt thrilling to be in Turkey.

We followed Naciye upstairs to a raucous restaurant where half the clientele had abandoned their seats to dance to a violin and drum. In high spirits we feasted on a mezze entrée of deep-fried mussels on skewers, aubergine ratatouille, humous and ice-cold Doluca wine from Anatolia, then launched ourselves on to the dance floor, where Batterby kept adjusting his bow tie while Naciye did her best to teach him Turkish dancing.

Across the street, in a mirrored hall that spoke of grander times, we followed up with several plates of baklava, sticky Levantine pastry stuffed with almonds and pistachios then seeped in honey. The night was still young so we piled on to a nightclub on Hurriyet Street, drank more, danced more and somehow found ourselves careering round the darkened, empty streets at three a.m. in an old Chevrolet with a ropey cassette-player, driven by someone called Osman. I have no idea where we went – probably straight home. I only remember sticking my head out of the window into the warm night air and glimpsing a skyline of floodlit minarets and moonlight on the Bosphorus, before tumbling into bed in a cloud of Anatolian wine fumes.

Süleymaniye Mosque from the west,
Istanbul, May 1986

8

USSR

Minus-30 Moscow

IMAGINE A COLD SO INTENSE YOUR URINE FREEZES BEFORE IT hits the ground. In the winter of 1986/7 reports were coming in from Siberia of exactly that, of schoolchildren freezing to death on the walk home, of drunks found stiff as a board on benches in Gorky Park. It was, my girlfriend Carrie and I decided, the perfect time to visit Moscow, although admittedly neither of us fancied testing the urine theory. Carrie's job in a London advertising agency was probably more exciting than my new-found banking career in a City dealing room, but she still shared my twenty-something yearning to get as far away as possible from office life as soon as the holidays came round. She had put up admirably with Batterby's buffoonery in Romania the previous winter, but now the idea of a romantic break on the edge of Red Square rather appealed to her, and this time Batterby was not invited.

For my part, I had always wanted to visit Russia in the

depths of winter; at school I had studied Russian history, even learned some basic Russian and the Cyrillic alphabet, while the extraordinary ice-cream swirls of the sixteenth-century St Basil's Cathedral on Red Square had fascinated me even as a teenager. Now, though, history was on the move. There was a new leader in the Kremlin called Mikhail Gorbachev and he was trumpeting something called *glasnost* – openness. For decades this country had been so secretive that in neighbouring Poland they used to joke that the only way to find out if another Soviet leader had died was to look at the weather report and see if Moscow was 'minus 1'. But today the Soviet Union seemed to be on the cusp of change and we wanted to see it.

Since neither of us could afford a holiday I phoned the *Daily Telegraph* travel editor and got her to commission an article. 'Moscow in winter? I like it,' she said and put down the phone; it was that simple. Through a Regent Street travel agency I found us an all-in package for a few days: £210 for a return airfare on BA, with hotel, meals, visas and tour of the city sights with the infamous Intourist, the USSR's state-run travel organization which had a monopoly on all in-bound tourism.

So on the day after New Year's Day we flew east into a white, frozen world. Beneath us passed Baltic islands encrusted with ice, and then, three hours from London, we crossed into Soviet airspace over Riga. Within seconds a patrolling MiG fighter streaked past below the wing, leaving a trail of vapour. As dusk gathered, the bleak forests of Latvia came into view, stretching out to every horizon, a landscape of unending grimness broken only by the wriggle of a frozen river coiling away into the twilight. There was no discernible colour, only varying shades of grey; for once, I had brought the appropriate camera film: black and white.

At the spotlessly clean Sheremtyevo Airport, twelve miles north of Moscow, we stood in line while soldiers of the Border Guards Regiment inspected us and our passports. Using angled mirrors that allowed them to peer at the top of your head, they stared at each face for nearly a minute, as if willing you to break into a sweat, occasionally reaching for a telephone while never taking their eyes off the passenger under scrutiny. I watched several people's Adam's apples go up and down like yo-yos. And then we met Ludmila. Waiting for us behind Customs, she was our official Intourist guide: short, podgy and swathed in white furs, she exuded an unstoppable energy tinged with wit.

'So, welcome to the Soviet Union,' she barked into the microphone on the bus to the hotel. 'As you know, Russia is only one of fifteen autonomous Soviet Republics. As your guide, I am a very important person and if you do not like me – well, it is very difficult for you to get rid of me.' Several passengers exchanged knowing glances; she was probably speaking the truth here. 'You thought you were going to the Cosmos Hotel,' continued Ludmila without drawing breath, 'but in fact you will be accommodated in the Russiya Hotel. You will not grumble.' More glances, and one package tourist began to scribble in a notebook; his travel agent would be hearing about this later. 'The Russiya Hotel has six thousand rooms and is the main of the mainest. It has a very nice restaurant. Be sure to come in proper time for your meal or someone else will eat it. So. That is all.' With that, Ludmila was gone, alighting from the bus in a hiss of pneumatic doors and a swirl of furs, vanishing into the night like a character from an opera. I missed her already.

We had expected Russian food to be fairly spartan, so the desiccated chicken wings that landed on our plates that first night at the Russiya came as no surprise. But we didn't care, we abandoned dinner to push our way through the hotel's revolving doors and out into the night. The cold hit us like a hammer in the face; a thermometer on the wall read minus 27°C. Moving quickly to stay warm, we trudged through the streets to Moscow's most iconic landmark – Red Square – a thrilling sight at night with the fabulous snow-covered onion domes of St Basil's Cathedral rearing their convoluted whorls into the sub-zero air.

Red Square was vast, much bigger than we had expected, but it was surprisingly busy, with groups of muffled Russians huddling together on the cobbles, eyes narrowed against the cold, faces pinched and bloodless beneath fur hats tinged with frost. Beyond the crenellated walls of the Kremlin Palace a giant red flag hung illuminated by spotlights, its yellow hammer-and-sickle motif clearly visible against a backdrop of softly falling snow. Through the massive gates of the Kremlin the shadowy figures of the guards marched past, returning from some frozen duty. On the hour, every hour, the two-man guard on Lenin's Tomb was changed in an impressive display of precise military drill. At a slow, rhythmic gait the replacement guards would come goose-stepping out of the Spassky Tower, skilfully balancing their bayoneted rifles

Above left: On the Arctic Circle, near Rovaniemi, Finland, 1980.

Above right: My fellow 'acutely infectious' patients, Limodon Hospital, Thessalonika, Greece, 1980.

Right: Igorot tribesmen in Guinaang, Philippines, 1980.

Below: Ifugao woman near Banauwe, Philippines, 1980.

Above: Sketching in my journal, Samosir Island, Lake Toba, Sumatra, 1981.

Below: Pride before the fall: posing at the rim of Gunung Merape volcano, Sumatra, shortly before getting completely lost, 1981.

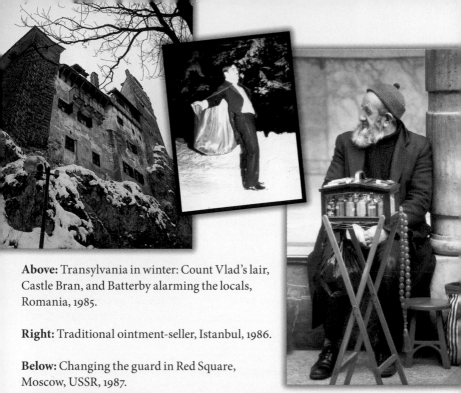

Above: Transylvania in winter: Count Vlad's lair, Castle Bran, and Batterby alarming the locals, Romania, 1985.

Right: Traditional ointment-seller, Istanbul, 1986.

Below: Changing the guard in Red Square, Moscow, USSR, 1987.

Above left: Esquipulas, Guatemala, 1988.

Above right: Guatemalan pilgrims at the Feast of the Black Christ, Esquipulas, 1988.

Below: Mass transit: travelling in Guatemala was certainly scenic if precarious, 1988.

The fabulous eighties Japanese guitarist in Yoyogi Park, Tokyo, 1989.

Something of a let-down: the 'Tokyo Tongue Bar', 1989.

Out on the town in Tokyo with John Donald (*left*) and friends, 1989.

Petra, 1989. A rare moment of reflection on the 'Boys' tour' of Jordan (I am second from right).

Xavier, our Quechua Indian boatman on the Rio Putuimi, Ecuadorian Amazon, 1990.

Toasting the jungle: with James Maughan in Quito before setting off for the Amazon, 1990.

↑ S.P. ATACAMA
C O Y O →

Hitch-hiking at 10,000 feet on the Chile–Bolivia border, 1990.

Left: In South America, a continent that enthralled me since childhood.

Above: Boatman on the idyllic Moucha Islands, Djibouti, 1994.

Left: The Rift Valley: French convoy heading north for a 'picnic militaire', Djibouti, 1994.

Above: White-water rafting with Amanda on the Zambezi River, Zimbabwe, 1994, before the incident with the shorts. I am second from left.

Right: My parents, Grace and Neil, in the Dolomites, Italy, 1993 – still mountain walking well into their seventies.

on the palms of their hands, holding them at the vertical with barely a waver as they negotiated the ice-covered cobbles. At the mausoleum the guard commander inspected his men, turned down the fur collars of the outgoing guards and ceremoniously turned up the collars of the new pair. It may have been all for show, but this was definitely what we had come to see.

'I don't believe it,' said Carrie the next morning. 'Someone must have rifled through my bag last night when we were out.' OK, we thought, so this was Cold War Russia, perhaps they were looking for subversive literature. 'Is anything missing?' I asked. 'Yes! But they must be desperate.' The cleaning lady, it transpired, had helped herself to certain feminine toiletries, which we supposed was hardly surprising in a country where women were said to use industrial wool during their periods. We turned our attentions to matters cultural. On a short trip like this, we had been warned, it was highly unlikely we would get our hands on tickets to the Bolshoi Ballet. Sure enough, the wax-faced harridan at the hotel's Intourist office greeted our request with a well-practised '*nyet*' – no, she said, they were all sold out. But I had read somewhere that you could get standby tickets at the National Hotel on Gorky Street, so we raced over there before breakfast. 'Yes. How many you want?' they said. Ballet tickets for foreigners were supposed to have leapt up that month from one pound to fifteen pounds each, but news had yet to reach the National Hotel. For the price of a coffee we bought two balcony tickets for the evening performance of Prokofiev's *Ivan the Terrible*.

Back at our hotel, Ludmila was clapping her hands in the lobby. 'It is time for tour. Please. To the bus quickly.' I have to say that a conducted coach tour is about as far from my idea of travelling as it is possible to get, but this time I was happy to go along since we had little time and much to see.

We began at a viewpoint across the frozen River Moskva, clambering out of the bus to gaze across the ice at the Kremlin walls, where Ivan the Great's sixteenth-century bell tower reared its golden dome beside the building of the Supreme Soviet. The bell tower, Ludmila informed us, was 250 feet high and was the tallest building in Moscow when it was built. 'Anyone caught making a higher construction lost their head,' she said with what I thought was a certain grim satisfaction. 'Now look please,' she continued, 'at the British Embassy. It has nice position on the river because Britain was one of first countries to recognize the Soviet State after 1917 revolution.'

The coach ground on, past Gosplan, an Orwellian monolith housing the State Planning Committee, midwife to all those unfulfilled five-year plans, and thence to some exquisite eighteenth-century mansions in Arbatskaya, all lemon-yellow-and-white friezes in the pale winter sun. 'As a special treat,' announced Ludmila, now warming to her task, 'and because I am such an incredibly nice person, I am extending this tour a little to show you the Novodevichy Convent – the New Maiden Convent.' If someone had asked me back in London if I would pay to spend my time going round a convent I suspect the answer would have been no. But this was worth every rouble. In a breathtakingly beautiful courtyard, white-frosted silver birches concealed old churches where once unloved tsarinas were banished into internal exile by their ruthless husbands.

We drove south, past the enormous Lenin Stadium that could house 103,000 spectators, to the grounds of Moscow University, perched on the Lenin Hills. One by one, many of the twentieth century's Kremlin leaders had been discredited and Russian school textbooks altered to de-idolize their names. Josef Stalin, Leon Trotsky and Nikita Khrushchev were no longer considered heroes of the Soviet Union, but the one name that still endured was that of the godfather of the 1917 Bolshevik Revolution: Vladimir Ilyich Lenin. There was an entire museum dedicated to his life and times, while his embalmed body lay in state in the mausoleum beneath the Kremlin walls on Red Square, where queues of patriotic citizens filed past in reverential silence. We got used to seeing and hearing his name several times a day.

Standing on the Lenin Hills above the capital, it was easy to concur that Moscow was experiencing one of its bitterest winters since the Second World War: today it was minus 30°C and the view across the city was obscured by a frosty haze. Behind us, young ski-jumpers clambered up a wooden tower to hurl themselves down a steep chute, vanishing against a wintry backdrop of sombre pine trees. Up on the observation terrace newly wed couples were posing for photos with glasses of Georgian champagne in their hands, the brides dressed in little more than they would wear on a summer's day in England. Russian women, we concluded, were impressively tough. Along the River Moskva solitary fishermen sat huddled over the holes they had cut in the ice, proving, said Ludmila, 'that we have no pollution in our river'. But the cold was too much for the wheezing Intourist tour bus and we broke down when the carburettor seized up.

Ludmila took advantage of the hiatus to feed us some more statistics. 'The USSR was the first country to establish free medical care and all operations are free,' she boomed. 'On retirement the State still pays out 70 per cent of everyone's salary without their ever having to contribute to a pension scheme. One month's vacation is obligatory every year.' She omitted to mention that all but a handful of Russians were forbidden to travel outside the countries of the Warsaw Pact, i.e. the USSR and its Eastern European allies, but she was in full flow now. 'The rent for flats in Moscow is unchanged since 1928. The two-bedroomed apartment I live in costs just 8–10 roubles (£8–10) per month. Families will be proud to tell you that they spend no more than 3.5 per cent of their family budget on rent.' The poor Russians; not even the all-knowing Ludmila could have predicted, on that chill winter's day in 1987, that four years later they would be catapulted out of their comfort zone as the Soviet Union and the whole State welfare system they had grown up with would disintegrate around them.

The Intourist bus coughed back to life and we ploughed on with the tour, pulling up at the headquarters of the Committee for Mutual Economic Assistance. Who dreams up these names, we wondered? 'I don't want to bore you with statistics,' chirped Ludmila, 'but 10 per cent of the world consists of socialist peoples yet they contribute one-third of the world's industrial output.' But by now no one was listening; lunch was the priority, and back at the Russiya Hotel we charged past the doorman to gorge on bowls of hot borscht and cheese blinis. Outside, Moscow smelt of diesel fumes and coal dust, exacerbated no doubt by the huge grey cloud of dirty smoke that came billowing out of a four-chimneyed factory across the river that still bore the revolutionary Communist slogan 'SLAVA TRUDU!', 'WORKERS ARE HEROES!' The smoke was drifting north, blotting out the weak winter sun, so that almost the entire area around Red Square was in permanent shadow. A long queue of patient Muscovites wound along Gorky Street, waiting to buy – what, Levis jeans? An imported computer? No, a consignment of Nefertiti oranges from Egypt.

We descended for the first time into the well-lit caverns of the Moscow Metro, where everything we had heard about it was true. The stations were spotless, beautifully designed and decorated with marble tiles and friezes, yet devoid of any advertising posters. They bore more resemblance to the interior of a palace than a transport hub. I thought back grimly to the wind-blown, litter-strewn Tube station at Clapham South.

Later we ducked into a restaurant, where raucous laughter erupted from a wedding party; they were all shouting '*Groika! Groika!*' at the newly married couple. Apparently it meant 'bitterness', something that needed to be sweetened with a kiss. As the couple obliged and their lips met their friends counted out aloud like referees at a boxing match.

It was time for the Bolshoi Ballet. Our seats, predictably, were up in the gods, in fact our heads very nearly touched the ceiling, but we still had a clear view of the superb choreography and constantly changing backdrops. It was a thrilling performance, and the plush red upholstery and massive chandelier formed a strangely opulent setting for so dramatic a ballet. In the interval the bar sold chilled vodka, smoked salmon and canapés of caviar from the distant Caspian Sea.

There must have been something funny in that vodka because the following morning I appeared to lose my mind. Along with two others from our group from England I got up before dawn and set off to run a complete circuit around the walls of the Kremlin before breakfast. In minus 30 degrees. Clad only in my father's 1950s vintage ski pants, a T-shirt and a sweatshirt, I was nearly knocked over by the cold when I stepped outside; the one sensible precaution I did take against the cold was to coat my ears in Nivea cream.

We were up before all but the early-shift civil servants, flashing their ID cards to the guards on the Kremlin gate towers, the crunch of their shoes on fresh snow echoing around the walls. The only other sound was the rasping scrape of the old babushkas shovelling snow off the pavements, enveloped by blue clouds of their own frosty breath. It was as if we had Moscow all to ourselves. We completed the circuit in under thirty minutes, stopping at last to catch our breath as our steaming bodies sagged against the rough bricks of the Nevsky Tower. The Kremlin guards eyed us with a mixture of consternation and suspicion, but did nothing.

After breakfast Carrie and I strolled down to Gorky

Park, where speed skaters swung down the frozen paths to bracing music that blared from tannoys. Dark silhouettes flitted through the trees, vanishing behind clouds of drifting steam seeping from a hot-air vent in the ground, while boys played ice hockey against the backdrop of Lenin's eight-foot-tall face. We walked over to Dzerzhinsky Square to take a look – from a discreet distance – at the headquarters of the KGB and the adjacent Lyubyanka jail, home to countless dissidents in their time. The blank exterior gave nothing away, but bizarrely, the headquarters of the USSR's feared secret police sat right next to a toyshop called Children's World.

It was time to go for a swim. Moscow's public swimming pool, not far from the Kremlin, was not perhaps an obvious draw in midwinter, but the Russians love their outdoor sports and here they had turned the weather to their advantage. Open to the elements yet heated, the pool created an extraordinary pocket of steam that melted the snow on the surrounding trees and lampposts, so that when it refroze they became encrusted with great globs of heavy ice. We bought our tickets for fifty kopeks, then got dispatched to separate male and female changing rooms. I changed under the continual gaze of a burly babushka, showered and tiptoed blindly down a steam-filled corridor until my feet touched water. This was the time to take a deep breath. The water was a balmy 27°C, but to reach the pool I had to swim under a flap into the bitingly cold air beyond. Suddenly I found myself beneath Moscow's grey, snow-laden skies with my freezing shoulders sticking out of the water. Only then did I realize why everyone wore a bathing cap: with your head unprotected, the water froze on your hair in an instant. The Russian bathers were a stoic bunch: not content with splashing around with just their heads above the water they were giving each other piggy-backs, lifting their near-naked bodies clear into the sub-zero air or clambering up on to the side and staging short races. The steam was so dense you could barely see the person next to you, which evidently suited courting Russian couples just fine. It was a thoroughly eerie experience, seeing heads looming out of the swirling mist then vanishing with a Slavic cry. By now I was mildly concerned that I could not locate Carrie. It later turned out that we had each been circling the pool clockwise looking for the other, so we didn't meet up again until we were back in the café, nursing steaming bowls of borscht.

In the days before the Channel Tunnel connected London's Victoria station to the rest of Europe, I always found train stations on the Continent irresistibly exciting. In Britain you could not take a train to another country – you had to fly or board a ferry across the Channel – but in Europe a whole world of destinations opened up from a single railway station. At times I have stood spellbound in Paris's Gare d'Austerlitz, staring up at a flickering timetable that announced the imminent departure of the express to Barcelona, Madrid or Lisbon. It always made me feel as if I was on the threshold of an unknown hinterland ready to be explored.

In Moscow I envisaged booted soldiers stamping their feet in the snow and muffled women fighting for seats on overnight trains to unpronounceable destinations. At the Kazansky station I was not disappointed. This was the terminus for the Trans-Siberian Railway and the departure point for all points east in the Soviet Union. Dozing Army officers in grey fur astrakhans were being woken for their trains by saluting privates, while the tannoy called everyone to attention with a constant stream of instructions. In the crowded departure hall men with high, Mongol cheekbones jostled through the crowd, wearing long, quilted black jackets bound round the waist with scarves of bright-blue silk. They seemed to be not just from another place but another time, belonging perhaps to the nineteenth-century world of the Great Game and the jostle for power in the vast steppes and deserts of Central Asia. Within four years, these men would no longer be Soviet citizens as the Muslim republics far to the east would win back their independence from Moscow, at least nominally so.

In the month before we flew to Moscow I had done something particularly geeky: I had bought a teach-yourself-Russian book, which contained stickers in Russian that I subsequently plastered over various household objects. I have to admit that I never actually needed to know the Russian for 'cupboard' while we were in Moscow, but I did need some basic phrases to get us around; taxi-drivers spoke no English at all in 1987.

That night we were heading for the Moscow State Circus, thirty minutes to the south, and I rustled up just enough Russian to get us there on time. The show opened with a couple of clowns going into the audience and picking on a stout, middle-aged, disgruntled-looking man and trying to get him to come down into the ring. He refused, but the clowns were persistent, tugging at the sleeve of his jacket in vain while he raised his voice in a stream of invective; people were not sure whether to be embarrassed or laugh. Suddenly the arm of his jacket ripped loudly then came off altogether. The man broke into a broad grin and somersaulted into the ring; he was, of course, all part of the act. For the next two hours the ring was filled with jugglers, tightrope-walkers, acrobats and trapeze artists, with each act accompanied by an infectious atmosphere of suspense and surprise. Few people there that night could have doubted the State Circus's proud boast to be the best in the world.

Our final act of tourism was to tour the Kremlin. As instructed by Ludmila the All-Knowing, we turned up at the Intourist office at the appointed time, but we were met with blank stares. 'Your guide has already left,' they said flatly. 'You will not catch up with her now. You must be here earlier.'

But we did catch up with the guide, a sulky and under-nourished individual who obstinately refused to talk to us until we had walked all the way to the starting point of the tour of the Armoury Chamber, which housed a unique collection of Imperial antiques and gems. She told us briskly to step aside as a group of drab-suited Communist Party officials swept past, all wearing little red badges, accompanied by a tall soldier with an unsheathed bayonet clipped to his belt. After climbing a broad flight of marble stairs, we were ushered into the Room of the Carriages. Tsarina Elizabeth I, we were told, never rode in the same carriage twice and during her reign she amassed no fewer than four thousand carriages. 'Hardly surprising,' muttered a tourist behind me, 'that they had a revolution after that.' Behind glass doors hung decorous frock coats of the nobility. Before the time of Peter the Great these coats used to have unnecessarily long sleeves, extending twelve inches beyond the wrist, so a popular expression was coined: to say that someone 'worked with long sleeves' meant they did no work at all. We passed Tartar helmets, strangely spiked and set above fur-trimmed shields and suffocating suits of chain mail. Peter the Great's boots were here, enormously long since he was six foot seven inches tall (and evidently fond of eating huge feasts then farting loudly before his guests). A hush then descended as we came to the priceless Fabergé eggs, each exquisitely crafted and inlaid with precious stones. The hinged top of one had been left open to reveal a perfect miniature model of the Winter Palace in Leningrad that measured just two inches across.

Coats, hats, scarves and gloves back on, we emerged into the snow to trudge past the House of the Supreme Soviet, then left into the courtyard below Ivan the Great's Bell Tower. Ivan ran up against a religious decree that forbade anyone who had more than three wives to walk up the steps to the adjacent church. He had eight wives, so he had a new set of steps built so he could get into the church by another route. We filed past the Czar Bell, a massive structure weighing over two hundred tons, which was said to have glowed red-hot during the Great Fire. Firemen tried to cool it by throwing buckets of cold water over it, causing a huge segment to crack and split off; it now lies quietly beside the rest of the bell. The Tsar Cannon was an equally impressive sight, so huge that it was never fired, but it served its purpose as a psychological weapon against

Moscow's enemies. At this point I noticed a wide open space adjoining the building where President Andrei Gromyko worked. The cobbles were lined with neat rows of the official black limousines of the Soviet leadership, and it was sobering to think of the momentous, world-shaping decisions being made in those well-guarded rooms.

Afterwards we went to GUM, the famous department store on Red Square, with its multi-tiered labyrinth of shops linked by passageways and narrow, wrought-iron bridges. Food here was cheap – 45p for a large tin of sardines – but clothing was surely way beyond the means of most Russian shoppers: over £50 for shoddily stitched dresses and jackets. The queues were serpentine and, like everywhere else in the Communist bloc, you had to queue twice: first to hand over your money in exchange for a receipt, then again to trade the receipt for the thing you were buying. It made me almost nostalgic to discover, twenty years later, that Argos still practises this Soviet-style system of shopping.

On the drive back out to the airport the next morning the bus was full of nodding heads, but my eyelids fluttered open when we passed three enormous X-shaped tank traps – placed beside the road, so Ludmila told us, to mark the spot where Hitler's army was turned back from the gates of Moscow by the terrible Russian winter of 1941. Over twenty million Russians died in the Second World War, a sacrifice which Russians still feel has never been sufficiently acknowledged by Britain and America, although Stalin killed just as many of his countrymen in his infamous purges.

At Sheremtyevo airport there was plenty of time to kill, so I cornered Ludmila to sound her out on what she really thought about her country. Looking back on it now that so much of Moscow has been transformed by oil wealth and capitalism into a glitzy world of customized four by fours, burly bodyguards and state-of-the-art nightclubs, those dreary days in the 1980s seem impossibly drab. Ludmila thought about my question and then surprised me with her honesty, saying, 'Nobody takes any notice of these rooftop slogans that say "Communism will be victorious!"' But she admitted that she preferred showing round groups of older Western tourists, who, she said, came with fewer hostile preconceptions about Russia. And what of Gorbachev's *glasnost* (openness) and *perestroika* (reconstruction), I asked? 'Yes, it is taking hold slowly, but against much opposition. There are powerful people here who do not want things to change.' Dissidents like Andrei Sakharov, who had returned from exile only the previous week, she hoped would now be allowed to criticize the Government openly. Then suddenly, as if remembering some longstanding order from on high, Ludmila reverted to type. 'You must know, of course, that pages three and four of our newspaper *Pravda* [Truth] have always, always carried sweeping criticisms of anything corrupt in the Government or the economy. We have freedom here, you see.'

As we shook hands and departed, almost friends, Ludmila dispatched us with a request. 'Please – for me – when you go home to England, tell your friends that Russia is not such a bad place after all.'

9

Honduras and Guatemala

The Feast of the Black Christ

IN SAN PEDRO, HONDURAS, I STARED AT A PAINTED MURAL on a whitewashed wall. Crudely and in vivid primary colours, it depicted two men having a gunfight: one man's revolver went 'Bang!' while the other's went 'Klik, Klik' and his face wore a look of despair. The wall belonged to a busy workshop that repaired guns. Customers got the message – they were streaming in. Welcome to Central America.

There had always been a certain something about Latin America – although certainly not the guns – that intrigued and excited me. After Moscow, Carrie and I had spent a holiday in America's south-west, renting a car and briefly driving south of the border into Mexico at Tijuana. In San Diego, where we had set out from, Tijuana had had a reputation for being a tacky, tawdry place, a stag-night pit-stop for young, partying Californians in search of cheap tequila and an uninhibited nightlife. 'So you're going down to Tijuana?' they would say with a knowing smirk. 'Well, you folks take care down there, don't know what you might get yourselves into.'

I found my pulse quickening the moment we caught sight of the green-uniformed Mexican border guards and the Spanish street signs, heard the lilting rhythm of salsa music and saw the Indian women with high cheekbones and psychedelic skirts hawking flimsy necklaces and plastic donkeys. It hit me then that this was the gateway to the Pan-American Highway, the road that stretched south all the way down through the Central American republics like El Salvador and Guatemala, past towns with names like Quetzaltenango, on through Panama and down the western spine of South America – practically all the way, in fact, to the southern tip of Chile and glacier country, just a short hop on the map from Antarctica. Knowing that was somehow a huge thrill.

At school one of my classmates had come from Honduras. 'What's the capital?' we used to ask him. We already knew the answer because we had asked him count-less times before, but we just liked to hear him say the name. 'Tegucigalpa' (pronounced Tay-goosey-gulper) he would reply with a grin, and I tried to imagine what it looked like.

Now, years later, on a wintry evening in New York, where I was working as a trainee investment banker, I strolled into my favourite bookshop just off Wall Street and picked up a guidebook to Honduras. I knew little about the country except that its economy was propped up by the United States to the tune of $250 million a year and it had so far escaped the crippling insurgencies that had plagued some of its Central American neighbours. The bookshop had a whole wall dedicated to Latin American destinations and I wanted to go to all of them, but I had to choose one. My banking course was finishing soon and I had two weeks' leave coming up before I returned to London and the humdrum buzz of a dealing room in the City. New York had been fun, but I was craving some adventure south of the US–Mexican border. Airfares were ridiculously cheap from New York – you could fly down to Puerto Rico in the Caribbean for the weekend for just $99 return. I made a half-hearted attempt to persuade some friends to come too, but for them a fortnight in Honduras just didn't cut it; they were either off skiing in New England or heading home to London. I was on my own for this one.

Flying into Tegucigalpa was like coming upon a city by accident. One moment the aircraft was banking over low, bare, volcanic hills, the next it had landed in a valley on what must surely have been one of the shortest runways in the Western hemisphere. I got out, queued up for Customs and caught a bus into town.

In the central plaza, flanked by a white colonial Spanish cathedral draped in bougainvillea, the banyan trees were alive with the chatter of roosting birds. In the shadow of their drooping branches a woman was fretting over a barbecue that was fuelling some indescribable sausage creation. The lottery-ticket-sellers, those indispensable pillars of Latin American society, were gathering up their pink, fluttering sheets from where they had pinned them to the paving stones with rocks. Men in white sombreros and cowboy boots lounged by the fountain, yawned, stretched,

La Iglesia Catedral, Tegucigalpa, Honduras

then got up and wandered away. You had to look carefully to see the gun-toting soldiers, quietly smoking beneath the trees. 'Honduras,' a US diplomat later told me, 'has something of a benevolent military.' I was soon to see this for myself. As the light faded I spotted some graffiti on a wall saying '*Fuera Contras y Gringos*', 'Go away, Contras and White Men'. Hmm. Perhaps this really was not such a good time to explore Tegucigalpa, especially as the place seemed to be emptying rather quickly.

Since it was now practically dark, I decided to return to the hostel the way I had come, but I had no sooner turned down a cobbled backstreet than I ran slap into a Honduran Army patrol, complete with machine gun, bandoliers, radios, antennae, the works. The patrol commander demanded to see my 'papers'. The fabled stiff-backed British black passport, now long since replaced by floppy Euro-maroon, seemed to have a positive effect that night; once it was established that I was neither a CIA spook nor an Israeli gun-runner, just a dumb English tourist who was blundering around Tegucigalpa on his own, I was welcomed warmly. Now that I was under their protection I must join them for a drink, they said. A drink? Really? What, with all these machine-gun belts and stuff? 'Yes, why not?' they said. It seemed churlish to refuse.

The patrol commander pushed his way through the saloon doors of a cavernous dance hall alive with salsa music and gyrating couples. This was about as far from the ordered and sequinned world of *Strictly Come Dancing* as it is possible to imagine. Everyone was drunk, yet moving with a natural rhythm and lithe sexuality devoid of any self-consciousness. The barman greeted the soldiers with a familiar shout and placed eight glasses of tequila on the bar; whether these men were on-duty or off seemed to make little difference, this was obviously their regular haunt. The soldiers responded by plonking the squad machine gun on the bar, the cartridges jostling for space with the tequila glasses; it seemed more of a statement than anything else.

The patrol radio crackled into life: someone back at base was demanding a Situation Report, but the men ignored it and called for more tequila. Luís, the patrol commander, asked if I wanted to dance. What, with him? 'No, stupid, with a woman!' he replied, turning to his troops and roaring with laughter. I looked across at the crowded dance floor. Everyone seemed to know all the steps perfectly, the men, in sombreros and cowboy boots, leading the women with a hand round their waists, their pelvises locked together as they moved in time to the music. A squat, smiling Hondureña with wide cheekbones suddenly appeared at my side and led me to the dance floor, where I did my best to keep up. I must have passed some kind of unwritten test because when I returned to the bar the patrol commander gave me a hearty whack on the back and toasted me with a glug. Come to think of it, he would probably have toasted a comatose iguana by this stage, but I took advantage of his bonhomie to ask for a military escort back to my hostel. 'Carlos! Suarez!' he shouted, and two of Honduras's finest fighting men put down their glasses and shouldered their M16s, and we tottered out into the night.

Fifteen minutes later I was thanking them profusely and trudging up to my room. I could not help noticing that when we came out of that salsa bar there had been a shifty-looking militiaman loitering on the street corner, still wearing his reflective aviator sunglasses even though it was well past midnight, along with jeans, leather jacket and casually slung machine gun.

Late morning in Tegucigalpa and I decided to head north by bus to Comayagua, the former colonial capital where a seventeenth-century cathedral housed one of the oldest clocks in the world. Built by the Moors for the Alhambra palace in Spain more than eight hundred years earlier, it was said still to keep perfect time. That month Comayagua was also housing 1,200 US servicemen, flown in from Texas to a base just outside town to deter any incursions by the Sandinista Army in Nicaragua. I was unaware at that point that the Americans had recently got into trouble in the town when they went out on the lash one night, and were now banned. So as I drifted round the marketplace and makeshift open-air casino, I was the object of a lot of curious attention: what was a lone Americano doing? Who cared? He must have money. '*Hola Gringo!*' squealed a drunken prostitute as she squeezed her way towards me between the gaming tables, and I rapidly took cover in a beef restaurant. I opened up my small canvas rucksack and unfolded my map to decide where to go next. Just off the Caribbean coast there was a string of islands with the attractive name of Las Islas de Bahia – the Bay Islands – and I resolved to visit them.

One hour north of Comayagua the jungle began abruptly. At one time the whole country had been covered in rainforest, but centuries of slash-and-burn agriculture had reduced much of the landscape to naked, cropless hills. At a roadside stop-point in the jungle, almost identical to the ones I had seen on the other side of the Pacific in the Philippines, the bus shuddered to a halt beside a kiosk and pandemonium broke out. Food was offered up like a sacrifice on long sticks, windows slid open, skinny hands emerged to grab packages and scarlet banknotes fluttered down. The shouting reached a peak and then, seconds later, it faded away as we set off once more on our way.

San Pedro Sula, the second city of Honduras, was the epitome of a Central American commercial capital: hot, humid, garishly colourful and chock-a-block with traffic and neon shop signs. 'Crocodil Discos' flashed above a music shop, next to 'McJean Shop' and 'Dunkin' Donuts'. In a market square couples were dancing merengue, an impossibly fast Afro-Latino rhythm that I could not hope to mimic. Here, so close to the Caribbean coast, I noticed, faces were darker, more African than Spanish; many people spoke English. Built on profits from the surrounding banana plantations, San Pedro was the fastest-developing city in Central America, which was why I wanted to leave it as quickly as possible. I spent the night in a ramshackle fleapit just up the coast, listening to the rain drumming on the corrugated-tin roof, which helped drown out the grunts and groans from what was almost certainly a bordello next door.

'Picturesque' would be a generous word to describe Utila Island's landing strip as the tiny four-seater Cessna circled above it the next morning. I had bought a ticket for next to nothing, flown out of a jungle airstrip and was now beginning to see why the ticket had been so cheap. The flight lasted about fifteen minutes and the destination was really just a rough track, pitted, furrowed and liberally sprinkled with rocks. We bounced, bumped and then came to an abrupt stop beside the carcass of an old DC3 cargo plane that looked as if it had leapt straight from the pages of a Tintin comic strip. It had shed most of its fuselage on to the grass, butterflies flitted in and out of the empty cockpit and a two-foot-long lizard basked on its broken wing. Already I liked this place.

Within an hour of landing I was settled in a hammock beneath a coconut palm, watching an emerald-green hummingbird as it hovered and probed amidst the hibiscus blooms. In the turquoise bay beyond, pelicans fished by soaring over the water then suddenly plummeting into the waves beak-first, to emerge gulping down their catch. Nothing stirred save for the gentle nodding of rocking chairs on white verandahs along the street.

That evening I got chatting to the owner of the local grocery store who, like most people on the island, was called Morgan. 'We is all descended from pirates, you see,' he said, fixing me with his rheumy eyes. 'I expect you'll have heard of Captain John Morgan? Well, he spent plenty time here. These islands were like a safe haven for his folk when they went raidin' the Spanish Main.'

Utila Island today seemed to me to be the most tranquil place in Latin America, but apparently there were all sorts of hazards lurking beneath the surface. A banana planter told me he had been stung by scorpions every day that week; someone shot the mayor in a land dispute; an Austrian drifter who lived on the island showed me where a shark had taken a lump out of his leg; and snorkelling one morning in the coral reefs, we were harassed

English Church on Utila Island, Bay Islands, Honduras, January 1988

continually by a large, mean-jawed barracuda. The island measured just seven miles across, but when I spent a day exploring it I still managed to get lost and run out of water, ending up drinking rainwater that had collected on plants and crashing home through a mangrove swamp in the moonlight. In that eerie, silvery light, my imagination turned every crab that scuttled past my feet into a tarantula, every beetle into a scorpion.

Within a day of leaving Honduras's Caribbean coast I reached the Mayan ruins of Copán on the Guatemalan border. Unlike the better-known sites on Mexico's Yucatán Peninsula, Copán was well off the beaten track, and hidden away as it was in the jungle and partially overrun by vegetation, I had the place to myself. The ancient temples exuded a strange, primeval aura, compounded by the drooping creepers, the raucous parrots that flew from the top of the jungle canopy and the swathes of cloud that clung to the surrounding hillsides.

I sat down to sketch some of the stone friezes. The Mayans, who were eventually overrun and subdued by the Spanish conquistadores, were incredibly advanced. Despite having no metal tools they were able to measure the stars, and invented their calendar and used the number zero a good thousand years before the Old World did so. Now facing me across the grass, their ruined pyramids were full of haunting faces, stone jaguars and grotesque smiling skulls, all carved in painstaking detail. I felt there was something sinister about this place too, though I could not quite put my finger on it. Perhaps I was having trouble blacking out thoughts of bloody ritual sacrifices with hearts being ripped out of living victims on altars, which we had read about in our O-level history class. The Mayans certainly loved their spectator sports: a millennium ago travellers had come for miles to stand where I was now, to witness one of the most famous spectacles in Central America: the Ball Court. Before thousands of spectators, the Mayan athletes at Copán had to bounce a solid rubber ball weighing 5 kg up the slanted walls of a stone enclosure. The aim was to hit the stone goals at the top fashioned as bird heads, using no hands, only their feet and bodies. Whoever let the ball touch the ground lost the game, but there was a sinister catch. Whoever scored the most points was the winner, a tremendous honour which unfortunately was rewarded by execution.

There is something uniquely thrilling about crossing a land border into a new country for the first time. I used to feel this way even as a child, crossing from Germany into Switzerland, or even from Holland into Belgium, two countries which looked pretty much the same to my seven-year-old eyes. Sitting in the back of the Hillman Hunter as we slowed down to hand over our passports, I always detected an infectious frisson from my parents, an intangible tension perhaps born of their previous diplomatic postings behind the Iron Curtain.

Now I was nearing another border, alone, grown-up and joyously in charge of my own destiny. At El Florído the Honduran–Guatemalan border was a token boundary – just a passport stamp in a tin shack humming with flies, then a splash across a muddy stream – but this time the contrast between the two countries was dramatic. Where

Honduras's villages had been neat and trim, with white-washed walls and gardens of bougainvillea, in Guatemala the first village I came to was distinguished by a half-starved mongrel worrying at a dead bird, a black sow snuffling through the garbage in the gutter and a tiny Indian woman bent double as she hoisted a massive bundle on to her back, screwing up her face and tottering down the hill on flat feet. A boy whose legs had long been wasted by polio limped past, an expression of pain and self-pity etched on his prematurely ageing face. The poverty hit you immediately.

I hitched a lift on the back of a pickup truck to the town of Chiquimula, jolting along with half a dozen home-going Guatemalans past tiny hamlets of palm-thatched huts, with chickens scratching in the dust and hammocks slung up alongside. There always seemed to be a mangy dog crossing the road, narrowly avoiding getting run over with inches to spare. We reached Chiquimula at dusk, just in time to catch the last of the day's market. An old man with a face like a Mayan carving (90 per cent of Guatemalans, I learnt, are ethnic Mayan Indians) insisted that I try some red, mushy fruit with a skin like a potato. '*Es delicioso*,' he assured me, but it looked disgusting and sure enough, to my taste it was.

The Fodor guide to Central America had mentioned 'the ever-present military in Guatemala' and now I was here I saw it for myself: the market square was liberally sprinkled with soldiers in jungle fatigues, continually climbing in and out of jeeps and fondling their Israeli-made assault rifles. Three burly paratroopers were guarding the Banco de Guatemala too; one of them, dressed in full combat kit, was carefully watering a pot plant in the foyer. But the Guatemalan military had a well-documented reputation for appalling human-rights abuses and I did not care to imagine what went on behind the walls of their fortified police station. The soldiers looked permanently ready for trouble, but when trouble did erupt they did nothing about it; neither did the police, who wore their revolver cartridges on the outside of their leather belts, sheriff-style.

One moment the market square was a picture of peaceful activity, the next everyone was sprinting to one corner to gawp at a street fight, with no one attempting to intervene. Before long the loser stumbled away, his face covered in blood from a knife slash, while the policemen studiously looked the other way. Someone, I felt certain, had been paid off.

The following day, the temperature topped 40°C. The heat came off the red earth in waves, making the cacti wobble in the haze. Beyond the cobbled backstreets men cantered through the dusty valley on horseback, dressed in spurs and sombreros and carrying three-foot machetes. This really was the epicentre of machismo, I concluded, noting that the women did not seem to have quite such a good deal as they padded past with bundles the size of washing machines on their heads. How did they cope in this heat, I wondered, with so many layers of clothes?

In the local cantina, which I quickly realized doubled as an all-day drinking den, I sat down at a formica-topped table and opened a bottle of Sol beer, tapping my feet subconsciously to the salsa music on the jukebox. A partially drunk Indian came over and sat with me; I noticed he was drinking something that looked and smelt like raw paraffin. '*Hola, amigo!*' he said, leering conspiratorially as if we were both members of some underground cult. He moved to clink glasses with me but missed by a mile, spilling his kerosene and laughing loudly. No one looked up – it was that kind of place. I was about to make my excuses and move on when he said something that caught my attention. Was I going to the Feast of the Black Christ? This sounded intriguing enough for me to buy my new-found pal a beer and ask him to tell me more.

Every year at this time, I learnt, thousands of pilgrims from all over Central America converged on a Guatemalan town called Esquipulas to celebrate and kiss the Black Christ. Apparently, four hundred years ago the Spanish colonists were finding it hard to convert the local Indians to Christianity, which was hardly surprising given that they associated a white Christ with the hated con-quistadores. But when a Mayan had a vision of a dark-skinned Christ, the Spanish ordered a statue of Christ to be carved out of dark wood. The Black Christ was believed to have miraculous healing powers and to have cured the Archbishop of Guatemala of blindness, helping to convert thousands to Christianity. It was a hit then, said my inebriated friend, and it was a hit now. 'You will not believe your eyes, señor.' But if I was going I would have to hurry to make it by 15 January, the climax of the festival. I thanked my informant, left him enough money to keep him drinking all day, and headed for the bus station.

Soon I was heading south, through a landscape of

parched earth, villages in a perpetual state of siesta, giant cacti and those ubiquitous men on horseback with machetes. Ten miles short of the El Salvador border I knew we had reached Esquipulas: people were streaming towards the great white colonial cathedral and the streets were seething with costumed Indians in patterned shawls and necklaces. I was stiff and sore after a cramped bus journey, during which five of us had been squashed up on a seat built for two, on a hairpin descent from a pass from which you could see three countries: Guatemala, Honduras and El Salvador. But I was immediately swept up in the colour and atmosphere of the festival. The air was thick with incense mixed with woodsmoke from cooking fires outside tents, while the sun bounced off the white walls and illuminated the Indians' dazzling jewellery.

The scene in the main square was hard to take in: pilgrims were crawling the last mile on their hands and knees, blindfolded, and dripping blood from their self-inflicted cuts and grazes on to the steps of the cathedral. I had never before witnessed such mass religious devotion outside the Muslim world. Riding high on the occasion, the whole town was a market, with stalls selling everything from leather saddles, Christian icons and Indian weaving to Taiwanese bras and posters of Samantha Fox, the last two actually side by side. In a bookshop an official pamphlet was on sale entitled *Información y Prevención sobre El Sida* – Information and Prevention against AIDS. Right next to it was a rather more popular publication, a cartoon paperback named *Desire*, which depicted a scantily clad woman with voluminous breasts being manhandled by several men. The AIDS pamphlet was not selling well.

Outside the cathedral a queue of several thousand had formed, waiting patiently for hours for their turn to kiss the Black Christ. I looked around to see if there was some kind of religious supremo directing all this mass devotion and was surprised to see three American priests. 'We're from Louisiana,' they drawled as they looked me up and down. 'So where y'all from?' They were busy dousing pilgrims with holy water, but their leader seemed happy to talk while he worked. Wrongly assuming that I was Roman Catholic, he shared what was troubling him. 'We've had a real problem with Protestant aid workers here,' he said, mopping his brow in the midday heat. 'They've been handing out contraceptives to these people and we can't have that, so my folks have been working hard to counter that message.' Whatever I might have been tempted to say was nipped in the bud by a blast from a nearby brass band. The mariachi musicians were in town, dressed like Mexican bandits in their black embroidered tunics and contour-hugging trousers. They played on late into the night at whoever threw them money, to the accompaniment of yelps of appreciation and the odd bottle being smashed drunkenly against a wall. The Feast of the Black Christ may have been a religious festival, but this was a town that loved a party. There was even a circus in town, patronized, it seemed, by prostitutes and off-duty policemen. At 30p a seat I reckoned it was worth a visit, but not everything went according to plan: the trained poodle that dutifully trotted into the arena on its hind legs suddenly made a beeline for a member of the audience and peed all over her leg. But the circus redeemed itself with its amazing motorcycle act. Two motorcyclists rode their machines into a large spherical cage, like the one in the Simpsons movie, and the door was closed behind them. Working up a speed, they then rode around and around the walls of the cage and upside-down along the ceiling, timing it to perfection so that each time they passed each other they avoided disaster by a split-second. It seemed to me to be a fitting metaphor for this whole region, where joy and suffering are often separated by the narrowest of margins.

Leaving Central America two days later, I met a home-bound New Yorker on the flight. I asked him if he had enjoyed Honduras. 'Are you kidding?' he replied. 'Forty-seven people died in San Pedro at New Year when they all fired their guns in the air and the bullets came back down to earth. People are crazy down there. Those guys just ain't playin' with a full deck of cards.'

Stone figurehead guarding the Jaguar Stairway of the Eastern Court, Copán Ruinas, Honduras, January 1988

10

Tokyo

One Weird Weekend

AFTER LIVING IN MANHATTAN THEN ROAMING AROUND
Central America, it felt distinctly strange to be returning to London. Everything about New York had been
larger than life: the skyscrapers, the look-at-me extra-
vagance of the Trump Plaza, the outrageous costumes of
the Halloween Gay Parade in Greenwich Village, the
telephone-number salaries on Wall Street, the casual
reporting of murders in Harlem and the Bronx. By
contrast, life in London seemed initially humdrum and
banal, and when my Territorial Army unit deployed to
Cyprus for a two-week exercise I welcomed the chance
to go too, splashing ashore at Akrotiri by landing craft at
night, flying along dried-up gullies in Puma helicopters,
then sweating up the sun-baked hills in the full heat of
August. One particular corporal was so solidly built he
was known as Spud (an unspoken rule dictates that every
battalion must have someone by this name), but Spud did

not take kindly to the heat of Cyprus. Eventually I tired of his continual whingeing and confronted him as he flung down his weapon in the dust. 'OK, Spud, that's it. If there's any more ticking from you I'm sending you back to camp and we'll get the stores corporal to replace you.' It was a calculated insult: the stores corporal was a famously fat knacker deemed unfit to carry any kit on exercise and about as unmilitary a figure as it was possible to find. Spud's eyes narrowed and I could almost hear his brain whirring as he decided how to respond: whether to thump the officer, or not to thump. After a few seconds he grunted, picked up his weapon and shouldered his kit.

Days later, back in camp, he came up to me. 'I don't think you realize, Captain Gardner sir, how fucking close I came to punching your lights out back there. But you got me off my arse and back with the platoon, so I owe you a drink. Cheers, sir.'

Loyalty can crop up in the strangest places, because on the final night's piss-up Spud came charging to my defence. We had had a couple of Paras attached to us for the duration of the exercise and when it came to standing up and singing rude songs these lads calmly started throwing their empty beer bottles at me and my fellow officers. 'Oi!' roared Spud. 'Wotchoo think yer doin?' The Paras paused in mid-hurl. A look of genuine bemusement crossed their faces. 'Wassit look like? We're throwing bottles at the officers. We always do that on the last night of camp. It's tradition, innit?' Spud squared up to them, his sixteen stone of brickie bulk shining with sweat in the humid Cyprus night, a trickle of blood rolling down his temple where he had recently smashed a light bulb on his forehead as part of some delinquent song. 'They may be Ruperts,' said Spud, using the squaddie slang for young officers, 'but they're our Ruperts and we don't like you throwing bottles at them. Understand?' The Paras backed off, shaking their heads in disbelief; clearly a regiment that didn't believe in bottling its officers was no fun at all.

Back in my civilian job in the City, life had settled into a familiar routine: markets had largely recovered from the turmoil of Black Monday the year before, colleagues were getting headhunted, leaving in triumph then getting made redundant as soon as business slowed down again. I had still not worked out what I wanted to do in life: I still liked the idea of becoming a full-time journalist, but I knew this would mean a serious drop in salary and like so many of my peers in the dealing room I was already hitched to a mortgage.

Determined to find some outlet for my writing, I rang my old schoolfriend John Donald who was living in Japan. 'Come to Tokyo and write it up,' he suggested. 'But I've used up all my holiday allowance,' I countered weakly; John could sense I was looking to be persuaded. 'Well, just come for the weekend then.' 'I can't afford it.' 'Yes you can, I'm paying for everything once you get here. But on one condition . . .' There was an ominous pause and I could tell that John was taking a long drag on his cigarette. 'You have to do everything I say for twenty-four hours. I mean *everything*.' John and I went back a fair way: we had sat the scholarship to Marlborough College together when we were twelve, spent five years there, then shared a shambolic house with other students at Exeter

University. Now he was living the lotus life in Tokyo as a market expert on the electronics sector, working for an investment bank and living in Roppongi, the heart of the city's party district. 'OK,' I replied, 'it's a deal.' I put down the phone and booked myself on an Aeroflot excursion flight for that weekend.

Dawn. With the glutinous taste of cheap Aeroflot caviar still in my mouth, I touched down at Narita airport in pouring rain. During ten hours of flying through the night across Arctic Siberia the sun had never set, and I had never slept.

'Welcome to Japan,' purred a strangely American accent over the tannoy. 'The quarantine rooms are situated on the left.'

The shuttle bus swept down the forty miles of expressway, past a grey vista of paddy fields and pylons, to Tokyo's Central Station. Inside it was organized pandemonium with a thousand men in suits – Japan's infamous 'salarymen' – rushing in all directions. I called John. 'How can you live here?' I asked him. 'Everyone dresses the same and they're all in a hurry. This does not look like a fun city.' 'Be patient,' he replied. 'Here are your first instructions: go get something to eat, then have a massage, and I'll join you as soon as I get out of the office.'

I headed to a twenty-four-hour stall that was serving skewered chicken and noodles. I had spent much of the flight swotting up from a Japanese phrasebook, in between watching the drunken Russian hockey team chat up the very large and rather masculine Aeroflot stewardesses. But now the two Japanese girls next to me in the noodle bar were in fits of giggles at my botched attempt to order tea. They took over the ordering for me and introduced themselves as 'life-insurance tele-saleswomen'. I pegged them for the Japanese equivalent of the dreaded cold-caller, but they were proud of their profession. Perhaps they could help me with my first mission: the Japanese massage. The girls led me to Tokyo Kur, an apparently popular health centre beneath the station. Was this going to be sordid, I wondered, as the two girls left me at the door, bowing and giggling, in a hurry to get back to phoning those punters.

I then committed my first major infringement of Japanese etiquette. Halfway to the ticket counter I got turned back with a scowl and was asked to remove my shoes. Right. Sorry. Won't happen again. For 5,000 Yen (about £25) I opted for the 'Silver Service' and got ushered through to the locker room, jostled by some of those same Japanese salarymen now busy changing into skin-tight polyester shorts. As the only foreigner in the place, I followed the crowd and headed straight for the sauna, where thirty flabby men were already sitting cross-legged watching television while the sweat poured off them. One old man had most of his body covered with violent blue tattoos of men fighting. I later learnt that this marked him out as a *yakuza*, a Japanese gangster.

Out of the sauna and face-down on to a slab, where I was doused with cold water. This was not fun, although I noticed it was being done to everyone else and no one was complaining. A middle-aged woman with a face fixed in a permanent grimace then set about me with a stiff sponge, scraping my skin from top to bottom. It felt like a close encounter with a Brillo pad, as I watched tiny grey flecks of dead skin float past me on the water-logged tiles.

Into the jacuzzi to recover and to wait for my number to be called. Roused from my jet-lagged torpor, I was escorted to the *shiazu* room. 'You'll love it,' John had said. 'It's Japanese fingerpoint massage, so much more relaxing than all that oily Swedish stuff.' Well, he's entitled to his opinion, I decided once it was over, but that's the last time I pay to be poked in the kidneys and have my ankles trodden on by someone heavier than me.

One p.m. and it was time to meet up with John at the bar of the Imperial Hotel. Outside, in the shadow of the Imperial Palace, the air was buzzing with the sound of insects; inside it was all air-conditioned hush and the soft clink of expensive drinks. I told John he was looking 'prosperous', which was a polite way of telling him he'd put on a shedload of weight. He was clearly loving it out here, speaking fluent Japanese and getting paid to indulge his passion for researching new electronic gadgets.

We emerged from the hotel and walked through a passageway where the bullet train passed overhead to Kyoto and where the air was thick with the smoke of a dozen *yakatori* grills, lending it that same surreal atmosphere as in the film *Blade Runner*. John paused outside a restaurant where half a dozen live turtles were paddling around in shallow tanks. 'Hungry?' he asked. 'Not really.' With a sinking feeling I noticed that John's eyes had alighted on a row of glasses containing a bright-pink fluid that looked like washing-up liquid. 'Turtles' blood,' he announced brightly. 'It's used as a stimulant here by old men. Let's go in.'

Inside, we folded our lanky European legs awkwardly

under a low table while John ordered two glasses of turtles' blood. Down in one, leaving a strange aftertaste of strawberries. A china jar of hot sake was brought to our table, along with tiny bowls of raw whelk, all spotted and streaked with black. But something had gone horribly wrong with John's Japanese and instead of the chargrilled chunks of cooked turtle he thought he'd ordered we were now presented with an exquisitely arranged platter of raw turtle, complete with innards, raw squid and – oh, as if this made it all fine – some chopped chrysanthemum petals. There was no turning back, though, a deal was a deal, so I piled in with the chopsticks, feeling the squid form an oily film around my mouth. Getting mercifully drunk on the sake, we then ordered a plate of roast baby crabs. They arrived lacquered with a sweet coating and we crunched them whole. Already I was trying hard to forget the raw turtle.

Three p.m. and we staggered out into the warm May afternoon. Up the road, in a district called Shibuya, we came face-to-face with a musical Tower of Babel. Here in the park were dozens of raucous Japanese heavy-metal and punk bands, all performing at top volume to circles of swaying teenage groupies. They were, almost without exception, unburdened by talent, but their costumes were colourful and imaginative: patterned fans stuck behind headbands, waist-length green hair and one-piece leopard-skin jumpsuits.

Even here, though, in this charged atmosphere of faux rebellion against society, I noticed that Japanese etiquette prevailed. The performers bowed politely before coming on to play and at the entrance to the park everyone waited obediently for the lights to change before crossing the road. In Tokyo, said John, the penalty for being caught crossing against the lights was being made to cross the road ten times under police supervision.

Five p.m. and the heat was subsiding as we strolled through an old Shinto temple, where some medieval pageantry was being acted out in front of a grinning audience. Near by, a window displayed a collection of what appeared to be trolls. 'Tanukis,' explained John. Apparently the *tanuki* is a mythical Japanese animal akin to a naughty satyr. It is always depicted as having unfeasibly large testicles since tradition maintains that its scrotum is the size of six *tatami* floormats. The lustful *tanuki* uses this outsize appendage to throw over damsels in woods, ensnaring them so it can have its evil way. Down the coast at Kamakura, I learnt, there is another temple where there are thousands of tiny statuettes, each one representing an aborted foetus. 'Don't they use the Pill here?' I asked. 'Not much,' replied John. 'The rubber companies are so powerful that nothing is allowed to threaten condom sales.'

At dusk we started knocking back sun-downers on a balcony overlooking the Russian embassy. By now I should have been exhausted, but John was right, there was something about this weird city that made you want to stay up all night. We picked up his video camera and headed for the bars of Roppongi. Out on the street, all inhibitions gone, we pretended we were from a major foreign news network and started to interview people (I was still six years away from joining the BBC). We induced polite giggles wherever we went until we picked on the wrong customer. 'Jeez! He's a *yakuza*! Let's get out of here!' hissed John, breaking into an unaccustomed run. 'How could you tell?' I asked him when we finally caught our breath several streets away. 'Half his little finger was missing. If the *yakuza* commit some breach of gangster honour they have to go to the boss and chop off their own finger in front of him to reaffirm their loyalty to the clan. Believe me, you do not want to mess with these guys.'

I committed my next faux pas as we climbed into a taxi. 'Never shut a cab door behind you here,' commanded John authoritatively. 'The driver does it automatically with his foot and if you close it for him it can ram his knee up against the dashboard. Which he won't thank you for.' 'Ah. By the way, where are we heading?' 'Kabuki-cho. It's the red-light district. Now you're going to see Tokyo,' replied John with a self-satisfied smile.

I glanced out of the window at the ever-flowing stream of neon that passed by in a psychedelic blur. Not one sign was in English; I would be completely lost here on my own.

'In the early eighties,' began John, warming to his theme, 'the big craze here was "no-pan kissas", short for "no-panties *kissatens*" or coffee shops. The waitresses used to wear miniskirts with nothing underneath, sashaying between tables while little fans wafted warm air up from the floor, Marilyn Monroe style. But since then . . .' he paused, choosing his words, 'things have progressed – or perhaps regressed, depending on your point of view. OK, this street looks promising, we'll get out here.'

Within minutes we got pulled into a club to watch an S&M show. The place was packed full of salarymen all gawping at a svelte girl onstage. She was dressed in black leather and was parading a man around the stage in chains, with a choker round his neck. His mouth was smiling but his eyes suggested he might have been having second thoughts. One of the chains was attached to a keyring which in turn was fastened to a very sensitive part of his anatomy. With a deft flick of her wrist, the girl locked him on to a pulley suspended from the ceiling and produced a whip. At this point it has to be said that the volunteer salaryman began to look as if he was not having such a good time after all. The crowd began to chant '*Mo-to!*' meaning 'More!' John and I exchanged glances and decided to leave while our consciences were still intact. Just.

Four thirty a.m. Tumbling out of a club called Java Jive, I was surprised to find that it was already getting light. What happened to the night? I could never get used to long-haul flight: yesterday I had been in London; now I was watching the sun come up over the Pacific. Surely it should be time to crawl into bed? But no, a mischievous smile was spreading slowly over John's well-pampered features. My mind boggled as to what further diversions and perversions he could think up. 'Up here,' he said. The city was still very much awake at dawn and I loved that. We took a lift up to – get this – a 'Tongue Bar'. John refused to tell me what lay within, remaining tight-lipped as I speculated as to whether this was one of those in-famous businessmen's dives I had heard about where you all sat around pretending to read the *FT* while beneath the table . . . yes, well.

In we went, to find ourselves facing row upon row of

. . . dried cows' tongues. This was gross, they were even still attached to chunks of jaw. It was like a private viewing in the backroom of a butcher's. I commented on how rough and bristly the surface of the tongues looked and my curiosity was mistaken for enthusiasm. Seconds later two plates of raw tongue were set before us, all sliced up into finger-shaped chunks ready to be chopsticked into the mouth. I looked imploring at John, who glanced meaningfully at his watch. The twenty-four hours were not quite up yet – I was still bound to do every blasted thing he said.

'What's the Japanese for "enough"?' I said, but John was milking this for all it was worth, and proceeded to order us bowls of something white and chewy with two little tubes running through it. It looked like squid but it wasn't. 'All right, I give up, what is it?' I asked. 'Just try it,' he replied. I popped a couple of slices into my mouth – it tasted and felt like a chopped-up rubber band marinated in vinegar. 'It's time to tell,' I said to John. 'What is this stuff?' John took his time, savouring the moment. 'It's pig's uterus,' he replied. 'Very popular here.'

I stared at him in disbelief, gagged into my napkin and called him every name I could think of, but John was unstoppable. 'If you think that's bad you should try *na-to*. It's fermented cabbage and it really stinks – most Westerners can't handle it. In fact, there's a thought. Waiter . . .?'

'John! Enough! I'm leaving for my flight. You can keep your fermented cabbage, and your raw turtle's innards and your missing-finger gangsters. I'm going home.'

11

Jordan

Five Go into the Desert

IN 1989, MARRIAGE WAS APPROACHING. NOT MINE – I HAD another eight years of bachelordom ahead – but for a lot of my university friends, who were starting to feel that with 'the big 3-0' approaching they really ought to be doing the grown-up thing and settling down. Certain conversations between us began to take on a sort of eleventh-hour feel: some male friends who were secretly getting quite broody would pretend they were being dragged kicking and screaming to the altar, while others were determined to embark on a final fling of all-male antics that bordered on the ridiculous. One such friend was Guy Bonser – even his name sounded like a frisky Labrador panting for a walk – and one day he rang up with a suggestion. 'How d'you fancy coming on a boys' tour?' he asked. 'Sure,' I said. 'Where do you have in mind?' 'Jordan.' '*Jordan?*'

I could not quite see this desert kingdom being up there

with Amsterdam and Dublin as a top-ten lads' destination. I was also unsure if this was how I wanted to return to the country. Three years earlier I had spent some of the happiest weeks of my life living with a Bedu tribe in the burning sands east of Wadi Rum. I had had time to kill before starting my first job in the City, so I thought I would reimmerse myself in the Arab culture that had so entranced me at university. Commissioned by *Time Out* magazine to write a travel piece, I got the Jordanian Tourism Ministry to deposit me with a sheikh and his extended family from the Huwaitat tribe who were still living a nomadic life in black goats' hair tents. It had been a magical time, a glimpse into a world of desert feasts beside the campfire where craggy-faced tribesmen recited ancient poetry beneath the stars, where one day blended seamlessly into the next as we wandered for miles through sunlit canyons, shepherding the tribe's precious flocks of sheep and goats. By day I would marvel at the dazzling blue lizards that skittered amongst the ochre rocks; at night we would take off our slippers and swat at the hideous yellow camel spiders that lurked around the campfire, and once the tribesmen had killed a viper they called 'the one that gives you ten minutes to live'. I had parted from their company reluctantly, having been briefly accepted into their vanishing world thanks to my Arabic and the fact that I had come alone and uncluttered by any of the trappings of Western culture. Although the sheikh had promised I could always return, I would have to think long and hard about whether I really wanted to do so with a group of friends who did not speak their language, and when, because of our number, we could be seen as something of an intrusion.

But Guy was persuasive; he had it all planned out. This would be 'the *Viz* tour of Jordan', named after the Geordie adult comic that was all the rage at the time. There would be five of us going and Guy had T-shirts printed with our characters from the comic on the front. We would rent a jeep and explore Petra, Crusader castles and the desert of Wadi Rum, and swim in the Red Sea. I was in.

But later that week I groaned when I realized we would be going out with Egyptair. I had not had good experiences with Egypt's national airline, with its endemic delays, its inexplicable cancellations and, worst of all, its smokers' paradise of a hub in the form of Cairo airport. (A sign in the terminal used to read YOU ARE WELCOME TO CAIRO AIRPORT, which I thought summed it up pretty well.) But this time Egyptair did us proud: £330 to Amman and back, with a complimentary overnight stay in a Cairo hotel thrown in.

Lifting out of Cairo on a cloudless October morning, we watched the Suez Canal sneak past the wing. Far below us, a shoal of tankers nibbled like minnows at the mouth of the Gulf of Suez. Then we banked right towards Asia, skirting the Sinai coast to avoid Israeli air space, and descended to Amman's middle-of-nowhere, state-of-the-art airport.

Few tourists came to Jordan just to see the capital. With its clean, orderly streets built on seven hills, I rated it possibly the Middle East's least exciting capital at the time, although it did have a fine Roman amphitheatre; journalists, I was to learn later, dubbed it 'the capital of the Hashemite Kingdom of Boredom'. We took a quick

straw poll amongst the team: 'Who wants to see Amman?'
I asked. 'Nope', 'Nah', 'No', went the chorus. Fine. Within
hours of landing we had duly rented a four-wheel-drive
land cruiser and were heading west for the Dead Sea,
driving full tilt into the afternoon sun with a cassette of
Prefab Sprout's *From Langley Park to Memphis* playing
on the stereo, until I messed up the map-reading and
realized we were now heading towards Syria instead.

I decided to keep quiet so long as nobody noticed our
tortuously wide detour and soon we were losing height,
coming down off Jordan's three-thousand-foot plateau
and entering the lush valley of the River Jordan. Military
checkpoints sprang up behind the date palms like
obstacles in a computer game; they were manned by
unshaven teenagers in toyshop helmets and crotch-
hugging fatigues. This close to the Israeli border they were
nervous. Jericho was just across the border and already we
could see the lights of the Jerusalem suburbs twinkling in
the dusk. Israeli Special Forces reconnaissance patrols
were known to have sneaked into Jordan near here, while
Palestinian gunmen had slipped past the checkpoints heading in the other direction. It certainly seemed to be a
porous border. The Jordanian soldiers took one look at
our *Viz* T-shirts and incompetently tied Arab headdresses,
decided we did not look like illegal migrants and waved us
through.

We slept in a vine-covered guest house on the shores of the
Dead Sea, then in the morning I made a big mistake.
Important safety tip: when about to go swimming in one
of the most saline lakes in the world, do not have a

haircut just before entering the water. But the sun was out and it felt like a good idea at the time. Not clever. Even the haircut itself was a joyless experience: in the airless barber shop flies settled continually on my lips, nose and eyelids while the expatriate Egyptian barber hacked and snipped at random, apparently learning on the job as he went along. A bit off the front, a quick go on the electric trimmer to see if it worked, now for a few snips down one side but not the other. I emerged to hoots of derision from Guy and the others, who were already floating in the blue water.

Swimming in the Dead Sea is everything they say it is: you bob around, trying to find your balance, standing upright with your feet nearly a yard off the seabed, or loll on your back pretending to read a newspaper and praying you don't get the salt in your eyes. In my case, five minutes after plunging into the Dead Sea's saline slime the freshly shaven back of my neck felt like it was on fire. I raced barefoot to the shower room, where an immovable obstacle blocked the doorway in the form of a tattooed old crone demanding an entrance fee. With no money on me, I pleaded and implored, dancing from one foot to another in pain, but to no avail – this lady was accepting cash only that day. By the time I rejoined the others my neck looked like something from the Chernobyl nuclear disaster.

From the lowest patch of dry land below sea level on the planet, we ascended six thousand feet to Kerak, a fortress town perched on the crags that straddle the King's Highway, the ribbon of road that runs from north to south through some of Jordan's most spectacular scenery. Far below us, almost lost in the haze, we could just make out a column of mountain bikers sweating their way up the hill. The Crusader castle of Kerak, built in the twelfth century, had had its fair share of grisly history. One occupant, we were told, had had a particular penchant for throwing his enemies off the ramparts attached to primitive parachutes, which were ineffective to break their fall but just sufficient to allow them time to contemplate their imminent deaths.

'You like the view, yes?' said a voice just behind us. A young Jordanian in a smart blue uniform flashed us a perfect smile, a laminated 'Tourist Police' badge pinned to his well-ironed shirt. Mahmoud was charming and only too happy to earn a few extra dinars on a quiet day by taking us under his wing, showing us knowledgeably around the castle's labyrinthine corridors and windswept ramparts. The tour over, he took us to a restaurant, plied us with mountains of falafel and Amstel beer, then gave us his opinion about places in his country. 'Do you know what they say about the people who come from Tafila?' he asked. 'Tequila?' repeated our friend Duncan, suddenly taking an interest. 'No, no, my friend! Not tequila – Tafila. It is a town near here. Very stupid people from there, I tell you. Always we make jokes about them.' We all waited to hear a joke at the expense of the hapless Tafilans, but Mahmoud had turned his attention to Duncan, who was displaying an excessive amount of hairy chest for such a conservative country. 'You know, I must tell you, there was a Lebanese lady back at the castle who is liking you very much.'

Duncan beamed with pride, while the rest of us tried to

think who this could be. Lebanese women were well known for their good looks, but the only individual we had encountered that afternoon had been the Nora Batty of Kerak, a stout matron with laddered, calf-length stockings. Did he really mean her? Surely not.

Mahmoud had more to say on the subject. 'Have you never tasted a Lebanese woman? It is a must!' His eyes blazed with sudden passion and Duncan was all for going back to the castle to investigate. Somehow we managed to talk him out of it, but for the rest of the trip we felt compelled to keep reminding him that he had 'yet to taste a Lebanese woman'.

The next day we barrelled into Petra in a swirl of dust. A quick bout of haggling and we were off on horseback down the Siq, the narrow canyon that leads to the ancient Nabataean city of Petra itself. In the fading evening light we had the place to ourselves, our voices rebounding off the towering cliffs of red sandstone. These Nabataeans knew they were on to a good thing here, holding out for centuries in this mountain stronghold while they levied and plundered the caravans heading north to Syria. The Romans, however, were more than a match for them, and after taking the city by storm in AD 106 they called in the planners and installed baths, an amphitheatre and a magnificent colonnaded street, much of which still survives.

At a gift shop a gap-toothed salesman offered us postcards and 'genuine relics'. 'This stone very old, maybe two thousand years, see, with picture man and woman, yes? For you special price, ten dinar.' 'This thing's only just been made,' countered Pete. 'No, no! Not lying, my friend . . . perhaps just little lies . . . OK, one dinar then?'

*   *   *

From Petra it was downhill all the way to Wadi Rum, the starkly beautiful desert from where T. E. Lawrence and his fearless Bedu laid up and raided the Turks at Aqaba in 1917. We stopped off for supplies in Quweira, a rather desolate town on the Desert Highway, where a large man with a long beard tried to convince us that all women were 'unclean' and would the youngest and blondest member of our group like to stay the night as his guest? John (who was a different John from my Tokyo soulmate) was oblivious to beardo's advances, since he had his Walkman clamped to his ears, and I am sorry to admit there was a brief moment when we contemplated stitching him up.

Further south, the village of Rum, so enigmatic when I first caught sight of it three years earlier, was now infested by a coach party of tourists, all posing for pictures on swaying camels while the driver hooted his impatience with an air horn. 'Let's leave,' said Duncan. 'Wait!' I insisted, 'you haven't seen the desert yet.' I had decided to chance it and introduce my friends to the wonderful Bedu family I had stayed with last time I was here, hoping that if I briefed them beforehand none of them would commit some faux pas like plunging an 'unclean' left hand into the communal bowl of rice.

After asking around the village I duly found Hamad, a young Bedu who remembered me, and he jumped into the passenger seat to lead us to his family's tents beyond a range of low hills. John was driving, doing his best to steer the vehicle through the soft sand but managing to collide with several bushes in quick succession. Hamad was not impressed. 'Your friend,' he said bluntly,

'I think very weak driver, yes? Perhaps better I drive.'

An hour later we were all sitting cross-legged on the sand beside a black goats' hair tent, sipping the bitter cardamom coffee that had been my daily fare for weeks. The old sheikh who had been Glubb Pasha's guide in the 1950s was still there and greeted me like a long-lost son, while his seventeen-year-old granddaughter, who he had trusted me to go shepherding with three years ago, was now married and a mother.

At twilight the five of us scaled a sandstone crag and sat there in the deafening silence watching the stars blink on, one by one, in the purpling sky of northern Arabia. Back in the tent it was a noisy, disturbed night, with the camp dogs baying to ward off two prowling jackals; when sleep came in the small hours we all dreamt of snakes and scorpions, which was probably my fault since I had not held back on describing the delights of desert creepy crawlies.

In the morning, though, there was a very embarrassing discovery for which Hamad was rightly demanding an explanation. John, who had been guzzling biscuits all the previous day, had felt the call of nature in the night. Terrified of venturing more than a couple of feet from the tent flap in case he was bitten, stung or eaten, he had relieved himself inside the camp. He had then made a poor attempt to cover up his efforts with sand. 'What this?' demanded Hamad, pointing at the offending pile, now black with flies, adding with some understatement, 'This is not our custom.' We were at pains to point out that it was not our custom either, and John was duly ostracized for the rest of the day.

Marked on our map was a drunken dotted line inscribed with the magical words 'Lawrence's desert route to Aqaba'. Hamad saw us studying the map and read our thoughts. 'You want to go that route? It is possible. My brother Ibrahim he can guide you.' I had a feeling that after John's unforgivable sin, Hamad was quite keen to see the back of us and I could hardly blame him; I was beginning to think it had not been such a great idea to bring friends out to this Bedu camp after all.

We turned our attention to Lawrence's exploits and the route ahead. Back in 1917, the Turkish garrison in Aqaba had thought themselves largely safe down on the Red Sea coast, protected by the desert at their backs. But Lawrence had taken them by surprise, exploding out of the desert with his small force of hardy Arab fighters and routing the Turks. It was a journey they had thought impossible, but today, in our land cruiser, we covered it rather less romantically in just three hours. Since there was not enough room for all of us inside with Ibrahim, I spent most of the trip riding outside on the tailboard, just as I had done in the highlands of the Philippines, clinging to the roof rack and bouncing up and down with each pot-hole, which gave me a wonderful 360-degree view of the landscape of southern Jordan: crimson rock massifs, blackened volcanic outcrops and soft, shifting dunes of pure white sand. This to me was travelling at its very best, going somewhere new, while passing through scenery of mesmerizing beauty.

We did have one awkward moment when we drew up at a military checkpoint and the Jordanian soldiers made us all dismount for questioning. 'What are your jobs?' they wanted to know, more out of boredom, I suspected, than for any pressing reasons of national security. 'Architect,' replied Guy, a slight twist on the truth since he was a surveyor. 'Banker,' said Duncan and I in unison. 'Computers,' said Pete. The soldiers turned to look at John, who appeared to be having an identity crisis at this point. 'Um ... marketing,' he finally announced. 'Marxism?' echoed the soldiers, gripping their M16s in outrage. These were God-fearing folk down here and they had no truck with godless heathens of a Communist bent. It took some explaining to convince them that John was not in fact an emissary from the Kremlin, but a humble sales and marketing assistant from Blackheath.

Aqaba was busy. There were very few tourists to speak of but the hotel pool area was full of large, rangy Americans with very short haircuts. Exercise Bright Star had just ended, a series of joint US–Jordanian military manoeuvres designed to strengthen compatibility between two not very compatible allies. (Nine months later, when Iraq invaded Kuwait in 1990 and most of the Arab world was outraged, Jordan's King Hussein refused to condemn Saddam's invasion, a slight for which the Gulf Arab rulers never forgave him.) The US paratroopers lived up to their stereotype that night, getting very drunk on quite small amounts of lager then throwing the white plastic furniture into the pool. Poor John. Not having the strongest of heads for alcohol even back in genteel Blackheath, the sun, the heat and the lager all got the better of him and the next day he could remember little of the night before. So Pete sidled up to him with a shocked expression. 'John!' he hissed. 'Do you realize what you did last night?' 'No. Why? What?' 'Well,' continued Pete, shaking his head ruefully, 'you see that US paratrooper sitting nursing a hangover at that table over there? You were so drunk you tried to stick your tongue in his ear. I think you'd better go and apologize.' For the record, let it be said that Pete did intercept his friend just before he reached the said serviceman, and no one got punched.

The return drive back north up to Amman was not fun. On the potholed asphalt, worn down by the constant trundling of cargo bound for Baghdad, we experienced triple overtaking by tankers marked 'highly flammable', driven by deathwish Filipinos racing against some hidden clock. Random herds of camels and goats also meandered at will across the highway in the sand-coloured heat haze, but somehow we did not mind them.

In Amman we came down to earth with a jolt. In the hotel bar a grim East European couple were playing synthesized Frank Sinatra, complete with electric drum effects. Fortified by Jordan's ubiquitous Amstel beer, we seized our moment when the band stepped down and got up onstage to treat the bewildered audience to a stirring rendition of 'Rawhide' from the Blues Brothers film. In sedate Amman, this was not in the hotel's entertainment programme and a tubby hotel security man in leather jacket and shiny shoes was quickly summoned, windmilling his arms in protest. We checked out the next morning under a bit of a cloud; Leather-Jacket Man was there to make sure we headed straight for the airport. But just then the hotel receptionist approached us in a whisper.

'This is not usual behaviour for English guests. But I am glad because I am hating this synthesizer rubbish. Welcome in Jordan any time!'

There was no question that this had been a very different experience to my first time in Jordan, and in retrospect it was easy to see how travelling in a group can alienate you from your hosts. Since it's far less effort to chat to your fellow Brits in your own language than wrestle with Arabic when your throat is already dry with thirst, you inevitably spend less time getting to know the locals, and the insights, stories and jokes they might otherwise have told you get left unsaid. While I was proud to have shown my friends a taste of Bedu life in the desert and they enjoyed it, I don't think we made a great impression on our hosts. In fact, years later, when I happened to be in Rum with other friends in 2002 and I ran into one of the sheikh's sons, I noticed he was in no hurry to invite us out to the camp. Selfishly, perhaps, I have been lucky enough to see Jordan from two very different perspectives: first as a lone traveller, completely open to the local culture and happy to adapt to local ways and casual discomforts; then later with mates, on what was more of a holiday. I find it hard to say which I preferred since they were utterly different. I learnt and experienced so much the first time round – my brief time with Jordan's Bedu will always be one of my most memorable travel experiences – but my goodness it was hard work. As for the *Viz* tour, it was a barrel of fun and I would go again any time, although perhaps only after John had completed some intensive training in the finer points of desert etiquette.

12

Ecuador

Sulphur Springs and Ocelots

IN THE SUMMER OF 1990, WHEN THE MIDDLE EAST WAS about to experience a major upheaval as Saddam Hussein's forces prepared to invade Kuwait, I was very far away from the action. Soaked by rain, straining to see more than a few yards ahead in dark and tropical undergrowth, I was spending my twenty-ninth birthday hiding in a bamboo grove on the Hong Kong–China border. I should explain that this was not some perverse stag-party game of hide and seek, but one of my last stints in military uniform: a brief attachment to the Gurkhas, the legendary regiment of Nepalese hill men who had been part of the British Army for over a century.

The Gurkhas were engaged in what was known as 'I.I. Ops' – Illegal Immigrant Operations – and as a Territorial infantry officer in my final year with the Royal Green Jackets I managed to wangle a very brief stint with their troops up on the Chinese border, thanks to a mate, Dan, who was serving with them. Hong Kong was and still is one of the most crowded patches of real estate in the world, with over six million people crammed into just a few square miles. To poor, illiterate farm workers living in the People's Republic of China across the border, it was the pot of gold at the end of the rainbow. So the Gurkhas' job was to patrol the border to stop, catch and return any illegal immigrants and to prevent smuggling. This was not easy, since there had been reports of whole shipments of luxury cars getting an armed escort out of Hong Kong and into Chinese waters.

The Gurkhas were hard, squat, mountain men, with a passion for goat curry. They were incredibly fit and they expected a lot from their officers, not least a working knowledge of their Nepalese language, Gurkhali. There seemed to be a genuine bond between them and the Brits, and I suspected they did not tolerate fools lightly.

In the late afternoon Dan and I piled into a Land Rover and drove over to Man Tok to report to the Operations Room for orders for the night's operation from the Company Commander, Major Sean Crane. The Ops Room was housed on a hill with a large Union Jack hanging limply from a mast. At the bottom of the hill ran a wire-mesh fence – the Chinese border – and just across on the other side, the boom town of Shenzhen. The Intelligence Officer reeled off his assessment. 'Based on the pattern of activities in our sector so far this month, we can expect a concerted effort by several groups of I.I.s to try and come over tonight. We know from documents found on captured individuals that they are mostly coming from this district here –' he said, stabbing at a map of southern

China. 'They will have walked a long way, so don't expect them to give themselves up easily.'

The other officers were quick to fill me in on some recent dramas, like the stabbing of a Gurkha soldier the week before by a desperate would-be immigrant. 'That's nothing,' interjected a subaltern with a jutting chin. 'I hauled myself up through a bamboo grove chasing one of them and came face to face with a King Cobra!' I then made the mistake of asking how he knew it was a King Cobra. 'It just was,' he said, turning his back and clearly marking me down as a smartarse.

Major Crane then showed me round the control room, where they monitored the entire length of the border. 'If someone cuts the fence here –' he pointed to a map line on the wall, 'then a red light starts flashing at the nearest sensor. We've got static OPs [observation posts] strung out at intervals along the fence, but the I.I.'s guides have got wise to them, they know where they are and how to avoid them. But we've got a few hours left before they start coming across. Come on, let me show you the border.' The OPs were large, permanently manned wooden structures, and they looked right across into China. Their metal-rung ladders stretched vertically upwards for fifty feet but Crane shinned up ahead of me like a monkey in a hurry. 'Take a look through this,' he said at the top when I'd got my breath back, indicating a heavy night-vision thermal imaging scope mounted on a swivel. It was fully dark now, but through the scope I could see about a hundred Chinese soldiers of the People's Liberation Army drilling and exercising just across the border, shouting instructions to each other. They wore floppy green tunics and Mao caps with red stars and behind them stood heroic posters glorifying the Communist party and the Revolution; I felt as if I was peering in on a day from 1966. It occurred to me that some of these Chinese troops were probably watching us too, while somewhere out there in no man's land small groups of illegal immigrants were gathering in the gloom, waiting for the moment when they would try to launch themselves across the border into the territory of Hong Kong.

'What about this OP over here?' I said. 'How come there's nobody in it?' 'Ah,' said Crane. 'You may find this hard to believe, but the Gurkhas don't dare go near it.' 'Why on earth not? They don't seem to be afraid of anything.' 'They're not,' said the Major, 'except ghosts. One of them says he saw a banshee going round and round the tower one night and now they won't go near it. We don't force the issue.'

It was time to get kitted out in the Ops Room: webbing, water bottle and bamboo stave, more for keeping balance on mountain paths I found than brandishing at illegals. Major Crane had come up with an ingenuous way of trying to second-guess the I.I.'s intentions and now I was to be a part of his plan. Since the illegals knew where the very obviously positioned OPs were, they always tended to try and break through in the jungly undergrowth between them. A patrol road ran the length of the border, some distance back from the fence, and using a well-spaced convoy of Land Rovers Crane ordered us to drop off in twos and threes so we could conceal ourselves in the dark, unlit undergrowth between OPs. The illegals and their guides would be watching and listening for engine noise, alert to anything that sounded like a vehicle stopping, so to keep them guessing we never actually stopped. Instead, each time the Rover slowed to negotiate a bend in the road a pair of us would leap silently out the back and slither into the foliage. When my turn came I tried very hard not to think of King Cobras, or even knife-wielding farmers from Guangzhou Province, but within seconds we were adjusting to our new, dark, damp environment.

It had rained recently and the ground was moist and mushy. Something scuttled over my hand, then there was silence save for the zing of cicadas. This is a weird way to spend your birthday, I thought, three thousand feet up a jungle hill, but then decided it was actually quite exhilarating. Here I was, on the other side of the world, a blip on the underbelly of China, hiding out close to midnight in a covert OP in tropical undergrowth, waiting for the frenzied burst of activity we knew was coming.

Hours went past – or so it felt – then, in the darkness beside me, there was the faintest of static clicks on the radio. Contact. The fence had been breached. I.I.s were coming across to our left. We leapt from our cover and set off in pursuit, running full tilt through the rain-sodden foliage, tripping, recovering and lurching forward. My friend Dan, who was serving in the Gurkhas, had lent me his spare *kukri*, the regiment's traditional crooked knife, which was now strapped to my side in its camouflaged scabbard. Unused to carrying one, let alone running with it, I felt as if I had a heavy metal boomerang clattering against my thigh and that if I wasn't careful I could see myself impaled like a kebab on the pointed scabbard.

Up ahead the illegals broke cover; it was a group of three Chinese, dressed all in black, zigzagging quickly away from us. As soon as they saw us they split into a starburst, each running in a different direction, having obviously agreed this was their best chance of getting through. We did likewise, each marking the man in front, but they were fast. And clever. More than once they crossed over each other, ducking and weaving through the undergrowth as if they had trained for this moment, which they quite possibly had. I lost the man I was supposed to be following. 'Hard luck,' said King Cobra Man afterwards at the Command Post, 'I got mine.' Honestly, this felt like school sports day all over again.

In an empty warehouse near by, the Gurkhas were standing guard over the captured I.I.s, armed only with picks. I went over to talk to them. 'We found this on their group leader, sir,' said a sergeant, handing me a crumpled sheet of paper with a map covered in Chinese characters. I couldn't read Chinese but it was clearly a precise, detailed map of this whole border area. Our OPs were marked, together with our communications road, the best routes in and where to fan out; someone had been watching us very carefully over a period of time.

'I wouldn't feel too sorry for them,' said a subaltern beside me, seeming to read my thoughts. 'They'll be back soon enough. We hand them back to the Chinese authorities, they get a bit of a hard time, then they're released. Once they've saved up enough dosh they make contact with the people smugglers and they set off again. That's how a lot of people get into Hong Kong.'

But it was hard not to feel sorry for them. The failed

immigrants were a pathetic sight, clad in tattered black shirts and thin trousers held together with a drawstring. They huddled together, waiting for whatever fate was decided for them, pale, malnourished, having walked for days across southern China only to fall at the final hurdle. With the exhilaration of the chase now over, there was a collective feeling of anti-climax; the Gurkhas were only doing their job guarding the border and they did it with professionalism and restraint, but there was something rather distasteful about soldiers catching unarmed peasants. I was glad to have had an insight into what went on along that border at night, but I would not have cared to be assigned to that job for months on end.

While I was thrashing around in the sodden undergrowth on the Chinese border the Iraqi Army was consolidating its stranglehold on Kuwait. By November that year there were over forty thousand British troops in the Gulf, and around half a million others, mostly Americans, were making final preparations to drive the Iraqi divisions out of Kuwait. Most people suspected that war was on the horizon, but it was taking rather a long time coming – over five months, in fact.

I, too, had several months left before I had to move out to Bahrain to take over the running of the Middle East office of the merchant bank Flemings. I was craving adventure somewhere very different and Ecuador fitted the bill. My travelling companion was James Maughan, whom I had met at the company urinals two years earlier. Working for the Saudi International Bank at the time, I had just been on his interview board and since there was now no one senior to overhear us I had given him my best advice. 'Look, James, you're a Cambridge graduate, aren't you? If you come and work here you'll have quite a lot of fun, but you're unlikely to ever get rich. If you're ambitious you'll go and work for one of the big American banks.' To my surprise, he ignored me and for the next two years we went to the same parties, flirted with the same girls and attended the same training programme in New York. James was a tall and tanned Yorkshireman with an annoyingly healthy complexion, so that he always looked as if he was just back from holiday. Once, when he and his pallid flatmate Simon had gone skiing together, James returned to the bank's dealing room with a glowing tan while a Saudi friend looked at Simon's blotched face in horror. 'Bloody hell, Simon!' he exclaimed. 'Where have you just been on holiday – Chernobyl?'

One day after leaving London, our Iberia Airlines flight made its final approach to Quito airport. This high up in the foothills of the Andes, the cloud was so thick we could see almost nothing. As we turned away from the windows, our conversation returned once more to the news we had heard that morning. 'It's the end of an era,' said James. 'I can't believe she's out.' With just weeks to go before Desert Storm, the Iron Lady, Margaret Thatcher, was out of office and a new man with silver hair and big glasses was now our Prime Minister. I remembered seeing John Major coming into the bank when he was Chancellor of the Exchequer; he seemed harmless enough.

Quito airport was almost deserted. This didn't seem right. Where were the teeming crowds of emotional relatives? Where were the hustling taxi touts? Where *was* everyone? 'Ah, señor,' exclaimed a policeman. 'Today is census. Everyone must stay indoors to be counted.' As if to reinforce the point, a pair of shiny-booted paramilitary types paced up and down the arrivals hall in dazzling blue fatigues, cradling assault rifles and squinting at us suspiciously.

So why Ecuador? Well, we'd wanted to go to South America, specifically an Andean country, but we had heard too many horror stories about Peru: travellers doubled up with diarrhoea, trekkers systematically robbed of everything on the way up to Machu Picchu, or gassed to sleep – then robbed – on the train up to Cuzco, back-packers getting taken off a bus and castrated by the Maoist rebels of Sendero Luminoso. So Ecuador appealed to us as 'safe adventure'. So safe, in fact, that I decided to forgo all vaccinations while James took the lot: cholera, typhoid, hepatitis, malaria tablets, you name it. In scientific terms, you could say that he was the control and I was the experiment. James, I am sorry to report, fell ill.

As we rattled into the capital on a government bus, blood-red graffiti screamed out at us from cracked and crumbling ochre walls where men in sombreros dozed like extras from a Western. 'FREEDOM FOR POLITICAL PRISONERS!', 'ENOUGH OF THE SAME', 'DOWN WITH GRINGOS!' And then, bizarrely, 'KUWAIT IS IRAQ!' At 9,300 feet above sea level, Quito was a bracing city, all cobbled backstreets built on hills, with whitewashed walls and wrought-iron balconies, and colonial churches in the old quarter. It felt more like a cosy village than a city.

We slept, then headed straight out the next day for the

Indian market at Otavalo, Ecuador's most celebrated weaving town close to the Colombian border. Like all the best South American bus drivers, ours swung his vehicle along the muddy road, gunning it around the bends, honking furiously at passing farmers and their pigs. Squashed in the back with our rucksacks, we felt as if we were on one of the more demanding rides at Alton Towers. One final bend and then a shallow valley opened up beneath us.

Colombian militiaman, Bogotá airport

Down in Otavalo, a seething multitude of pigtailed Indians had flooded into town for the weekly weaving market, *el mercado de los ponchos*. The women were adorned with layer upon layer of gold necklaces, the men dressed in rakish white boating flannels, flared and ending abruptly at the calf, beneath dark-blue ponchos and banded felt hats. Filling the market square was a bewildering display of tapestries, ponchos, sweaters, gloves, balaclavas, wristlets, bracelets and earrings. We had found the Camden Lock of the Andes. In a nearby sidestreet a whole roast pig was turning slowly on a spit, fanned by young girls who waved clusters of filthy pigeon feathers at the glowing embers. Someone was selling a framed placard with an inscription in English that would have appealed to the late and controversial comedian, Bernard Manning: '*When White Man came here the Indians had no taxes, no debts, and the women did all the work. White Man thought he could improve on a system like that.*'

We had heard there was currently a plague of giant rats in the coastal town of Guayaquil, so we thought that on balance we would probably give that a miss. Instead we opted for the fishing village of Manta, travelling the last few miles clinging to the back of a minivan as we chugged past a stunted forest of curiously tumescent baobab trees.

On the beach we watched the cold waves of the Humboldt Current come crashing in, then lent an un- solicited hand to the fishermen as they reeled in their catch, fending off the marauding frigate birds as they dived screaming around our heads. James impressed the locals at beach football so much that one-litre flagons of beer were fetched, but try as he might he never quite man- aged to translate 'I come from a place called Bradford' into Spanish. Then at dusk, further down the beach we found Inés. She was young, dark and pretty, but she was in- consolably sad. As the day faded she sat there gently rocking herself beside a single, flickering candle. Eventually, she told us her story. 'There is a boy here in the village that I love, but now I am facing disaster.' James and I exchanged glances; we both guessed what was coming next. 'Yes. I am pregnant by him and if my family find out I don't know what they will do. Maybe even they will kill me. So now I must leave him and this place where I grew up and go to Quito. I have a friend there who will help me to finish the baby before anyone knows and that is why I am sad.' Inés was adamant, she had made up her mind. The prospect of being a young, single mother in the tiny Pacific village of Manta was clearly a bleak one. We offered to pay her bus fare, but she would have none of it. 'I have got myself into this situation,' she sighed, 'and now I must get myself out of it.'

We thought about Inés all the next day, as we rattled eastwards up over the mountain spine of Ecuador and down to the spa town of Baños. 'I still say we should at least have paid her way,' said James, whose naturally generous nature was constantly at odds with his commercial instincts as a banker. In contemplative silence we continued our journey down the Pan American Highway, past the snowy cone of Cotopaxi volcano. Once again, the valley opened up below us to reveal the thermal town of Baños and boy, did it stink. It may well have been famous in the world of guidebooks for its restorative thermal baths, but what greeted us that afternoon was a collection of foul-smelling, suspiciously rust-coloured pools, thick with floating algae, as a brisk wind from the mountains blew dust into everyone's face.

We got down from the bus and slung our rucksacks into the first hostel we could find, a refuge for German back-packers and their self-laundered underwear, strung out on washing lines for all the world to see. A stocky Fräulein gave us a defensive look and snatched her greying bras from the line, hastily stuffing them in her rucksack in case we were tempted to pilfer them as trophies, and slammed the plywood door to her room.

Outside, in the gathering gloom of a chilly evening there were festive, twinkling Christmas lights in each window down the street. '¡Feliz Navidad!' they proclaimed, beside nodding plastic Father Christmases, but there was little cheer to be had here. Within a few minutes we had quartered the village and found that every bar and café had shut at seven in the evening, the streets were deserted and every house door was locked and bolted against the outside world, prompting James to coin the phrase 'eking out a good time in Baños'. We returned in low spirits to the Germanic hostel and the greying bras.

Things could only improve in the morning and they did. Yards from our hostel was a sign advertising trekking in the Amazon – 'The Magnificent Jungle'. So we went and introduced ourselves to Xavier, our Quechua Indian guide, and his ten-year-old son and apprentice, Isaiah, then plotted our escape from backpacker hell, buying up a week's rations that night by candlelight. In the grey, clammy dawn that followed we all boarded a bus bound for the alluringly named Oriente province and the jungle. For mile after twisted mile we shadowed the River Pastaza as it roared through a canyon hundreds of feet below. Clouds clung to the dripping, fern-clad slopes; at times we drove straight through them, the giant fronds looming eerily at us through the mist. Waterfalls cascaded down through the foliage like streaks of mercury, while up ahead a row of ridges receded in hazy ranks down the valley until the horizon blended with the distant blur of the greatest rain-forest on earth. We were heading for the Amazon.

The mud road levelled out at last and we pulled up at the town of Shell – no prizes for guessing what the main-stay of the economy was here. In a sunlit arcade of shops we stocked up on water from a girl with jet-black hair and a revealingly tight T-shirt. This was a chance for James and me to wheel out our cheesiest chat-up lines in Spanish. 'So what are your jobs?' she asked politely. '*Somos medicos de corazon*,' we replied. 'We are doctors of the heart, we cure heartache.' It was a ridiculous thing to say but she loved it and went and called her sister to come and meet the funny gringos. But our poor command of Spanish meant we could not push past second base and we were soon back to stilted phrases and eyebrow-raising misunderstandings. We were secretly relieved when Xavier came and retrieved us.

Half an hour later we were trudging past the Army's Jungle Brigade outpost to arrive at the local version of the Indiana Jones rope bridge. A swaying three-hundred-foot cable spanned a muddy, churning river; suspended from it was a flimsy-looking wooden platform on which we now jostled for space. Xavier gave a shove and there followed an exhilarating swoop down over the foaming waters. 'What if we fall in?' asked James. 'You drown,' said our guide flatly.

On the opposite bank he led us through the under-growth to a thatched hut adorned with jaguar pelts. Here we dumped our cold-weather mountain clothes and changed into gumboots while an Indian girl appeared with a plate of freshly chopped papayas. 'There will be a lot of mud,' warned Xavier. Outside the hut I spotted a tiny movement on the ground: it was a coral snake, pencil thin with red and black bands. As we walked slowly over for a closer look the snake sensed our movements and froze, contorting itself into the strangest shape I have ever seen an animal adopt. Instead of hugging the earth or slithering off to safety, the snake arched itself into a stiff hollow ball, its body forming the sides about three inches off the ground.

Refreshed from the papayas, we moved out into the fierce tropical sun that beat down from directly overhead and trekked until dusk, when Xavier brought us to the self-explanatory Laguna de los Crocodilos. While brilliantly plumaged parakeets cackled demoniacally from the treetops, Xavier displayed his jungle knowledge: a medicinal tree whose bark was good for stomach ache (we dutifully chewed some); an armadillo's freshly dug burrow; a column of army ants pouring over a log; a sprig of *palupanga* – a weed that can be chewed as an antidote to cobra bite; a four-inch scarlet millipede; a powdery termites' nest. Now he hacked methodically at the under-growth, skilfully building a lean-to shelter of giant palm fronds.

Unfurling my sleeping bag in the dark, I debated whether to remove my boots or not, only to turn and see a startling sight. James had quietly changed out of his clothes and into a pair of hummingbird-green pyjamas. 'What on earth are you wearing, James?' I asked incredu-lously as something scaly scuttled across the leaf floor of the shelter. 'I mean, we're in the jungle! You brought pyjamas to the jungle?' James denies it now, but I am certain that his jungle pyjamas actually bore a mono-grammed motif of his initials on the breast pocket. Xavier put down his machete and looked from me to James, his pyjamas, and back again, shook his head, and carried on hacking at the palms.

We dined that night by candlelight beneath our canopy of fronds, listening to the cacophony of whooping monkeys, chirping cicadas and persistently burping tree frogs. When it was fully dark we descended to the Lagoon of the Crocodiles, James now wearing gumboots below his pyjamas like an extra in a Christmas panto, and followed the glowing eyes of the crocodiles with our torch beams. Where Xavier had calmly swum earlier, he said, a twenty-foot anaconda now lurked beneath the surface.

At first light I was woken abruptly by a pain in my foot. Something had bitten me during the night. Damn, I thought, I knew I should have kept my boots on. Xavier came over and inspected the bite. 'Ah! Conga Ant! This is very painful!' he announced triumphantly, and he and Isaiah burst into laughter. I didn't get the joke myself but Xavier soon found some leaves which he moulded into a compress and the pain subsided.

As we set off that morning in a large canoe that Xavier had arranged in advance with the local Indians, the heavens opened. In sulphur-smelling Baños we had taken the precaution of buying a couple of telescopic umbrellas and these now proved invaluable. We must have made a laughable sight: two Englishmen being paddled upstream in the rain, reclining in the centre of the canoe while holding our umbrellas at a jaunty angle as thunder rumbled in the distance.

When the sun re-emerged a few miles later, the river was transformed. Swollen by the rain, it had become a dangerous animal, rushing and swerving, sapping the boatmen's strength. On either side of us the jungle foliage closed in, trailing great hundred-foot aerial roots into the water while hand-sized electric-blue butterflies danced above the banks and pied kingfishers shot past, flying just inches above the swirling current.

We set up camp that evening on the riverbank, then after dark the moon rose above the tree canopy and we drifted downstream by canoe to catch fish with a spear. Xavier stood motionless in the shallows like a bronze statue, his arms tense, his eyes scanning the moonlit water, then striking downwards with the speed of a cobra. On the opposite bank the fireflies blinked intermittently, as if sending out some secret message in Morse code, while bats skimmed the water. From the dark depths of the jungle behind us, an ocelot called softly to its mate. For me, it was a time of perfect peace.

When we emerged from the jungle a few days later, we found there was no bus back to Quito. But Xavier had an answer to everything. He took us to the gates of the nearest Ecuadorian Airforce base in a clearing in the forest, and after a few brief words a deal was struck. For a handful of pesos we could hitch a lift in the cargo hold of a turbo-prop Twin Otter that would soon be heading up to the capital.

I have to say it was one of the least comfortable but

most memorable of journeys. There were no seats, naturally, but we found a place on the metal floor, littered with peanut shells, beside half a dozen Quechua Indians and their belongings. Beside us a toucan hopped about in its cardboard box, oblivious to the bone-jarring vibrations of this flimsy craft. As we taxied for take-off a thunderstorm erupted and rain lashed the runway in sheets, yet somehow we rose shakily into the purple sky, banking crazily over the treetops for one last glimpse of the Amazon. The co-pilot grinned at us, a half-chewed biro tucked behind his ear, then leant over with that endearing smile so typical of Ecuadorians and shouted above the howl of the engines, 'I think you are happy in our country, no?' We were.

Chiquimula market, Guatemala, January 1988

13

Djibouti

A Picnic with the Foreign Legion

AS A STUDENT IN CAIRO, I HAD A MAP ON MY WALL. IT WAS the Michelin road map of north-east Africa, which really wasn't much use to me because I didn't know how to drive at the time. But it did serve as an incentive, a needle to prod me to go and explore the world beyond the crenellated walls and dusty suburbs of the great city I was living in. To the south lay the whole of Egypt, then Sudan, a wrinkled brown desert on the map, until it turned a lush green at the border with Zaïre. The Michelin map spurred me go to Khartoum, a three-day journey spent mostly on the roof of a train, but there was one country that both fascinated and eluded me. Right down on the bottom right-hand corner, tiny, shaped like a wobbly pizza with a slice missing, sandwiched between Somalia and what was then Ethiopia before Eritrea won its independence, lay Djibouti. The desert home of the French Foreign Legion and labelled in brackets on my map as 'Former French

Territory of the Afars and Issas', it sounded to me like the acme of exoticism and I wanted to go there. My student friend Peregrine and I investigated flights, which were way beyond our budget, then looked into getting a ferry, but couldn't find one, so we gave up. As if to console me, Peregrine waved a medical book at me that he had found in Cairo's Madbouly bookshop. It had a picture of some terrible venereal disease caught by a legionnaire in Djibouti. 'There,' he said triumphantly. 'Imagine if you had gone there and caught that!'

But I was determined to get to Djibouti one day; I just had to wait another twelve years. My chance came when I was a banker living in the Gulf, shuttling continually between the client-infested business centres of Kuwait, Abu Dhabi, Riyadh and Jeddah. As manager of our little regional office in Bahrain, I had a fairly free hand and although I was scrupulous about expenses I certainly pushed the boundaries when it came to tacking on a few extra days somewhere interesting. A morning meeting in Muscat meant I would probably stay on for the weekend and head up into the Jebel Akhdar mountains; Riyadh in Ramadan saw me exploring the wild borderlands along the Yemeni frontier. Until I met my future wife, Amanda, I had little incentive to spend the weekends on base in Bahrain, which was fun but all too developed compared to these wild places that drew me to them. And so after a couple of days of doing business in Jeddah I arranged to fly the short hop across the Red Sea down to Djibouti. For the first time in my thirty-two years I was going to Africa south of the Sahara, and I couldn't wait.

* * *

'Djibouti?' snapped the Saudi airport official. 'You're too late. We've closed the flight.' Hampered by the Ramadan traffic jams, I had inched northwards out of the city, arriving at the airport a full hour before take-off but apparently still too late for the Air France transit flight from Paris. Self-important officials were dashing around with clipboards, muttering into walkie-talkies and shaking their heads at passengers. The thought of returning to Bahrain, having failed to get to Africa by five minutes, was too much to bear and I had to summon my best classical Arabic proverbs to induce a reluctant smile of compassion. '*Al-'ajl min ash-shaytaan*,' I told them. 'Haste is from the devil.' 'All right,' said the Saudi official. 'We'll let you on, but there is no catering for you. You will have to go without food!' The look on his well-fed face was one of utmost repugnance, as if he might as well have been telling me I would have to spend the entire flight locked in the loo. 'Fine by me,' I said, and within minutes of take-off I was guzzling smoked salmon and champagne.

As the Red Sea coast of Arabia fell away beneath the port wing I got chatting to the Frenchwoman next to me. Christine was visiting her brother, a French naval officer stationed in Djibouti. She confirmed the rumour I had heard, that due to rebellious Afar tribesmen in the north most of the more interesting landscapes were out of bounds, sealed off by government checkpoints. 'But you know, Frank,' she added with a conspiratorial smile, 'tomorrow we are all going on an excursion with the Légion. We are going to try to reach Lake Assal in the north-west. If you like, we can take you with us.'

Djibouti airport in 1994 looked as if it had come

straight out of the Humphrey Bogart film *Casablanca* – I might as well have been looking at it through a black-and-white filter. French naval ratings and crew-cut legionnaires stood around in long socks and camp, impossibly tight shorts, looking tanned and fit, while lanky African baggage-handlers loped across the arrivals hall, cheap cigarettes drooping from their lips. Djibouti had only recently gained independence from France, but you wouldn't have thought it; this place gave every impression of still being a colony.

Outside the terminal it was very dark and very hot. Local boys scampered mischievously amongst the passengers while French soldiers shouldered their way through the throng and hefted their seamen's bags on to waiting trucks, bound no doubt for some fly-blown camp in this desert republic. Not sure quite what to expect, I had booked a room at the only international hotel, the Sheraton, on the beguilingly named Plateau des Serpents, but the promised transport had not materialized so Christine and her brother gave me a lift into town. Together we drove along potholed roads with the night sounds of crickets coming in through the window. Moths flickered around the few functioning streetlamps and skirted men sat around in sleepy groups, beneath peeling, colonial facades. I was in Africa at last.

At the Sheraton I was the only tourist, the other guests being all French aircrew and German military in transit from Somalia. Being something of a rarity I was invited to dine with the general manager on a terrace by the sea, candles flickering in the breeze. Han, from Holland, recounted how he had been skilfully pickpocketed in his first week here. 'I was easy meat,' he admitted, shaking his head as he poured himself a cold Kronenburg. 'Someone came up to me in the marketplace and thrust a tray of cigarettes beneath my nose. By the time I could get them to take it away his friend had slipped his hand beneath the tray and lifted the money out of my breast pocket.'

Han's dire warnings of pickpockets failed to put me off; the night was yet young and I was itching to get into town and see this place. It was, admittedly, perhaps not the best night to head into the heart of Djibouti. Two thousand French marines and sailors were already spilling ashore from the visiting Navy assault ship, the *Jeanne d'Arc*, but I had no intention of malingering in my hotel room and within minutes I was riding into town in a bright-green rust-bucket of a taxi.

You can picture the scene: a large, dimly lit square ringed by crumbling whitewashed walls with unstable balconies and flaking arches, children in filthy shorts hawking cigarettes and chewing gum, beggars in rags, a handful of seedy bars with sputtering purple neon signs above the doors. The town bore an air of casual menace.

I headed straight for the least dodgy-looking café, Le Café Bon Coin, to sink a cold beer from behind a low wall that kept the pedlars at bay; after years in the conservative, crime-free Gulf, I needed to find my bearings. Quaffing a chilled Kronenburg, I was vaguely aware of intermittent hisses from the other side of the wall. 'Psst . . . monsieur . . . cigarettes . . . cartes postales . . . mesdemoiselles,' and a face would be watching me with imploring eyes.

The French military were all over town: in stark con-trast to the Djiboutians they were, of course, clean-cut, well-fed and well-dressed. Tall and tanned naval officers in pressed white ducks sat at café tables, leaving the more raucous bars to the ratings and marines. Djibouti had its own Hard Rock Café, where I mingled with over a hundred sailors on R&R as they clinked beer bottles in endless toasts, pawing the Ethiopian waitresses with their braided hair and purple lipstick, then spilling drunkenly on to the dance floor. I had a sudden image of that terrible medical book in Cairo with its colourful genitals ravaged by Djiboutian VD.

At that point a fragrant beauty wafted up to me with a coy smile. Did I fancy a dance? I did, but I sensed it came with bells on. 'I live close by,' she added. There may have been a great party atmosphere in here, but this was clearly a pick-up joint too. This girl had not come all the way down from the Abyssinian highlands to make smalltalk with an Englishman. As I smiled and shook my head, I noticed that not everyone was joining in the fun in this place. Leaning against the bar and staring dead ahead with one of those thousand-yard stares was a chisel-jawed, shaven-headed legionnaire in immaculate service dress, with a bright-blue scorpion tattooed over his jugular. He flinched when someone pushed past him, then seemed to control himself. I could see that trouble was brewing and sure enough, the Military Police were already climbing out of their open-sided jeeps, truncheons swinging as I left. It was time to head back to the rattly air-conditioning of my hotel room, riding bleary-eyed through the dormant litter-strewn market and patting my pockets down.

Kept awake by the sheer thrill of being in Africa for the first time, I slept fitfully. As dawn broke, I pulled back the curtain to see a pair of flamingos flap low over the bay beneath my window. The sky was mostly still dark, but this close to the Equator I suspected the day would soon become scorching. The night before, I had arranged with Ahmed Assoweh, Djibouti's foremost diving instructor, for a day of scuba-diving off the remote Moucha Islands in the Gulf of Djibouti.

Down in the hotel lobby, the only people up were a handful of German soldiers, preparing to ship out the last of the German contingent from UNISOM, the UN's largely failed mission to save neighbouring Somalia from anarchy and famine. They were using Djibouti as their forward operating base, flying sorties into Belet Huen and Mogadishu just down the coast, and they looked exhausted.

At breakfast I met my fellow divers, a German medical crew on R&R, and together we drove down to the port in their white UNISOM van, then piled on to a boat crowded with French divers, its hold full of oxygen tanks and several crates of beer. Two hours out of harbour, where the French warship *Jeanne d'Arc* lay at anchor glinting in the sun, we reached the coral-fringed islets of Moucha, close to the narrow Bab el-Mandeb straits that separate Africa from Arabia. I was paired off to dive with Alain, a Frenchman, while the Germans, as novices, went down with Assoweh. It was at this point that we discovered that the dive equipment was basic, to say the least. There was no Buoyancy Control Device – the inflatable jacket you fill from the tank with just the right amount of air to control your depth – and there was no 'octopus' or second string, the reserve mouthpiece you are always supposed to carry in case your dive partner runs out of air at depth. In fact the equipment consisted of nothing more than a weight belt and an oxygen tank attached to a mouthpiece. OK, I thought, this is interesting, so how exactly are we expected to control our depth without a BCD? I looked at Alain and he gave me a well-practised Gallic shrug. He dived here every week, he assured me, it would be fine.

And it was. With a final glance at our watches we back-flipped over the side of the boat and used our fins to propel ourselves downwards. In warm seas and no current we worked our way slowly along the face of the reef, stopping to peer at fluttering venomous Lionfish from a discreet distance, then grazing the drifting tendrils of a purple sea anemone. From a rock crevice fifteen metres below the surface a brown moray eel opened and closed its jaws at the world, as if showing off its fearsome set of teeth. A turtle flippered past.

Back on the boat, we chugged towards the shore, a place straight out of a Bounty advert: a long, pristine white beach fringed by palms and mangroves and lapped by the gentle waters of the Arabian Sea. A pair of Osprey sea eagles was hunting close to the shore, gliding low over the beach to the fascination of the German Army medics, who borrowed my binoculars then quickly refocused them on the French girls from our group who had set up beneath a date palm and changed into bikinis.

While the Djiboutian crew waded ashore with cool boxes of beer and began cooking lobster over a charcoal fire, I chatted to Jurg, the chief medical officer in the German UNISOM team. The German mission in Somalia had been, he said, a disaster. Not having sent troops abroad for half a century, the Germans were ill-prepared for this job, in his view, and many of the soldiers had become demoralized, not understanding why they had to be there. The only German troops getting anything out of the operation were the Paras, he said, as they were using Somalia's open country to get in plenty of drops.

'But hang on a minute,' I interjected. 'I thought the whole idea was to save the Somalis from famine?' Jurg gave a snort and twiddled a piece of driftwood in the sand. The infamous Blackhawk Down incident just four months ago was still fresh in everyone's minds here, when Somali gunmen had shot down a US Army Blackhawk helicopter, killed eighteen Rangers in the rescue attempt and dragged American corpses through the streets. 'The Somalis' attitude to us, the UN forces, has degenerated into opportunistic pilfering of supplies,' he said. 'They have long ago become disillusioned with the Americans because they don't disarm the gangs, so now they are only interested in extracting as much material as possible from the foreigners before they leave.' Jurg grumbled that every time the Americans captured an arms cache they would get a delegation coming to them from the local tribe saying they needed the arms for their own protection against other raiding tribes, so the Americans would end up handing back half the weapons. He sighed. At least the combat casualties they were treating were not as bad now as they had been in October.

Combat casualties? I was having a hard time getting to grips with conversation like this: just twenty-four hours ago I had been sitting in a business meeting in a five-star hotel in Saudi Arabia, talking portfolio management, and now here I was sitting on a desert island off the Horn of Africa, sipping a cold beer and salivating over chargrilled lobster while a German soldier told me about the war just down the coast in Somalia. Djibouti was largely peaceful and it was impossible to imagine the horrors of the Somali conflict, which were so close and yet a world away from where I was now.

The next morning I was back in the hotel lobby at dawn. 'You are fortunate today, no?' said a voice behind me. It was Michel, the French naval officer, and his sister, whom I had met on the plane, come to collect me for the promised picnic with the Foreign Legion. 'This is the first excursion into the north for many months,' he said. 'Your timing is perfect!'

It seemed we were to be part of a big convoy, all French military and their dependants, led by a heavily armed escort of French Foreign Legion; there were six truckloads of off-duty sailors, no doubt the worse for wear after the last few nights' activities. From the port we drove west up on to a dry plateau, passing a desperate-looking Somali refugee camp partially hidden by a wall, which the French called '*une cache-misère*' – a misery-hider. 'There's cholera over there,' remarked Michel, keeping his foot on the accelerator. Djibouti was one of the poorest countries I had ever visited and yet these Somalis were clearly so desperate to escape conditions in their own country they had chosen to flee here. Things in Mogadishu must be truly dire, I thought. Coming from the Gulf I found such poverty a shock, even glimpsed as it was through a car window at speed. Years later, on a return visit for BBC's

Newsnight in 2003, I noticed the camp was still there; nothing seemed to have changed.

We drove on through a suburb called Bal-Balla, where a boy threw a desultory stone at our car, then shrugged his shoulders and turned away, not even bothering to run. The landscape was exactly what I had expected for the Horn of Africa: rolling, burnt-looking hills covered in stunted thorn bushes, dried-up wadis lined with acacia, camels moving slowly through the bush tended by stick-thin men with orange henna in their grizzled hair. We passed a train of camels loaded down with bundles of branches, the struts for building *dayoutas*, traditional Djiboutian nomadic huts of animal hide laid over a conical frame-work of interwoven branches. Nomad women with drooping bead necklaces, shepherding the camel train with wooden staffs, tossed stones at us as we passed. This was clearly a national pastime. It seemed impossible that this place was almost next to super-rich Saudi Arabia on the map, two countries separated by a thin strip of sea, yet worlds apart.

Drawing up at a junction, we found we were the first civilians to reach the expedition's convening point for the convoy, but already green-bereted legionnaires in reflective sunglasses were marshalling the troops off the trucks and corporals were lining up the vehicles in perfect formation. There were shouts in French and answers back in English and German; the Legion attracts all sorts. As the convoy gathered, a problem occurred. The Djiboutian Army was unwilling to let us through because they said no one had let them know in advance. 'It's all about money,' shrugged Michel. 'They want a bribe.' But the legionnaires had

other ideas: in a display of macho bravado they accelerated in their jeeps towards the Djiboutian position, braked
in a flurry of dust, got out and explained that government
permission had already been granted and that now they
would be moving through. It was the behaviour of a
school playground bully, but I can't say I was disappointed
when the convoy moved forward, the legionnaires riding
shotgun out in front with their hands on their heavy
mounted machine guns. 'I'd like to meet some of them
when we stop,' I ventured out of curiosity. Michel kept his
eyes on the road and did not say anything at first. 'I would
not advise it,' he said eventually. 'They don't welcome
questions. You know, some of these guys have dark pasts
and they don't like meeting strangers. Maybe they will
think you are a journalist or something.' Heaven forbid.

Skirting the western shore of the Gulf of Tadjoura,
which cuts Djibouti in half, we entered a dramatic and
awe-inspiring landscape. This was the Rift Valley, which
runs all the way from Central Africa up to the Sinai
Peninsula and beyond. The mountains were black and
volcanic, almost prehistoric in appearance; their peaks
were shrouded in cloud, their valleys plunged into the sea.

Another checkpoint and more waiting. This time the
Djiboutians sent an escort of a dozen soldiers to go with
us. There had been occasional attacks on traffic by the
local Afar tribesmen, and more than once we swerved to
avoid a crater blown in the road by a mine. As we rounded
a bend, the road simply fell away to one side. Hundreds of
feet below lay the Ghoubet Kharab, the westernmost bay
of the Gulf of Tadjoura, where the distant blue waters
glittered and sparkled invitingly. Just offshore stood a

strangely shaped island, l'Ile de Diable, Devil's Island, which looked as if it had once aspired to be a volcano before a giant fist had punched it hard from above, making it crumple in on itself.

'Jacques Cousteau came here,' announced Michel. 'He discovered some monstrous deep-sea fish that pulverized a shark cage with a dead camel inside that they lowered into the depths.' I looked down at the bay and I could believe it.

Inland, and five hundred feet below sea level, lay the searing expanse of Lake Assal, a barren and blistered salt lake giving off such a blinding white glare that everyone scrambled for their sunglasses. Here there grew no blade of glass, and not one bird alighted on its shores. It must be one of the most inhospitable places on earth, as well as one of the hottest, and if that was not enough I learnt that within living memory the tribes here had castrated intruders. But while the legionnaires kept watch, inscrutable behind their sunglasses, the French sailors were already enjoying themselves, hard at work with pick-axes, hacking off great chunks of crystallized salt to haul off as souvenirs. The Djiboutian soldiers were strolling along the shore with their ancient Kalashnikovs slung over their shoulders, stopping to chat with the French commandos and stealing furtive glances at the bikini-clad females. The men had stripped to their skimpy swimming trunks and were treading warily on the sharp and brittle salt crystals. I changed into my baggy British surf shorts and joined them in the water, where Michel was handing out cans of chilled lager. As I sank back into this treacly morass, the water felt warm and heavy, like a damp blanket, so saline I floated without effort. This is the life, I thought – a dip below sea level in one of the hottest places on earth with a cold beer in my hand, a cloudless sky above and a lunar landscape all around.

The plan was to drive around the north side of the Gulf of Tadjoura to the mountainous Forest of Djanet, but the authorities were edgy about rebel ambushes and declined permission. Probably just as well, I decided, when I noticed a signpost riddled with bullet holes. After stopping to scald our fingers in some boiling springs that came bubbling out of the volcanic rock, the convoy broke up once we were back in government-controlled territory, and we headed for the Grand Bara, the larger of Djibouti's two deserts.

Living as I did in the Middle East, I had to try hard to look excited at the prospect of visiting yet another desert, but this was to be like nothing I had seen before. Stretching for miles on either side was an utterly flat piste of white sand. No dune, rock or vegetation interrupted its deadpan surface; only mirages, blue and quivering, broke the surface, along with the occasional dust devil, or *sorcier* as the French called them. Mini-tornados of sand, they would race across the desert, spinning crazily, then vanish suddenly into thin air. No wonder the Bedu once thought they were caused by genies.

In the mid-afternoon, beside a corral of military jeeps, we cracked open the mother of all French picnics. There were fresh baguettes, baked early that morning back in barracks, there was Brie, Camembert, pâté, red wine, pastis and chilled bottles of rosé, all spread out on mats in the blazing sun. Hardened commandos with razor haircuts and reflective shades sat about on folding camp stools, passing comment on the excellent pâté. It was, quite simply, surreal.

At this point I noticed that a mirage in the middle distance was slowly forming into a shape, then two shapes, moving steadily towards us with a strange, loping stride, which gradually revealed themselves to be two Afar tribesmen. Tall, emaciated and barefoot, they must have walked for miles across the desert, yet now they seemed uncertain what to do.

They stopped some way off to regard us in silence, unable to ask for food or water due to the fasting strictures of the Muslim holy month of Ramadan, which was now in force, but evidently consumed with curiosity as well, no doubt, as hunger. And who could blame them? For the French had now begun a game of boules in the sand, rolling the shiny balls past beetle burrows and calling out to each other in triumph. The younger of the two tribesmen seemed amused by this strange sport being performed in his back yard, but his older companion kept muttering darkly in Somali. One of the French marines asked, by miming charades-style, if it would be all right to take a photo of him. At first the tribesman did not react. Then, the instant the photo was taken, he emitted a high-pitched canine yelp, jumped a yard into the air and brandished his stick. And then he did absolutely nothing, just stared at us, as if waiting for us to make the next move.

I was baffled. For years my cultural compass had been anchored in the Arab world. I knew not to take pictures of women, to avoid pointing a camera near sensitive buildings and always to ask men before taking a photo of them (although even with all these precautions, I was once arrested in Saudi Arabia for photographing a rather shapely watermelon in a market). I had seen up-close how conservative Arabs can react when someone takes an unsolicited photo; they are usually either indignant, angry or simply offended. But this Afar tribesman's childlike reaction was not something I could get a handle on. I had absolutely no idea what to expect next – would the tribes-men attack the group? Would they demand money? Would they run away? Seconds passed as we all looked at each other. Then the French shrugged and went back to their boules and their Camembert, and the tribesmen drifted away, vanishing back into the shimmering mirage from which they had come.

The picnic over, we drove back to the Djiboutian capital, stopping in some scrub to watch a herd of gazelles grazing on acacia bushes, rearing up on their hind legs to reach the best leaves. Rather less picturesque was the charnel-house we passed on the outskirts of town. This, explained Michel, was where they incinerated the city's dead, and sure enough the surrounding trees were heavy with vultures, their bald heads craning in expectation.

That night, back at my hotel, I put on some music and took a long soak in the bath to wash the dust out of my hair. As I watched a gecko do its gravity-defying crawl across the ceiling, I pondered how little I knew about this place, the Horn of Africa. Without the protection and the company of the legionnaires – not, admittedly, a community I felt instantly at home with – I was completely lost here. I did not speak the language, I did not understand the customs. Djibouti had certainly been an enigma and it had been good to break out of the comfort zone of the Gulf, but I had to admit that I was completely out of my depth here.

14

Botswana

Camping with Lions

IN A WHITEWASHED, LINOLEUM-FLOORED ROOM, A WOMAN pushed up my sleeve, grabbed a hypodermic syringe, pulled back her forearm and struck hard, swinging the needle in a rapid arc into the flesh of my upper arm. Not surprisingly, it hurt like hell. I glanced up at my new girl-friend and mouthed: 'You're next.'

Inoculations for southern Africa were not perhaps the ideal Cupid's arrow to kick off a fresh relationship, but Amanda, like the nurse, was a Kiwi and she took it like a trouper. I had met her a few months earlier when she gate-crashed my party at the company villa I lived in in Bahrain. Having parted company with Carrie, who I had dated for much of my twenties, when the bank assigned me out to the Gulf for an indefinite posting, I had really not expected to meet the future Mrs G on this tiny, hedonistic island. But Amanda was fun and I was entranced by her radiant smile and her easy laugh. By the time my posting came to an end and the bank was making plans to recall me to a desk job at head office in London, Amanda and I had backpacked around Sri Lanka and gone camping in the dunes of Oman. So when I announced that I now had a few weeks' leave to spend I was not surprised when she said, 'Let's not waste it. Let's go somewhere neither of us has ever been.' Ten days later we were touching down in Bulawayo in western Zimbabwe, a country that, back then in 1994, was seen almost as an oasis of stability and which had yet to endure the agonies and deprivations of the latter years of Mugabe's rule.

In Zimbabwe we did what everyone did: we gazed in awe at the Victoria Falls, where the mist rose up from the tons of falling water and made rainbows of the afternoon sun. In the elegant gardens of the Victoria Falls Hotel we sipped Earl Grey tea and watched vervet monkeys scamper between the waiters, leaping on to tables to up-end glasses with their nearly human hands as soon as customers left.

Then we went white-water rafting, which I vowed never, ever to do again. At the height of the southern African winter, the Zambezi river was dangerously high, and far, far below the towering cliffs that hemmed it in, the water churned its way down towards Lake Kariba, plunging over more than a dozen rapids and rock-strewn waterfalls. Young, enterprising South Africans had long ago worked out that to canoe or raft down this would be both fun and profitable. Travellers in their twenties and thirties, like us, would be more than willing to part with a few Zim dollars for the thrill and challenge of 'taking on' the river, especially when the price included a videotaped record of the whole experience, filmed from vantage points along the shore.

So early the next morning we reported to the riverbank, gathering with a dozen other backpackers to try on our lifejackets and yellow plastic helmets, which looked as if they had come straight from a toyshop. The river looked like a docile, sleeping animal at this point, lazily coiling its way downstream, and indeed it was as calm as a mill pond as we practised our drills in preparation for the rapids. Dragonflies hovered and skimmed above the surface and midges danced in the sunbeams.

'All right then!' called out Hendrijk, the oarsman in the bows, a burly South African from Cape Town. 'Who's ready for the white water?' It was a rhetorical question – we were already in the raft and there was no backing out now. 'We call this one the Catcher's Mitt,' he said. 'Hold on to the sides and paddle like fury when I say so!'

I will never in my life forget the noise of the approaching rapids, a rising, deafening roar that seemed to suck us inexorably closer. Our inflatable dinghy picked up speed and suddenly we were over the lip of a ledge, flying through the air and tilting downwards at 45 degrees. 'Here we go!' I shouted. 'We're going to flip over!' But we didn't – quite. The boat nosedived over the rocks into the swirling white foam and just righted itself; there were cheers and back slaps all round.

'That was just the beginning,' warned Hendrijk. 'That one was a tiddler.' But already there was a problem. Even the Catcher's Mitt could be dangerous, and the force of the current as we had gone over the edge had wrenched one of the oars from Hendrijk's hand and dislocated his thumb; now it was swelling up badly. 'Sorry, folks, I'm damaged goods,' he announced. 'I can't take you through the big ones with this thumb. But don't worry, I'll get you a replacement.'

The replacement, it turned out, was a dud. The son of a local politician, he was retained on the company's payroll, we were told, to keep the authorities onside, but now he was insisting that he was ready to crew a boat down the river and the rafting company had acceded. Clearly nervous, though, the organizers offered everyone the chance to bail out, and as he hopped aboard all the girls voted with their feet and hopped ashore. I must admit I would have dearly liked to have gone with them: the river was not really my home turf, preferring as I do mountains and deserts. But by now there was a certain macho camaraderie amongst those of us left in the boat, mostly American backpackers – a sort of hell-yeah-I-wouldn't-miss-this-for-the-world attitude – and I was reluctant to break the spell. We were to be the politician's son's un-witting guinea pigs.

At first all seemed well. He grinned broadly as we approached the next rapid and exhorted us to row faster in all the right places, steering us through the foam and rocks without incident. But then came the rapid they called the Terminator, and from the sound of it as we approached we might as well have been tipping ourselves over the Victoria Falls. At the crucial moment the politician's son lost his cool and panicked, flailing around with the oars; within seconds the inflatable raft had tipped us into a boiling, seething cauldron of angry water that masked a dozen unseen rocks. We did not know it at the time, but already that year two crewmen had been lost in this rapid, throttled by the Terminator when a rescue rope got snagged on the rocks and drowned by the sheer force of the water. When a river is so churned up that it turns to white foam, we had been told, the lifejackets lose much of their buoyancy and cannot always save you.

Having had the breath knocked out of me by the force of being flipped over, I now found myself in a strange world. I rose to the surface to find myself trapped beneath the upturned raft. There was a sizeable air pocket so I had no trouble breathing, but the current was sweeping me along at a fair rate towards the next rapid and I needed to either get back on the boat or out of the water before then. I reached my arm out under the side of the boat so I could slap it to draw the attention of the rescue crew, but immediately it became stuck: by ill luck my wrist had become wedged between the rubber side of the raft and the spare oar strapped to it. Now I was truly trapped, being carried along beneath the boat, unable to extricate myself and gulping mouthfuls of air as the water washed in waves over my head. This was not good.

Suddenly I felt strong arms freeing my trapped arm, then hauling me up on to the upturned boat. I felt a surge of relief, followed by an inexplicable sense of panic. Something was not right. I was missing something, but couldn't work out what. My shoe was gone, but I could live with that. Then I saw the crowd on the riverbank, including Amanda, collapsing with laughter. At me. I glanced down and saw why. My swimming shorts had been torn off by the rapids and were now dangling precariously from my ankles: I was stark naked except for that yellow plastic helmet still loyally strapped to my head, and the video cameras were happily rolling.

Neither of us could dispute that white-water rafting down the swollen Zambezi had been an adrenaline rush, but Amanda and I had come to southern Africa to see the wilderness and wildlife, and for that we had to fly west across the border into Botswana, where the glittering expanse of the Okavango Delta spread out towards the Angolan border. Landing on a dusty airstrip in the Moremi reserve, our tiny turboprop Cessna narrowly missed colliding with a warthog. We extracted our rucksacks, put them on our shoulders and followed the directions through the bush to Oddballs Camp.

It made no pretence at comfort. Run on a shoestring by hardy young South Africans and Brits, this was a put-the-tent-up-yourself-and-don't-complain sort of place. There was a rickety wicker enclosure euphemistically called 'the shower block' and a low-roofed shack with a few essential supplies, like can-openers. The light and colour of the African bush were all around us, but on the first morning I ran into trouble. 'Elephant approaching!' went up the cry around the camp. The elephants, it seemed, had a passion for palm nuts, and Oddballs Camp just happened to be built around several palm-nut trees. I was not unduly worried since I was tucked out of sight in the shower block. But Amanda's frightened face suddenly appeared round the wicker wall. 'Get out now!' she screamed. 'He's heading this way!' I threw a towel around my waist and emerged; she was not exaggerating, the elephant was a huge male and I looked up to see him striding purposefully towards me, ears flapping, trunk swaying from side to side. It was then that I noticed that some bright spark at Oddballs had built the shower block all around a tree bearing . . . palm nuts. Amanda and I withdrew to a safe distance just in time to watch the elephant crash indiscriminately through the flimsy walls of the shower enclosure, trampling everything underfoot, all so he could smash his forehead against the tree and bring down his precious palm nuts. Amanda gave me a rather smug look: if I had stayed to finish my shower I would have probably been crushed to a pulp.

Despite the excitement of being nearly trampled to death, Oddballs Camp was only meant to be a staging post before the real adventure – a trip into the wilderness of the Okavango by dugout canoe or *makoro*. We had booked a guide in advance and we had rather expected him to be some grizzled ranger/tracker type, an experienced marsh man who knew every inch of the bush. Instead, that afternoon, we were introduced to Keke, a slender boy who looked fourteen, though he insisted he was seventeen. He spoke little English – just enough to assure us he had nothing to defend us with if we met a lion – but he had an easy smile and his confidence was infectious. As the sun danced on the ripples between the reeds, he stowed our rucksacks between us in the *makoro* and poled away from the camp.

Within minutes we were out on our own, gliding silently through the marsh beneath a vast blue African sky. It was August, the southern African winter, but by day the Okavango was warm, clear and sunlit – the rains would come in summer. A large bird, an African Fish Eagle, flapped right past us, its talons skimming the water, then snatched up a fish and withdrew to an overhanging branch to tear it apart. Kingfishers hovered over the water and emerald-green Bee-eater birds perched on the swaying reeds, while a discreet splash up ahead heralded a pair of river otters, twisting and diving in the shallows. 'What about crocodiles?' asked Amanda, as if reading my thoughts; along with hippos, crocodiles are one of the deadliest animals in the African bush and one glance at our flimsy dugout told me it could be snapped in two with ease. 'No,' said Keke flatly. 'Not in this part.'

We beached our canoe that evening on a shallow mud-bank beneath the spreading arms of a baobab tree. As we pitched our tent Keke prepared a fire, ferrying cans of water from the riverbank, then drinking straight from the river. 'No bilharzias here,' he announced. When the sunset came it exploded like a slow-motion fireball in the western sky, silhouetting the curious shapes of the palm-nut trees and turning the marsh into a sea of fire. Amanda and I sat on the riverbank, nursing mugs of steaming cocoa as the temperature fell, listening to the sounds of the bush moving from day into night: the whirr of cicadas, the chuckle of guinea fowl settling down to roost, the distant yelp of a hyena, the crash of elephants bringing down more palm nuts. Strangely, since we were hours by canoe from help if anything went wrong, we both felt completely at peace, two tiny specks deep in the Botswanan bush, our safety entirely in the hands of a seventeen-year-old with the body of a young boy.

We heard the first roar just as we were scooping the last of our supper out of our mess tins. Amanda looked up sharply while I feigned nonchalance to reassure her. The noise was some way off but there was no mistaking where it had come from. 'Lion,' pronounced Keke and grinned broadly as if this was some huge prearranged joke to make our trip more exciting. 'So . . .' began Amanda slowly, 'exactly how far away is he?' Keke looked down at his plate and considered for a moment; he had cooked himself something different to the tinned rations we had broken open that night and it didn't look too appetizing to us. 'About fifteen minutes,' said Keke, 'for us to reach him.' 'No, I didn't mean that,' said Amanda. 'How long for *him* to reach *us*?' 'Ah . . . Maybe five minutes.' Amanda and I exchanged glances – this did not sound good. 'Maybe we'd better pack up these things and get inside our tent?' I suggested. 'Yes, maybe,' said Keke mildly, with a little shrug of his slender shoulders. I suspected that if the lion came bursting into our little camp circle right then, he might accept this with a sort of bush fatalism. As we prepared to disappear into our little musty tent and zip up the flap there was another roar, this time much closer. 'How far now?' I called out to Keke as I fumbled with the zip. 'Two minutes,' came the answer.

And so began a terrifying night. Within minutes it became clear that there was more than one lion and that they were heading for us. There is something deeply chilling about the throat-trembling vibration of a fully grown lion's roar. It speaks of an immense, controlled power, like the noise given off with the nudge of the accelerator on a turbo-charged sports car. 'Turn that torch off!' we hissed at each other, huddled inside our tent. We knew that lions were supposed to be impressed by the profile of a creature, so that unprotected humans sitting up in a large jeep, for example, are meant to be perfectly safe; but our tiny tent was no taller than a warthog; one swipe of a clawed paw and the canvas would be ripped open and we would be dinner. Lying there in the darkness, clinging to each other in fear, we counted the seconds between roars. Despite the cold, my hands were sweating as I gripped my diminutive Swiss Army penknife – all two inches of its biggest blade extended – bracing myself for that terrible moment I thought would come.

'You want beans?' called out Keke. What was he on about? Beans? When we were about to be attacked by lions? Was this some time-honoured Botswanan trick to put them off the scent? Then I realized it was morning and Keke was cooking breakfast. We must have fallen asleep in the small hours, dreaming of rippling, predatory muscles and savage, slavering jaws. Keke was very excited and was beckoning us over. 'See here?' he pointed. 'And here . . . and here.' The soft dirt around our makeshift camp was a maze of footprints, all bearing the pad and claw marks of lion. 'This one is lioness,' said Keke. 'She is with cub, probably very hungry.' 'So where are they now?' I asked. 'Will they come back?' 'Lion sleeping now,' he said. 'But we should move from here.' Right.

It took us less than five minutes to pull down our tent and stuff it into my rucksack; the daylight may have taken the edge off our fear, but we were still keen to put as much distance between ourselves and the lions as possible. We set off on foot through the dry, brittle grass with Keke striding boldly out in front, armed with little more than a bent twig. It reminded me of that line in *Blackadder* where

Rowan Atkinson talks of his heroism when being 'attacked by a tribeswoman with a viciously sharpened mango'.

The landscape was dotted with curious red mounds like mud stalagmites and Keke now ran up one and invited us to join him. 'Termites,' he pronounced as he surveyed the view. 'They eat everything, but this one empty.' The view was enchanting: not far off we could see a herd of zebra grazing, their extraordinary pied camouflage working perfectly here in the bush, and at the edge of the treeline we could see a patrol of three marauding ground hornbills, large, fearsome birds as big as turkeys that stalked the long grass in search of tortoises to prise open with their massive casqued bills. Here too were giraffes that moved with elegance and poise through the taller trees, pausing to stare down at us before taking fright and cantering off with rather less grace.

We moved on, then stopped short at the biggest pile of dung I ever hope to see. Clearly a small herd of elephants had been this way recently. While I was about to give these football-sized pats a wide berth, Keke leant forward in fascination, eager to divine what they had been eating. Soon he had picked up their trail and before long he gripped our arms in restraint: the herd was just yards away, ambling and snorting their way through a grove of trees, pausing to blow dust over their backs. Yet if they saw us they showed no alarm, heading off at their own leisurely pace to go and batter some more palm-nut trees, no doubt. We loved this kind of foot safari, although I shudder to think of how unprotected we would have been if we had ever run into the lions. Thanks to the skill of Keke, the wildlife of Africa was brought right up to our faces, invading our senses and making us tune in to everything around us.

Days later, when we had eventually poled back to Oddballs Camp by canoe, and hopped on another Cessna to spend our last few days at a more substantial, comfortable camp called San-ta-wani, somehow we found the magic was missing. There was all the food we could eat – 'save yourselves,' said the matronly waitress, meaning 'serve yourselves' – and there were escorted trips by jeep into the bush to find herds of bad-tempered hippos wallowing in the swamp or dozing prides of lions. The guides would all know exactly where the animals were because they communicated with each other by walkietalkie. It was, of course, a privilege to see all this, but the ten-year-old American boy beside us in the jeep, holidaying with his parents, was bored and blasé. 'Impala,' he would drawl as the herds went by. 'Just more impala and zebra.' I resolved there and then not to take my future children on safari until they were old enough to appreciate it.

But on our final night there was a drama that impressed even Impala Boy. We had left the campfire and returned to our stone hut when it happened again, that mesmerizing, heart-stopping roar of a lion. This time it was followed by a trumpet and a bellow: the lions and the elephants were having a face-off down at the waterhole. It was pitch dark outside and we decided, on balance, it would not be a good idea to blunder on to the scene with cameras flashing. Even though this time we were behind stone walls rather than canvas, Amanda glanced nervously up at the gap between the wall and the edge of the roof. 'Could they get through that, d'you reckon?' she asked. We decided they could, so we spent our last night under African skies cowering in the only room with a roof – the loo. It was not the most romantic finale to our African holiday, but we would not have had that trip any other way.

15

Colombia

In Search of the Lost City

IN 1995 SOMETHING HAPPENED WHICH, ALTHOUGH A setback at the time, was to fortify me for later challenges, including the biggest one of all: surviving multiple gunshot wounds. I broke three ribs in karate – or, to be accurate, a friend kicked them in during training. I had been training two evenings a week down at the Budokwai gym in Chelsea, where the sessions were exhausting: an hour of warm-up exercises, followed by an hour of instruction and sparring. The sparring, called Kumite, started off as a gentle, non-contact exercise when we were just beginners, but as my friend Mark Hutchinson and I progressed over the months, changing the colour of our belts as we went, the training grew more intense, the sparring more realistic. By the time we had earnt our purple belts in Shotokan, the instructor started pairing us up with black belts to keep us on our toes. I found myself having to fight an unsmiling, well-built man in his late twenties called Guy, who seemed to have lightning reflexes and a natural aggression for sparring. 'I'm warning you,' he said in a coarse voice curiously out of place for Chelsea, 'I'm gonna getcha. If you don't speed up I'll catch you. I'll hit you full in the face.' Several years older than him, I didn't like to admit it but I was already at full stretch, deflecting his punches and kicks, which he delivered with effortless accuracy. He seemed to be enjoying himself. As I slowed he picked up speed, like an accelerating train, and the next thing I knew there was a bang and a flash as his knuckles connected hard with my cheekbone. I felt temporarily dizzy. Just when I thought, I can't keep this up, I'm going to get smacked in the teeth here, the instructor shouted that welcome word 'Change!' and we switched sparring partners. I later learnt that my former opponent was Guy Ritchie, martial arts enthusiast, husband of Madonna until 2008, and director of such Brit gangster flicks as *Snatch*, *Lock, Stock and Two Smoking Barrels* and *RocknRolla*.

But it wasn't Guy Ritchie who sent me off to A&E with three cracked ribs, it was my friend Mark. An ex-Guards officer, he had legs like tree trunks, and what he lacked in finesse he made up for in strength. We had joined the Budokwai gym together as karate novices, but although we were technically the same grade Mark had an animal cunning, a sort of primal instinct for which way I was likely to move. Or maybe I was just dead predictable. Either way, he was certainly a formidable opponent at sparring. When he feinted a punch to my face I blocked it with my right arm, twisting it up and sideways as we had been taught, trying to deflect the strike I thought he was making. But Mark was selling me a dummy; in an instant he shifted his weight on to his back foot, tilted backwards from the hips and kicked out hard, his outstretched leg parallel to the ground, the sole of his bare right foot connecting full-on with my ribs. Even through the thin padding of my white suit it hurt. A lot. There were still several minutes of sparring remaining so I resolved to carry on, but soon the pain became too much; it felt as if there was a cannonball lurching around inside my ribcage. 'Hang on, Mark,' I gasped between wheezes. 'I've got to take a break. Maybe I'm getting old but you knocked the stuffing out of me just then.' We were both in our thirties and Mark clearly saw age as no barrier to excellence, but he suspected something was wrong and escorted me to the sidelines, where I sat wincing in pain.

The following morning an X-ray confirmed that I had three cracked ribs. Mark was mortified, yet I bore him no ill will – this was just one of the hazards of karate; in fact, the next week he told me he himself had narrowly avoided getting his front teeth pushed in. For me, this was a sign that it was time to call it a day. Like parachuting, which I had tried to do three times, only to be thwarted each time by the British weather, I felt as if someone were trying to tell me that martial arts were not for me. I was willing to accept risk, but only so far.

As soon as my ribs had healed I began to think about travelling once more, this time to Colombia. I now had rather more time and rather less money at my disposal, having forsaken the lucrative world of banking for the fickle industry of freelance news journalism. I had at last embarked on the career I had always yearned for, starting out in my thirties as an assistant producer in the BBC World TV newsroom.

Freelancing had its ups and downs: no one paid you for holidays, but you could at least take them whenever you wanted. I decided to combine work with play by taking my new video camera to the jungles of South America, accompanied by James Maughan, who had been with me in Ecuador. We were both intrigued by the idea of going to Colombia, although it had long had a bad press with its multi-billion-dollar cocaine industry, kidnapping and pipeline-bombing Marxist guerrillas. In 1996 stories abounded of Colombian drivers getting casually shot in the face for hooting their horns at the wrong kind of car at the traffic lights, or waking up naked and penniless two days after accepting coffee from a stranger. Guns, crime and coke had become part of daily life for many Colombians.

But we did have a specific incentive for going to Colombia. A window of opportunity had opened up in the remote Sierra Nevada de Santa Marta Mountains, the world's tallest and steepest coastal mountains, rising up through the jungle to a snow-capped 19,000 feet. We had heard that the region's well-armed *marimberos*, the Indian marijuana farmers, had started allowing small groups of trekkers to pass through these mountains to reach the fabled Lost City of the Tayrona Indians. It was said to be a hot, arduous journey, days of trudging up through malarial jungle, traversing swinging rope bridges and sleeping in hammocks, all to reach the cloud-shrouded ruins of a five-hundred-year-old Indian civilization that had been lost to the world until it was recently re-discovered. With the ongoing battle to eradicate drug crops in the Sierra, and the local Kogui Indians' mistrust of intruders, the Lost City had been opening, closing and reopening to travellers with maddening unpredictability. We were keen to seize the opportunity before the Indians had second thoughts and closed the route once more. I was thirty-four, James was thirty, and we were raring to go. In retrospect it was one of the best travel choices I have ever made, blissfully unaware at the time that this would be my last visit to South America before I lost the use of my legs and that the next time I came to Colombia I would be in a wheelchair.

In Bogotá, the country's bloated Andean capital, we were met at the airport by friends of James's in an armour-plated limousine. 'Bit over the top, isn't it?' he remarked. 'Not at all,' replied our hostess. 'You can't be too careful in this city.' It turned out she was from a wealthy merchant family who had no wish to add to Colombia's kidnap statistics, but their gated, patrolled apartment complex already had guests so we were shunted off to a small hotel. The place was almost empty and the two girls behind reception were bored to distraction, swivelling on their chairs and twiddling their biros, so they jumped at our suggestion that we should all go out that night. Bogotá's mayor – a figure of some controversy after dropping his trousers at a public event – was trying to clean up the city and had ordered an early curfew. 'This will not be a problem,' said Adriana, who was doing reception work to finance her way through university. 'To avoid the curfew everyone is going to nightclubs just outside the city limits. Our friends are going there tonight. It will be fun.'

In a long, low barn on the crest of the hills looking down on to Bogotá, we found the city's most beautiful people at play. The infinitely tedious and overplayed song 'La Macarena' had yet to become a hit in Britain, but in Colombia that night it was all the rage. Girls in skimpy tops and miniskirts were dancing in a line on wooden tables, their tanned, slender arms twirling in sync and their smiles flashing at their boyfriends, who cheered them on.

Groggy, but still pleasantly buzzing, we flew down from Bogotá the next day to the tiny coastal airstrip at Santa Marta, where a hot wind was blowing in from the Caribbean. Within hours of landing we had found a small tour company in the backstreets that was setting off for the Lost City the following morning. 'You must be fit,' said our guides, although it was a bit late to be getting in any training now.

That night James and I toasted our coming adventure, clinking cold beer bottles, sweaty with condensation, in a bar with peeling posters of bullfighters on the wall and a comatose drunk slumped in the corner. We had no idea where we would be sleeping the next night; all we knew was that we were heading for the jungle.

At dawn we gathered at the bus stop with the other trekkers, a collection of European and American twenty- and thirty-somethings, plus a young Israeli straight out of military service. An open-topped lorry drew up, then another, and we piled into the back with our rucksacks, exchanging mumbled greetings as we considered the trip ahead. From Santa Marta our two-truck convoy wound rapidly uphill, jolting through the banana groves to a tiny village in the foothills where barefoot children leant against an abandoned pool table, watching us solemnly, and from where our Indian guides now emerged to join us. This was as far as the trucks could go; from now on we would be travelling on foot.

Within hours of starting the walk uphill from Colombia's northern coastal lowlands, the cloying, humid heat of the Caribbean gave way to a downpour, turning our steep track into rivulets of red mud that sucked and clawed at our boots, so that for every two steps we trudged forward we fell back one. We had not been going long before we came across a python, short, fat and dead, apparently killed by a dog. By the time we reached our camp for the first night – a long, open-sided hut fashioned out of bamboo and wood – everyone's kit was soaked and the rafters quickly became festooned with soggy sleeping bags. For the past three hours we had been walking in cloud, moving like ghosts across ridges and gullies, but now the perpetual twilight turned abruptly to night and we gathered round a fire to eat boiled meat and rice. I suggested to James that now would be the perfect time to put on his hummingbird-green monogrammed pyjamas, the ones that had so baffled our guide in the middle of the Ecuadorean jungle six years before, but to my disappointment he had left them behind in London.

But the party had already found other figures of fun. A new porter, hired specially for the trip, had slipped on the muddy track and smashed all the eggs, earning him the tag of Egg Man. Meanwhile, Norbert, a rather earnest German, had discovered that his designer jungle kit, all pouches, buckles and zips, was already starting to fall apart. He sat in a darkened corner of the hut, grumbling to himself. We slept that night in cotton hammocks, fifteen feet long and deep enough to encase us; the guides had draped mosquito nets over us like giant bridal veils and we dozed serenely as the rain drummed on the roof and the nearby stream gurgled comfortingly over the rocks.

The next morning we awoke to find Indians from the Arsario tribe in the hut, exchanging news with our guides. As the sun rose they sat around the camp on tree stumps, dressed in their traditional white robes, resting their hunting rifles on the ground, smoking cheap cigarettes and helping themselves to our Coca-Cola. Rodrigo, a guide, walked over to a clump of coca bushes growing nearby and picked some leaves. '*Por la energia*,' he explained with a grin.

After a breakfast of maize fritters, we humped our rucksacks on to our backs and wound up a trail that revealed a vast hidden valley before us, thickly coated in jungle. Brilliantly coloured macaws flashed between the treetops and smoke coiled slowly from a distant village campfire. The Arsario had overtaken us, powered by their hydraulic calf muscles, and were now busy chopping down a tree. I noticed that each time they rested they chewed coca leaves from their woven pouches, then licked some substance off the polished gourd they each carried, a sort of jungle version of a tequila slammer. They would sell the wood, they told us, to lowland traders who bought it for five dollars a plank after it had been dragged for two days down the mountain by mule.

By midday the sweat was pouring off us. Norbert was

cursing his ever-disintegrating equipment and Egg Man too was having problems: he had resorted to making a harness for his backpack out of his own trousers, while the taciturn Israeli, Ari, had sensibly wound an absorbent scarf around his head to soak up the sweat; he had learnt it in the Army, he said, as a commando medic. The track crossed a small river at a waterfall so we all peeled off our clothes and dived into the clear water of a rockpool. Dozens of swallowtail butterflies danced on the sunlit rocks, then alighted on our steaming socks as we soaked in the chill water that had plunged all the way down from the high peaks. Suddenly we froze as a terrifying, ear-splitting roar erupted from the jungle not far off. It sounded very loud, very close and very dangerous; in fact it sounded for all the world like some sort of large and aggressive predator. I wondered if it could be a jaguar. Our guides answered the question on everyone's minds. 'Howler monkeys. Not dangerous. But very noisy, yes?' Frankly I was more concerned about some horror insect the guides had warned us about, a fly that lays its eggs in your skin, producing yellow boils from which maggots later wriggle out. Tremendous.

Bloated that evening from large portions of Andean potato soup, we lay about in hammocks, chatting, reading and passing the time as the rain began. We slept badly, crammed together in a line: it only took one person to shuffle about in their hammock for us all to be set in motion like some executive desk toy.

I closed my eyes and thought about where we were heading. Although the sixteenth-century Spanish con-quistadores never found the mythical land of Eldorado, these were the very mountains they came to search, systematically relieving the highly advanced Tayrona Indians of their gold, copper and cornelian. Then, when influenza and other European diseases laid waste the Indians' once-thriving mountain stronghold, the jungle closed in and the Lost City of the Tayronas lay buried for four centuries under dense foliage at the northern tip of the Colombian Andes. It was only in 1975, after months of chasing false leads, that a party of grave-robbers stumbled across the ruins, which concealed gold beyond their wildest dreams. In their delirious and competitive enthusiasm to plunder the tombs they threw the ancient Indian bodies down ravines and shot wildly at each other. The place became known as El Infierno Verde, the Green Hell. It was months before the government in Bogotá woke up to the value of South America's greatest archaeological find since Machu Picchu, rescuing whatever gold it could find for the capital's Gold Museum.

I shook myself awake as a grey dawn crept over the camp. 'We must move now, at once,' said Rodrigo, our guide. 'The river is swelling and soon it will be too high to cross.' Two hours later we were thanking him as we inched our way along an Indian rope bridge, a real Indiana Jones job with knotted vines that swayed alarmingly above a white foaming torrent. We crossed at a snail's pace, lurching beneath the weight of our rucksacks, then braced ourselves to wade through the river upstream.

It was almost as if the ants were lying in wait for us on the other side: with everyone barefoot they had a banquet, teeming over our wet feet and up our legs, biting at leisure. James and I had bought some eco-friendly insect-repellent before we left London, but it was no more use against the ants than it had been against the mosquitoes which had been settling on our sticky skin in droves. Rodrigo called for everyone's attention; he had an important announcement to make. 'You must take fruit and make like this,' he gestured, rubbing a piece of freshly cut pineapple on to his skin. We nodded sagely in agreement. Of course, we thought, pineapples, an old jungle trick, the locals must know best, and so on. Within seconds the Colombians were rocking in laughter as the gringos went into a frenzy of slapping, with the sweet, sticky juice acting like a magnet to the ants. Egg Man was having a particularly bad day. While rummaging for something buried deep in his rucksack, his hands closed around a rough, heavy object the size of a large melon, but weighing rather more. It was a rock, placed there by his fellow porters, which he had been unwittingly carrying up the mountain for three days now.

It was the final day of the trek up to the Lost City and the afternoon became a tired blur of moss-covered trails that clung to the sides of impossibly steep ravines. Time and again we slipped on dark, treacherous boulders covered in green slime, grabbing wildly at creepers to stop ourselves from falling and tripping repeatedly on roots. At times the jungle would open up to reveal an expanse of sunlit scenery below us, a place where parrots flew and toucans squawked. At other times we were plunged into semi-darkness as we clawed our way up muddy banks, always climbing.

We drew breath at the upper reaches of the Rio Buritaca, close to the spot where the grave-robbers had rightly convinced themselves there was gold buried in the surrounding jungle. Above us stretched a 1,200-step stone staircase, laid at a perilously steep angle by the Tayrona Indians at about the same time as King Henry VIII was sending his wives off for execution. The anticipation in our group was almost tangible: we were approaching what many of us had come to South America to see. Norbert was determined to be first to the top: having lagged behind for the last few hours, he now stood poised like a runner on the start line, while the guides eyed him with amusement, calmly passing round a shared cigarette. There was a sudden flurry of excitement and fear as one of them spotted something slithering in the bushes. *'Es una pudidora!* A putrifier!' they cried, pointing at a purple snake which they said could bite without alerting its victim. In their heavily accented Spanish they described – almost gleefully, I thought – how the bitten flesh then slowly putrifies, leading to inevitable amputation. Somehow, in the ensuing confusion, Norbert lost his place and found himself once more at the back of the line.

Breathless, we passed through a dark passage in the undergrowth, humming with daylight-biting mosquitoes, to emerge into a clearing. 'This is incredible,' muttered James. After so many miles of wild, untamed jungle we were suddenly standing on a series of neat stone circles that ascended into the clouds like something out of a fairy tale. A jungle pheasant stood watching us as if we had intruded into a private world, as indeed we had. Six thousand feet above the coast, we had finally reached the Lost City, and save for a Colombian army outpost of six guards, we had the place to ourselves.

For two days we wandered, entranced, through a labyrinthine network of stone terraces, ancient burial chambers and sacrificial altars. Rodrigo, a veteran of many treks up here, explained to us how the Tayrona men and women had lived in separate huts, passing food to each other in a stone bowl across a clearing. 'Even husband and wife they sleep under different roofs,' he grinned mischievously. 'But then, they go into the forest when they feel like disturbing the bats.'

I sat on a carved stone slab and looked around me at this mysterious Andean ruin, thinking about the people who had built it and lived their lives here, all this way up in the jungle, so far from the coast and the marauding Spanish. At the height of its power, a thousand years ago, the Lost City had contained fifteen thousand inhabitants spread across several ridges, some of which had still to be explored. To drag boulders up from the river the men would have chewed coca leaves, just as they did today, and concentrated their minds to endure the pain.

Profoundly superstitious, the Tayrona slept beside constantly burning fires and quaked when they heard howler monkeys roar in the trees, as they did frequently during our stay. But it was the jaguar they feared most, casting for themselves gold masks of mythical beasts, half-men, half-jaguar. 'We are the people of the jaguar,' ran a Tayrona myth, 'and our land is that of the jaguar.' We never saw any jaguars, for they had all been scared away by the Army helicopters that brought supplies up to this beleaguered outpost, where unruly conscripts were sent for a four-month punishment posting. Worrying that the Indians' pigs would foul the neat stone circles and put off visitors like us, the government had paid the locals to stay away from their ancestral home, driving them down the mountain to live in jungle clearings, in thatched huts with twin peaks to symbolize the summits of the high sierra.

At dusk that night we sat beneath a palm-thatched roof, watching the mountain mist roll in across these ancient stones. A 'Four Mirrors Moth', as wide as a man's hand and all purple and green, landed beside me. Colombians say that if you touch it then someone close to you dies. By now our feet were sore and blistered and we were several pounds lighter. For a week we had lived off soup, rice and increasingly tough plantains while our bodies strained to cope with the gradient. We had drunk water from fissures in the rock and slept curled up like babies in our hammocks at night. All our belongings were sopping wet and we had grown used to pulling on wet shirts in the chill dawn breeze. Our arms were punctured with insect bites and some of us, including James, had started to hallucinate about plates of grilled lobster being cooked down on the coast at Cartagena. Yet not one of us wanted this trek to end.

On our way down the next morning, we caught a last glimpse of the world we were leaving. In thick jungle we paused at a bend in the track as a party of Indians marched past us in silence. Their faces were as taut and stretched as old parchment, long black hair fell to their waists and their clothes were in tatters. These were the Kogui people, last descendants of a pre-Columbian Indian civilization that resisted the Spanish conquest for seventy years before fleeing to the remote upper slopes of these Sierra Nevada mountains, desperate to stay clear of the chickenpox and venereal disease that were killing their brethren. The Koguis were the guardians of the final secret: only they are said to know where the rest of the city is buried. For a moment their eyes met ours in a look born of centuries of distrust, then they were gone. For a long time afterwards the sweet smell of marijuana hung in the air and nobody spoke.

16

Oman

A Forbidden Exorcism

Mention exorcism in arab society and you can hear a pin drop. It's just not done. Like infidelity and homosexuality, it is one of those things that everyone knows takes place, it is just better not to breathe its name. But the ceremonial exorcism of evil spirits from the body – or *zar*, as it is called in Arabic – does exist; it just happens to be one of the most secretive rituals in the Arab world. When someone is believed to be suffering from a curse, the tribe gathers to summon a jinn, or genie as it is known in the West, to drive out the bad spirit. The ceremony is usually held at night, in an enclosed space known only to a privileged few. Strangers are rarely invited. But one clear, moonlit night, I found myself at just such an exorcism in the Sultanate of Oman.

When the offer came to attend a Bedouin exorcism I had mixed feelings. As an aspiring TV journalist, I had gone down to Oman to make a 'soft' feature for BBC World's business channel on how a group of artisans were trying to preserve the country's traditional crafts – like dagger-making and basket-weaving – from an onslaught of cheap plastic products from China. The filming had gone well and we had made a passable film that even made it on to BBC1's *Business Breakfast*, which was something of a professional breakthrough for me at the time. I had sat cross-legged on the burning sand to interview a portly sheikh with his priceless curved silver dagger; I had interviewed heavily veiled weaving women, their faces hidden by hawk-like masks known as *qamamas*, the same word the Arabs use for gas mask; and I had poked a camera into the crimson furnaces of a potter's studio in the foothills of the Jebel Akhdar Mountains. So far, so good. But an exorcism? This was not in the script.

Camping out in the dew-laden sands of the Wahiba Desert was grist to the mill for me; I loved the peace and solitude here in the wilderness. But when Yousef, my Omani guide and trainee cameraman, had returned from visiting the local Bedu, he presented me with a dilemma. Did I want to come to a secret exorcism tonight? I would have to stay silent at the back, the camera would not be allowed, and I must not speak of it when we returned to Muscat, the capital.

I thought for a moment. The last time I had gone to one of these things, a hyperventilating Sudanese woman had thrown an axe through the air with her eyes tight shut and it had missed my head by centimetres, landing with a thunk in a wooden pillar beside my skull. This time, I was assured, there would be no such violence. Yet Yousef, with typical Omani hospitality and thinking of my wellbeing, strongly advised against going. We were deep in the Wahiba Sands, a vast, rolling sea of sand in the far south-east corner of the Arabian Peninsula, miles from the nearest town. This was Oman's largest desert of dunes, and despite his university education and Western habits Yousef feared that desert spirits, once summoned, could not be controlled. We debated for some time. 'Enough, let's go,' announced Yousef, with an authority beyond his years. Tonight we would visit a neighbouring tribe, he said. Three of their women were suffering from a mysterious affliction: they wouldn't talk, they wouldn't eat. Only by calling on the jinn to enter the women's bodies could they be cured.

So off we set, jolting across the moonlit desert in a jeep that creaked and wheezed with old age and poor maintenance. I gripped the doorframe as we side-slipped through deep sand then swerved to avoid the thorn bushes that loomed ghost-like out of the night. How the Bedu ever found their way through the desert at night was a mystery to me. To my urban mind, each bush looked identical to the last; this was surely a desert without landmarks. But I was in good hands. The engine coughed, the brakes squealed and we drew up eventually at a large hut built of nothing more solid than plywood, surrounded by miles of empty desert. A dozen pick-up trucks were parked haphazardly outside, as if abandoned in a hurry. Khaled, the driver, beckoned me inside.

Before my eyes could adjust to the sudden darkness, I almost tripped over a turbaned form, which shifted and grunted as I looked round the room. In the dim light of a paraffin lamp I made out forty or so seated figures: the men, in traditional mauve Omani robes, lining the walls;

the women, covered completely in loose, patterned veils, squatting together in a corner. The air was thick with the smoke of local frankincense which coiled upwards from incense-burners and at first it was hard to breathe. Against a wooden pillar sat a huddled figure, as stiff and as lifeless as a mummy, its head bent back, its eyes staring up. Only when the drumming began did it give any sign of life, emitting a croak then starting to sing in a thin, constricted voice.

'This man,' whispered the Bedu beside me, 'is a very big man. He is the sheikh of all our tribe.' The sheikh had a face like the Turin shroud, but it was the drums that caught my attention. Massive and booming, they lay balanced across three men's knees as they beat out a synchronized rhythm, summoning the jinn.

The mesmerizing beat filled the room like a living thing, while everyone sat deathly still. As if at some unspoken signal a shape detached itself from the women's corner and hurled itself, screaming, across the bare earthen floor. With pulsing, regular convulsions this amorphous form bobbed and swayed while the drums beat faster. Another figure joined it, then another, the three women rocking violently from side to side on their knees. Now, I was told, the jinn had entered their bodies and taken over their minds and their movements. They knew nothing of their actions and afterwards they would only remember entering the hut, nothing more.

The drummers were chanting now, their voices rising and falling in a strange chorus. A woman stood up behind one of the trembling forms and held her veil above her while she moved. This was the special *riddi* shawl which is brought out only for an exorcism. In the half-light of the paraffin lamp, in the choking, smoky atmosphere, I could have sworn that the cloth was moving by itself, as if possessed by some demonic force. I edged away from the circle, suddenly keen to distance myself from whatever forces were being stirred up here.

Abruptly the drumming stopped. With a gasp of expelled air the woman who had first leapt to her feet collapsed across the knees of the sheikh, her frail body exhausted, the jinn departed. With a shock, I saw that she was old and withered, yet when the spirit had gripped her body she had flung herself about like a teenager on a dancefloor.

People coughed, someone lit a cigarette, and a murmur of conversation dispelled the lingering sense of magic that filled that room. The full moon shone through the open door of the hut, painting the desert with an unnatural silver wash. A man appeared at the doorway, his loose robes flapping in the soft breeze, then he was gone. The ceremony was over, it was time to depart. I rose stiffly, my joints creaking after squatting cross-legged for so long. Curious eyes followed me to the door, as if surprised that a stranger had been allowed to witness this secret ritual. As we drove back to the camp I stuck my head out of the window, filling my face with fresh air, trying to make sense of what I had seen. Khaled turned to me, his face serene. 'The women are cured,' he said with satisfaction. 'The jinn have done their work.'

I was not to see another exorcism after that, I did not need to; the whole experience had left me feeling rather uneasy. But when I returned to London it redoubled my fascination for the Middle East and I resolved that we should move out there so I could report for the BBC. That year, everything changed for Amanda and me. We began 1997 as boyfriend and girlfriend, living in London with me working antisocial hours in the newsroom and getting reluctantly pigeonholed as a producer when what I really wanted to be was a reporter. By the end of the year I had become the BBC's 'Gulf Correspondent', a title I gave myself, we had moved to Dubai and were married, with our first child. The BBC had given me a letter of accreditation, no more, but I worked fast to put the region on the news map, jumping on and off US aircraft carriers in the Gulf, filming my own features and filing stories about the abuse of Asian guest workers.

Oman, probably the most picturesque of all the six Gulf Arab states, was to become a rich source of news feature films for my one-man-band operation, and few stories were stranger than that of 'Rain Tourism' in Dhofar province. Unlike the rest of the Arabian Peninsula, which sizzles in sky-high temperatures from May through to October, a short, sixty-mile stretch of the southern Omani coast around the town of Salalah catches something called the *khareef*, the edge of the Indian Ocean monsoon, and is drenched in drizzle for a few weeks each summer. While most Britons and northern Europeans will go to great lengths and expense to escape the rain for their holidays, I discovered that thousands of Gulf tourists were happy to do quite the opposite: they were, quite simply, paying to go to the rain. So I thought we might join them.

'Fancy a holiday in the drizzle?' I asked Amanda. If we had still been living in London she would no doubt have thought me mad, but we were not, we were living in Dubai, where the summer heat was like a sauna and the idea of rain was distinctly appealing. Our daughter Melissa was by now eight months old so we packed up her milk bottles, sterilizing kit and portable playpen, and flew down to Salalah, setting ourselves up in the Holiday Inn. Last time I had been here it had been a blazing-hot day in November, but now, as promised, there were lowering grey clouds and the sea was a heaving mass of brown waves, impossibly dangerous to swim in. The air was moist and heavy with the promise of rain and dazzling-yellow tropical Weaver birds clung upside-down to their nests in the hotel gardens. It did not feel like Arabia.

Leaving Amanda and Melissa in the hotel, I packed my camera kit into the hire car and drove north, directly away from the coast and up into the Jebel Qara Mountains, where the rain clouds clung darkly and mysteriously to the forested slopes. Up on the plateau, with visibility reduced to a few feet, I stopped the car and got out. A figure loomed out of the mist like a ghostly apparition and staggered towards me, clutching something to its stomach. This was starting to feel like something out of a Ridley Scott horror film. The figure fell panting at my feet, then got up and ran away, vanishing into the gloom. But it was just a child from the Emirates, nursing a football, and her face had told a story of pure, unbridled happiness.

Her father told me that they had driven down for days from distant Ras Al-Khaimah to revel in this dank and rain-sodden climate, where there was no chance of any Western tourist ever getting a suntan. 'We come here to cool down,' he said. 'We would happily drive for a week to be here.' Behind us a car splashed past in the mud, its headlights full on at midday. Near by another party of tourists from the Emirates squatted on a rain-soaked picnic mat, as if floating on a cloud. The fact that their Dubai-registered four by four was now bogged down in the treacherous mud of a Dhofari hillside was for them a small price to pay for this holiday from the heat. In fact, as I ventured further across this cloud-shrouded plateau, I found one group of Gulf tourists after another marvelling at weather they never thought possible in an Arabian summer. At the hilltop mosque of Nabi Ayoub, a Saudi tourist was gathering his family for a group photo in the rain. 'When I come to Dhofar in the *khareef*,' he said, stretching his arms expansively, 'I feel as if I have entered Paradise!' A teenager came out of the mosque with his brothers, a broad smile on his face. 'We are Omanis from Muscat,' he said, 'but we never thought that Dhofar would look so much like Europe.'

And it was true, it did look incredibly like Europe. Just below the cloudline, in a lush green meadow filled with cows and butterflies, I had to pinch myself to remember where I was: at the southern edge of one of the most arid and waterless land masses in the world. The *khareef* was so localized that just thirty minutes' drive landed me right back in the scorching desert. It was as if a great white woollen blanket of cloud had been pulled up over the southern edge of the Arabian Peninsula, creating a fantasy world of wooded valleys and gentle pastures that had no place in the Middle East.

17

Socotra

A Yemeni Galapagos

IN THE CRAMPED COCKPIT OF THE BOEING 737 I SQUATTED behind the Yemeni pilot and stared ahead. 'Do you see it yet?' he asked, drawing heavily on his cigarette. 'Do I see what?' 'The island. It's straight ahead.' I strained my eyes and squinted into the clear-blue void that lay beneath us to see a tiny distant speck grow slowly larger. We were two hundred miles out over the Indian Ocean, flying towards the remotest outpost of Arabia, the Yemeni island of Socotra. The horrors of 9/11 were still two years away and my casual request to visit the cockpit of this scheduled passenger flight from the mainland had been greeted with a smile and a beckon. Those were the days.

Of all the places I had yearned to visit in the Middle East, Socotra had long been my holy grail. Strung out in the Indian Ocean, a flake off the Horn of Africa, cut off for half the year by howling monsoon winds and until June that year accessible only by sea, Socotra was closer to

Somalia than it was to Yemen. Yet this sizeable island, measuring 1,400 square miles, belonged to neither. Having split off from the African mainland several million years ago, it had evolved geologically in near perfect isolation. Rare plants and trees that had long since died out elsewhere on Earth still thrived in the island's subtropical climate. Of all Socotra's 850 plant species, a third were endemic, existing nowhere else in the world; little wonder that when nearby Aden was a British protectorate in the 1950s, the Royal Botanical Gardens of Edinburgh mounted an expedition to survey its remote and misty slopes. I had read that there were unique birds on the island, like the nectar-sucking Socotra sunbird, chameleons and dazzling fish.

The name Socotra is said to derive from the Sanskrit *dvipa sakhadara*, meaning the Island of Bliss. The Portuguese once settled on it, then later the British, but now its forty thousand inhabitants were Yemeni, speaking a strange dialect called Mahri. They were said to exist in unusual harmony with their environment, taking only the fish they needed and rotating their livestock around new pastures. Socotra was dubbed by entomologists 'the Galapagos of the Indian Ocean' and to me it sounded like paradise. There were no poisonous snakes, no wild dogs, very little vermin – and what there was tended to get picked off by vultures, nicknamed 'the municipality' by the locals.

Yet the Yemeni government back on the mainland seemed determined to keep out journalists, and my repeated requests to visit it were met with rebuffs. 'It is a closed military area. You may not go,' said one chain-smoking official after another at the Ministry of Information in the Yemeni capital Sana'a. But I had a secret ally, the Health Minister, who happened to be an Anglophile and was Chairman of that august body, the Anglo-Yemeni Friendship Society. 'Of course you can go,' he said, snorting at the suggestion that it was closed to visitors. 'Give me your passport and I'll get you the visa by tonight, but don't tell anyone I gave it to you! Oh, and one more thing, they have malaria there, so as a doctor I had better write you a prescription for chloroquine.'

I had found out that there was a team of UN scientists on the island, frantically drawing up a plan to designate it a 'Man and Biosphere Reserve' so it could be saved from the otherwise inevitable unplanned and unscrupulous development by mainlanders. This was enough to convince the BBC to commission a film from me, so I made contact with the UN team and set off for Sana'a airport and one of the new, scheduled flights, accompanied only by my digital video camera.

Socotra's airport was a strip of tarmac, nothing more; there was no arrivals hall, no control tower. Instead, our plane was talked in by a man in a van, which now prowled like a predator around the taxiing jet. A crowd of several hundred had gathered to watch this great spectacle: a plane from the mainland meant a fresh supply of *qat*, the narcotic, hallucinogenic leaf chewed throughout Yemen and the Horn of Africa. Within minutes of the luggage being dumped on to the red earth every cheek was bulging with the stuff. The men spoke in incomprehensible sputters, impeded as they were by half a privet hedge stuffed into their mouths.

I now had a whole week in which to explore this place that few of my friends had even heard of. Better still, those paper-shufflers at the Ministry of Information did not even know I was here, so I would not be saddled with that blight of all Middle East journalists: the government minder.

'So, Mr Frank, I think you are not alone,' said a voice behind me. Oh heck. Minders, two of them, approaching fast. How did they get here? 'You surely didn't think,' said the first one, eyeing me up and down, 'that you could come to Socotra unescorted, did you?' I half expected him to add something like 'Nobody expects the Spanish Inquisition.' But one look at their clothes told me I would have no trouble here: dressed in dark, ill-fitting suits, they reminded me of Thomson and Thompson, the two detectives in the Tintin comics of my childhood. These were city boys from Sana'a and something told me they would not be joining me once I left the relative comfort of the hotel and headed up into the mountains with the scientists.

A white UN jeep arrived to collect me, and we bounced and jolted over a potholed road that meandered around the coast to Hadibo, the 'capital' and the only place on the island that resembled a town. Strange trees with smooth, sun-bleached trunks the shape of Coke bottles thrust up from the dry earth; a tiny, tropical sunbird flitted amidst the cacti; a school of dolphins coursed through the waves just offshore, while high overhead, beneath the clouds that clung to the limestone cliffs, I could see vultures soaring on thermals. I liked this place already.

In the turquoise waters of the bay, a couple of

prosperous-looking Arab dhows rode at anchor. 'Very important men,' said a Socotran in the back of the jeep. 'Also very rich – they come from the Emirates.' Socotra, I had read, had long exported its unique incense, aloes and medicinal resins to the Gulf and sea trade between them was still flourishing. But now we were drawing into Hadibo, whose one hotel was not a place to linger in. From the outside, the Summer Land Hotel had all the allure of a police interrogation block, and one of the nearest buildings was a clinic for tuberculosis victims. The hotel's barred windows looked out on to tottering cairns of crushed soda cans, while a collection of scruffy, ill-fed goats nibbled in vain at a fallen satellite dish that already looked well on its way to fossilization. Inside, flies circled the bare rooms in noiseless orbit. But the staff, all brought over from the Yemeni mainland, were amongst the friendliest in the world and they were only too happy to cook up steaming plates of shark and rice or let me sit out on the terrace with them, puffing on a *shisha* pipe. Thomson and Thompson, having checked themselves into the largest room, seemed to be losing interest in shadowing me already and in the late afternoon I bought them a large cooked fish to keep them busy for hours and went out to explore Hadibo on my own.

Despite the mounds of litter, the town did have a certain charm of its own: twisting, sand-filled alleyways wound between low, squat houses built of coral with thatched roofs and carved wooden doors. The air smelt at once of woodsmoke, drying fish and some unfamiliar Indian Ocean spice. Socotri teenage boys sat around in *futa*s – wraparound loincloths – or kicked a limp football around in the dust. I realized that my trousers were out of place here, and since no one was wearing shorts I decided to go bush and change into a local *futa* and flip-flops. I must admit it took a while to get used to wearing a skirt (David Beckham had yet to dazzle the world with his sarong-wearing habits) but it was surprisingly comfortable in the cloying heat. Women stood against crumbling walls and watched me go past, drawing their patterned veils across their faces so only their flashing eyes showed. When I unwisely complimented one on her child's bright eyes she gasped and covered his face with her hand, to ward off the evil eye of envy.

But I had not come to Socotra to frighten its women or to potter about its ramshackle capital, I was here to film with scientists in the hidden valleys and remote mountain plateaux. Early the next morning the UN team drew up outside the Summer Land in a small convoy of jeeps. 'Ready?' asked their leader, Eduardo, a newly married Italian scientist who appeared to be risking his marriage for the sake of preserving Socotra's fragile environment. 'What about your two minders?' he said. 'Don't they want to come?'

I glanced up at their bedroom window. Silence. Thomson and Thompson were sound asleep, probably still digesting that outsize grouper I had bought them the day before. 'It's not really their thing,' I said truthfully. 'Let's go.'

Eduardo shifted the jeep into gear and we set off for the mountains, driving up into the black bowels of a rainstorm. In the jeep behind, I noticed, there was a live goat. 'A present for our hosts,' he said. 'That will be our dinner tonight.'

When the rain eased off, the first of the Dragons' Blood trees began to loom out of the cloud and we stopped the jeep so I could get out and take a closer look. I had never seen a tree like this before. Endemic to the island, they were shaped like an upside-down umbrella, and produced a crimson healing resin known as cinnabar which was once exported as far as ancient Rome. There, gladiators are said to have plastered the resin on their bodies before a fight, partly to add a touch of gore, and partly to help heal the wounds that would soon be inflicted on them. 'Come on,' said Eduardo. 'We need to get up to the highlands before any more rain makes the track impassable.'

Two thousand feet above the Indian Ocean, we reached a hilltop village swathed in cloud where shepherds huddled, their beards trailing towards their navels. The Socotrans we met were invariably friendly, although I found their southern Arabian dialect hard to follow. They had a wonderfully quaint way of greeting each other, clasping hands then raising their joined hands to their lips, each kissing the back of the other's hand. It reminded me of some hearty Bavarian drinking toast.

We crouched to enter a stone hut with gnarled branches for a roof, our hosts encouraging us to sit down on rush mats and shelter from the rain while our goat was slaughtered. At first we seemed to be in complete darkness. From the corner came some whispering and then a curious rubbing sound. Eduardo clicked on a torch and I could hardly believe what I saw: the tribesmen were rubbing two pieces of wood together to make fire, an ancient skill I never thought I would see on the cusp of the new millennium. Our local guide seemed embarrassed. 'Of course we do have matches down in Hadibo,' he explained, 'but up here supplies are sometimes hard to come by.' I watched the man who was twirling a stick between his palms, his lined face a picture of concentration, his beard nodding with the exertion. As if by magic the room suddenly burst into light as a spark lit the wood chippings and a fire was born. 'Come back in ten years,' said Eduardo, 'and it will not be like this. Ah, here comes the goat.'

The carcass was duly borne into the hut with great solemnity, quite unrecognizable. Even in the genial light of the fire there was not a single piece of that goat I felt tempted to eat, and with some difficulty I managed to decline the offer of something resembling an old bedspring. I think it was part of the intestine. Another morsel that was pressed on me was so fatty that it shot out from between my fingers on to someone's lap. He promptly returned it to me with a gracious smile. Mercifully there was a bed of rice beneath the goat, so I ploughed through that and studiously avoided making eye contact with anyone lest more giblets were thrust in my direction.

The meal over, we sat around talking by the light of a hurricane lamp. Sheikh Ali, a kind and elderly Socotran with an orange hennaed beard, asked one of the visitors from mainland Yemen for his views on marriage. 'I would let my daughter marry any good Muslim,' came the response, 'except a barber.' 'A barber? Why not a barber?' intoned the Socotrans. 'Or a butcher,' added the Yemeni after reflection, 'because they would not be good enough for her.' 'And what if she married him anyway?' persisted Sheikh Ali, chuckling. 'Then I would have to kill her,' replied the mainland Yemeni, 'with a rope around her neck.' 'By God,' said Sheikh Ali, shaking his head, 'that is a little extreme.' At this point a goat from the village popped its head round the door, as if to check up on us, took a long look at everyone inside the hut, shivered and went on its way.

In the morning, under a white, sunless sky, we made our way up on to the verdant Diksam Plateau, a strange and silent world where the only sign of life was a man in a red cloak carefully slicing the leaves off a rare aloe and collecting them up for export. 'Feel it with your fingers,' he said in Arabic, barely looking up at me as if an Englishman with a video camera and tripod were an everyday sight up there in the mist. The aloe leaf was smooth and moist and it oozed a clear sap; I could almost sense its healing properties and it was not hard to imagine it being marketed in some organic boutique in London.

At the next village, the Socotrans made up an impromptu welcome poem to celebrate our arrival in the first week of the rains; apparently this was auspicious. The island had been suffering terribly from drought until just a few days ago, the lean, bony cattle testimony to the worst drought anyone could remember. Some two-thirds of the island's livestock were said to have perished. Yet now, after even just a little precipitation, there were lush green valleys where pink rose trees erupted from the ground in clumps and where green doves cooed and streams flashed past.

The headman, the sheikh, strode towards me, wanting to introduce his extended family. 'This is Salem Abdou,' he announced proudly, patting a young boy on the shoulder.

'He is fourteen and married.' Socotrans, I learnt, married very young and very often, and divorce was far more common than on the Arabian mainland. One of the doctors in the UN team told me he had recently treated a twenty-seven-year-old island woman who already had four divorces under her belt, so to speak. The first marriage, he said, was always arranged, but after that couples were free to choose, and often had little intention of staying together for life. Yemenis coming here from the mainland, with its far more conservative mores, were appalled at what they saw as the islanders' lax morals. Religious clerics were being sent down from Aden and Mukalla to try and impose some Islamic modesty, and the government had decreed that classical Arabic should be taught in all schools.

The clerics would certainly have had their work cut out with the young Socotran I met that evening. Ismail was already on to his second wife, the first having asked for a divorce after he kept getting drunk on the Russian vodka that had arrived by ship with a consignment of food. As soon as he was intoxicated, he told me proudly, he would get into his pickup truck and drive around the island until he found a wedding party to gatecrash. Then he would try to make off with any woman who would talk to him. Ismail had the annoying habit of tapping me on the knee each time he had a point to make, and I was about to make my excuses and go and sit next to the sheikh when he came out with a rare flash of insight. The Socotran language, he feared, would die out within a century, since it was only spoken, not written, and was now being squeezed out by Arabic.

Seated on rugs under a starlit sky, a crackling fire before us, we talked on into the night, the villagers' faces reflecting the flickering light. Dinner arrived: something warm, liquid and fiery with chillis, scooped up in silence with flaps of unleavened bread. From the semi-darkness came the sound of lips smacking, and figures rose one by one from the shadows to rinse their hands in bowls of spring water.

We slept that night beneath the rising moon and the first I knew it was daylight was when a goat trod on my chest. There followed an apologetic bleat as I sat bolt upright in surprise, and a vulture flapped heavily away from its perch on the wall above my head. I hoped it had not been getting any ideas.

'Psst!' said Salem Abdou, beckoning me over. 'What is it?' I replied, thinking that a nice cup of coffee would go down a treat. 'Do you want to see the *boumi*? It is very small.' *Boumi*? What did that mean? The word was familiar, but I could not place it. I followed Salem down a path into a thicket and there in the gloom, perched just feet away and staring at us blankly, was the smallest pair of owls I have ever seen, each no higher than a man's outstretched hand, watching us impassively from a branch with their swivelling heads. For the record, they were African Scops Owls, a reminder of how close we were to the Horn of Africa, but they were far from being the strangest creatures on the island. That morning I idled away a happy hour watching a mottled chameleon dance around on a thorn bush, occasionally shooting out its tongue to snare some bug which promptly disappeared into its scaly mouth. What outlandish creatures these are,

I thought, as it moved its limbs forward very slowly, one at a time, all the while swivelling its cone-shaped eyes.

We drove on, down to the Nugid Plain, a wide coastal belt on the south coast facing towards Madagascar. With the sun directly overhead we arrived at the main village of Abtaro, a pretty collection of coral huts where villagers offered to sell us exquisite woven rugs. But other visitors had been here before us, perhaps sailors, and the villagers jostled and pestered us until we left in a hurry.

For the journey back to the capital, Hadibo, I did what I loved doing most in a landscape like this: I rode on the back of the pickup truck, savouring the warm breeze on my face and a view unrestricted by car windows. Next to me stood Muhammad, one of the elders from a village we had passed. He must have been well into his sixties but I could see he was enjoying this as much as I was. I wondered absently if I would still be rattling around in the back of pickup trucks when I reached his age.

When we entered the final valley the magnificent skyline of the Haghir Mountains unfolded before us, the peaks all blue and mysterious in the last light of the day. Above this serrated ridge pink wisps of cloud zigzagged away towards the departed sun. To the north the Indian Ocean lay completely becalmed, and longboats manned by fishermen in loincloths ventured far out to the horizon, vanishing at the point where the mauve sea met the darkening sky.

At the airstrip the weekly plane back to mainland Yemen was reassuringly late – four hours late, in fact – so I passed the time drinking ginger coffee with a couple of conscripts sent to guard the new airport for a year. They seemed untroubled by this lonely prospect and when I left they asked me what day it was. Out there on this remote island, stranded between Africa and Arabia, I suppose one day must have merged seamlessly into another, with only the onset of the rains or the terrible monsoon winds marking time.

Days later, back home and with the mosquito bites on my arms already fading, Socotra seemed another world away. Yet for weeks after that I dreamt at night of a land of strange plants, a half-forgotten island where men rubbed sticks together to make fire and where they still killed a goat for a stranger.

18

Thailand

Adapting to Disaster

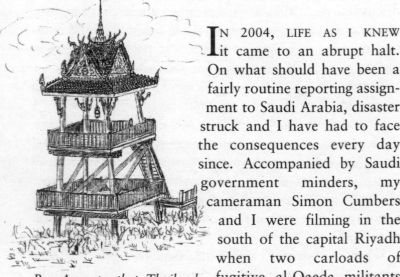

Ban Aranyprathet, Thailand

IN 2004, LIFE AS I KNEW it came to an abrupt halt. On what should have been a fairly routine reporting assignment to Saudi Arabia, disaster struck and I have had to face the consequences every day since. Accompanied by Saudi government minders, my cameraman Simon Cumbers and I were filming in the south of the capital Riyadh when two carloads of fugitive al-Qaeda militants happened to drive past as we were finishing and packing up. It was an ordinary, residential area and our unarmed escort from the Ministry of Information was strolling around smoking. But the gunmen had spotted that we had no police protection and they made the on-the-spot decision to murder us as part of their campaign to try and drive all Westerners out of the Arabian Peninsula. The first gunman got out, smiling as he approached me, called out in Arabic '*Assalaamu aleikum*' ('Peace be upon you') and promptly took out a pistol and shot me. The bullet passed clean through my shoulder and I ran on in search of cover. There was none. A second shot rang out and I fell to the ground, my leg bone shattered; the men had overtaken me in their van, cutting off my escape. I was now face-down but fully conscious, imploring these fanatics to spare my life. They had a quick discussion in Arabic while I strained to catch what they were saying, then one of them stood behind me and emptied the rest of his pistol into me at point-blank range, hitting me a further four times in the lower back.

To my astonishment I was still alive, but I knew I needed to play dead or they would come and finish me off so I held my breath, closed my eyes and stayed still as one of the gunmen came over and searched my back pockets, stealing a pocket Koran I had been intending to give someone as a present. (Some newspaper reports later said my life had been 'saved' by the discovery of this Koran. This is not true. By the time the gunmen found it they had run out of bullets.)

When the terrorists drove off, local residents began to appear on the street, but uncharacteristically for Saudis they offered no help, their sympathies in this particular case, I suspect, being firmly with the militants rather than with their Western victim. The police showed up and at first they too did nothing other than shield me from the crowd, standing with their backs to me, hands in pockets. By now I was in unspeakable pain from my wounds – I had been shot six times and some of the bullets were wreaking potentially fatal damage to my internal organs. Of my cameraman Simon there was no sign. Eventually the Saudi police bundled my broken body into the back of a patrol car and drove me off at speed, over rocky ground, to the nearest hospital. There my cries for painkillers were answered and I sank into sedation as an emergency trauma team led by a South African gunshot-wound specialist, Peter Bautz, raced over and tried to save me. For forty-eight hours it was touch and go, but thanks to his skill and the latest medicines, provided by the Saudis, I eventually opened my eyes to see Amanda by my bedside. I then received the devastating news that Simon had not survived; he had been fatally shot right at the start of the attack. Within months all but one of our assailants would be killed in subsequent shootouts with police and the sole survivor was captured the following year, but Simon was gone, killed by heartless thugs who never knew his decency or his profound humanity.

My repatriation from Riyadh by air ambulance was followed by seven months of slow, painful hospitalization back in Britain, a seemingly endless and depressing succession of injections, blood tests, tube insertions and extractions. Visitors and fevers came and went, but as the months went by a terrible truth began to dawn on me: I could not move or feel my legs. Some of the bullets that had hit my lower back had passed through the spinal nerves, leaving me partly paralysed. (Only later did it emerge that my spinal injury is what is called 'incomplete', meaning I have some degree of feeling and movement below the level at which the bullets did their damage.) When a nurse presented me with a wheelchair back then in hospital, I could hardly believe it was for me. Surely this sort of thing happened to other people, I thought. Bit by bit, the full enormity of it all hit me like a wave: if I couldn't walk then what sort of a life was I going to have? We would have to move house, to a flat with no stairs, but could I still be a proper father and husband? Could I ever drive a car again, or swim or ski or do any of the things I loved, like travelling to jungles, beaches and mountains?

In the first year after the attack, things looked very grim. While I realized that hiking through deserts was obviously now impossible, even being a passive passenger in a car was uncomfortable. Spinal-cord injury means you lose a lot of the muscle mass on your legs and backside, so that the bones of your sacrum are cushioned by only a thin layer of flesh separating them from whatever you are sitting on. In my case this meant that even an hour-long car journey became painful, so how on earth was I going to cope with a long-distance flight? But two months after I emerged from hospital and shortly before I was due to go back – at my insistence – to my job at the BBC, Amanda decided it would be good for all of us if I were to convalesce beside a pool in Thailand, and I was in no position to argue. Using some of the BBC compensation money, we paid for a business-class seat for me so that I could lie flat and take the weight off my backside. But whereas I once used to relish the menu coming round on a long-distance flight, I now had to virtually starve myself since I only had half my guts left and food passed through me at frightening speed. When I had no choice but to summon someone with an onboard aisle chair to get me to the loo, I found it was impossible to close the door on the aircraft wheelchair and hence the whole thing became a very public and embarrassing experience. I have yet to find an airline that offers wheelchair-access loos where you can do what everyone else does on a flight and shut the door behind you and retain some dignity.

Arriving in Thailand brought mixed feelings. This was a country I had backpacked around as a carefree teenager, sleeping in opium-hazed wooden huts up on the Laotian border, chugging round the islands in the south. More recently, I had run laughing into the sea with my family on a beach holiday at Hua Hin. Now I was back here as a virtual invalid, waving away people who wanted to push me through the concourse at Bangkok Airport, unable to carry any of our family's luggage, too low to the ground to even hand over our passports to the immigration officer who had to come out from behind his booth to check whether my face matched my photograph. It was all pretty humiliating.

My mood brightened when I caught sight of my brother-in-law Mike, who had come out to the airport to meet us. Mike lived in Bangkok, where he co-managed a hotel, and the previous summer he had been a tower of strength in Riyadh when he had flown out to be beside Amanda as she sat beside my unconscious form in hospital. The last time he had seen me I had been very ill and very weak in hospital, so this, at least, was an improvement.

Mike had organized a people-carrier to take us down to

Top: Sunset from our makeshift campsite, Okavango Delta, Botswana, 1994.

Above: Keke the boatman with a buffalo skull, Okavango, Botswana, 1994.

Right: Punishment duty for a Colombian soldier at the Lost City of the Tayrona, Colombia, 1996.

Below: Bedu girl in the weaving village of Sinaw, Oman, 1997.

Above: Traditional weaving in the remote Omani village of Qumzar, Strait of Hormuz, 1999.

Below: Rain Tourism: Gulf Arab visitors picnicking in the Dhofar monsoon, Oman, 1998.

Above left: Harvesting resin from a Dragon's Blood Tree on Socotra Island, Yemen, 1999.

Above right: Superstition: a Socotran mother shields her child's face from the evil eye, Yemen, 1999.

Below: Lighting a fire the prehistoric way, Socotra, Yemen, 1999.

Right: Back to the brink: resuming scuba-diving two years after getting shot, Red Sea, Egypt, 2006.

Below: 'Legless diving' off south Sinai, Egypt, 2006.

Left: Quadbiking in the Bahraini desert, 2007.

Right: Return to the desert: comparing mobile phones with a Bedu girl in the Sinai, 2006.

Top left: Not an optical illusion! Abseiling in a wheelchair, on the BackUp Trust activity course, Exmoor, 2007 .

Top right: At the Grand Canyon, Arizona, USA, 2007.

Bottom left: An object of fascination: my wheelchair in a Cambodian fishing village, 2008.

Bottom right: 'He needs professional help': training for BBC's Grand Slalom with Graham Bell, Courmayeur, Italy, 2008.

Above: Embedded at Bagram: with the BBC's Eddie Stephens (*left*) and Dominic Hurst (*right*) on the UAE base, Afghanistan, 2008.

Below left: Ta Phrom temple, Angkor Wat: something of a challenge in a wheelchair, Cambodia, 2008.

Below right: An undignified descent: at Colombia's Police Hostage Rescue Training Centre, 2008.

Above: A Tale of Two Surgeons: with Frank Cross (*left*) and Peter Bautz (*right*) who saved my life in Riyadh, on the roof of the Royal London Hospital, 2008.

Eyes on the horizon: dreaming up my next trip, 2009.

Hua Hin and as a former body-builder he was impressed that I was able to haul myself unaided up from my wheelchair and on to the raised seat of the van. It was a minuscule achievement, but I was happy to accept whatever compliments came my way.

Hua Hin was Thailand-lite. Not as raunchy as Pattaya, not as noisy as Bangkok, it was still quite a sleepy beach resort in 2005, more aimed at Thai family tourists than beer-swilling *farangs* (foreigners) from Europe. When we arrived at the hotel's car park a small mountain of steps separated us from reception, but someone found a way to get me through the bushes round the back to our hut. This meant wheeling myself over a rough and pitted stone track, which as well as being hard work was also painful. The gunshot wounds to my bladder and rectum had left me with a legacy of internal pain which would take years to subside, so that each time the front wheels of my wheelchair hit an obstacle, however small, the whole chair jolted, sending a spasm of pain through my body. The net result of this was that I essentially spent two weeks on a sun lounger, moving as little as possible, often only stirring to go to the loo or to sit up and eat a bowl of rice. I had never felt so lazy or useless in my life – this was not how I had pictured life even in my nineties – and Amanda had to constantly remind me that I was supposed to be convalescing. Our children had a great time, but still it was hard, raising my head feebly from the sun lounger to say no each time they asked me to join them in the pool; I was there in the background but I was a virtually silent member of the family, reduced to the basic bodily functions of a baby and little else.

On the one day we ventured into the town of Hua Hin there was another disappointment in store for me. One of the things Amanda and I had liked about Thailand from our previous trip was the reflexology massages: if you found a place where they knew what they were doing, these could be a mind-blowing experience, releasing all sorts of hidden tensions around the body as a hard-thumbed Thai woman kneaded the sole of your foot or expertly massaged your calf. In Hua Hin we had revelled in reflexology, strolling down a backstreet to lie back side by side in reclining armchairs and sip bottles of ice-cold Sing-ha beer as our senses were pampered and our bodies unwound. Now we decided to all go for a family foot massage, in the first place we came to that I could wheel myself into. But of course I could not feel a damn thing. The whole point about reflexology is that each pressure point on the foot is supposed to correlate to a different part of the body: the head, the chest, the heart and so on. But all the finger pressuring took place below the knees, which is where my paralysis kicked in completely. Amanda was in bliss, our children were ecstatic – although they sometimes said it tickled too much – but for me, lying there in the salon with them, it was like listening to an out-rageously funny joke when everyone else in the room gets it but you.

On the way back to the hotel we passed a local travel agent, still open at ten p.m., whose sign advertised jungle tours to a nearby national park. 'Reckon I could come along?' I said to the Thai standing smoking in the door-way; I was only half joking. He did not even hesitate, giving only the briefest of glances at my wheelchair. 'Sure, no problem,' he replied. 'We get you there easy and then we carry you.' Amanda was, quite rightly, having none of this – I was there to convalesce after seven gruelling months in hospital – but it certainly got me thinking: maybe the jungle was not beyond reach after all.

Eighteen months later we returned to Thailand once more and I was already a very different person. Still in a wheelchair, but now much stronger and able to stand for two hours at a time if I wore metal callipers on my legs and had a walking frame to keep my balance. Above all, I was rediscovering my thirst for travel and exploration, and was determined to see how far I could go despite my physical limitations. This time would be different, I told my family. There would be no malingering on the sun loungers for us this time, this would be adventure, great, green, dripping jungle adventure. Nature, red in tooth and claw. A wild, tropical safari in one of Asia's great rainforest reserves.

I was still telling them this as the taxi drew up at the carved wooden gates of the Kirimaya Hotel and Resort, where two butlers in silk costumes bowed as they handed us fruit cocktails and iced flannels. All right, so this was not turning out to be quite as rugged as I had planned, but there were no complaints from the Gardner family as we checked in beneath slowly turning ceiling fans and the children raced each other across wooden boardwalks that wound mysteriously between the reeds. A voice at my elbow breathed soothingly, 'Would sir like to see the menu for this evening?'

We had driven up that afternoon from Bangkok,

heading three hours north into the province of Nakhon Ratchasima which borders Cambodia and the mighty River Mekong. If we wanted to visit a national park, I was told, then we could do no better than Khao Yai. The oldest of Thailand's forty-eight national parks, this 2,000-square-kilometre patch of rainforest contained some of the last real wildlife in the country and was now a UNESCO World Heritage site. It was also delightfully off the beaten track. There were lodges and campsites, but just outside the park Amanda had discovered on the internet an oasis of comfort in the form of the Kirimaya, and it turned out to be a perfect base from which to explore the jungle. This was comfortable rainforest holidaying, with crisp white sheets, huge stone baths strewn with petals, electric mosquito coils and air conditioning to come back to each night after a day in the dripping heat of the jungle just up the road. It was a far cry from the sort of travelling I had done in the past, but I had to be objective about this: leaving aside the whole wheelchair thing, I was now in my forties, with a family and a regular job. My days of eating dodgy food in cockroach-infested hostels were well behind me, and if I am honest, I probably would have been quite happy staying here even without my injuries.

As the sun dipped below the distant limestone cliffs on our first day in the north-east, we were introduced to our guide. Nang was a thirty-something Thai with a passion for nature, she knew the names of everything in English and she had the biggest set of binoculars we had ever seen. She also came laden with bags of sumptuous custard apples and hairy rambutans, local fruits Melissa and Sasha soon developed a taste for. 'Are you ready for the bat cave?' she asked. The girls exchanged glances. At this stage in their lives, aged seven and eight, they were more into Hogwarts than Gotham City, but hey, a bat cave didn't sound bad at all. We piled into the back of Nang's open jeep and bounced along for several miles down rutted rural tracks, past grazing, sulky-looking buffalo with upcurved horns and clouds of insects that danced in clusters in the fading light. Beneath a low, tree-lined hill we pulled up and waited. Nang looked at her watch. 'OK, they coming now! Look! Look! Up there.' From the mouth of a black cave in the side of the hill spilled out into the air a black, twisting, airborne stream, coiling darkly like poisonous gas. On and on they came, over a million bats spewing out of the hillside without a break for nearly half an hour, then fanning out and hunting over the fields for insects. As abruptly as it had begun, the stream of bats ended, as if a secret tap had been turned off suddenly, hidden inside their cave.

As so often happens in south-east Asia, the next day dawned bright and clear, only for dark thunderclouds to start massing on the horizon. By the time we drove up to the wooden gatehouse that guarded the entrance to Khao Yai National Park the rain was falling in sheets, so we wrapped ourselves in waterproofs and savoured the cool breeze as Nang's jeep drove on up into the rainforest, which rises to over four thousand feet. Elusive Silver Pheasants, one of the 320 bird species here, said Nang, were hiding amongst the drifting mists and groves of giant bamboos.

Just then a strange whoop echoed from the treetops and the jeep slammed to a halt. 'Listen! Do you hear that?' cried Nang. 'That's a gibbon.' 'What kind?' chirped up our younger daughter, who, like her sister, had a curious passion for primates and had been quietly leafing through the guidebook. 'It's a White-handed Gibbon,' answered Nang. 'Who wants to come and find him?' From out of her rucksack she then produced some strange-looking canvas sleeves. 'Leech socks. We'll need them.' Ah yes, leeches, the uninvited guest on any jungle trip. Since the path into the forest was too steep and too muddy for my wheelchair I had to sit this one out in the jeep. I glanced at Amanda and she shook her head emphatically. To her, muddy jungle trails meant snakes, not something she was keen on, so she was not budging. Did we trust the guide with our children? We did, and twenty minutes later two very excited children came running back down the track. 'Daddy! Mummy! We found the gibbons! There was a whole troop of them up in the treetops and they had a baby that was pure white fur, you should have seen it! And when they saw us they threw fruit down at us but they missed! Ha!' As we peeled the waterproofs off them both girls complained of something itching on their backs. Sure enough, the leeches had found a way in, dropping down the gap at the back of their collars to feast on fresh British blood. Nang showed us how to remove them with her thumb and forefinger, and although we were all pretty grossed out by the sight of them Melissa coolly shrugged it off and from then on the children bore this incident as a mark of pride.

We moved on, deeper into the forest, until we came to the waterfall at Heaw Suwat, one of several in the forest but perhaps the most memorable. We recognized it immediately. 'Wait a minute,' said Amanda. 'Isn't that the one Leonardo di Caprio jumped off in *The Beach*?' Clearly there had been a bit of poetic licence here by the film-makers; we were a very long way indeed from the nearest beach, but it was easy to see why they had chosen Heaw Suwat. The water plunged straight down for 65 feet into a limpid pool. There were no Hollywood film stars there today, only the shrieks and whoops of gibbons in the trees. Monkeys, we had been warned, were everywhere and they were bold as brass. Before long we ran into a troop of Pig-tailed Macaques by the roadside, mothers carrying babies slung under their bellies, juniors picking nits from elders, grouchy old males standing guard. We made the mistake of stopping. Within seconds one animal ran straight up to us, stood up on his hind legs, reached his arm through the bars of the jeep, snatched our biscuits and was off. The whole operation took less than five seconds and was clearly a well-practised drill.

We drove on up on to a grassy plateau where a red earth salt lick scarred the hillside. 'This is where the elephants come,' announced Nang, before adding apologetically, 'in winter.' This was September and the elephants were now apparently deep in hiding. Khao Yai had somewhere between two to three hundred Asian elephants living wild in the forest but they are secretive beasts, pursued by poachers, and apparently the best time to see them is when they emerge to forage in January. Sasha, who had by now become hermetically joined to the binoculars my mother had given her, noticed a pair of soft brown eyes staring at us from behind a bush and she nudged my arm. 'That's Barking Deer,' said Nang. 'And over there, on the edge of the forest, that's a Sambar Deer.' A raucous croak then had us reaching for the binoculars. A pair of Indian Pied Hornbills swooped beneath the jungle canopy and settled on a lone branch, their grotesquely heavy bills clearly silhouetted against the storm clouds. It seemed there was wildlife all around us: beside the road, a large, multi-coloured spider clung to the centre of its web, challenging all comers and causing Sasha to recoil into the back of the jeep; a fluffy striped squirrel, looking like something out of the cartoon *Ice Age*, scurried around at the base of a giant fern; the air was alive with dazzling blue Morphio butter-flies the size of a child's hands, and from up in the trees an Asian Fairy Bluebird called out to its mate.

But this was still small beer: we had come to Khao Yai in the hope of seeing bigger things. That night we set out once more on a torchlit 'jeeptop safari', moving slowly through the darkness and scouring the undergrowth with our torchbeams for movement. Within minutes a civet cat showed up, then more deer. I had not forgotten my near miss with the Sumatran tigers as a teenager and the prize we were all hoping for was one of Khao Yai's last remaining tigers, or perhaps an Asiatic black bear or even a Gaur, a huge and reclusive jungle bull. But once again, South-east Asia's rarest wildlife eluded me and that night we had to content ourselves with one of nature's oddities: a pair of porcupines, moving rapidly through the bush. 'You know how they defend themselves?' said Nang. 'They run away, then stop suddenly so their enemy runs into their spines!' The children giggled and then yawned; it was time for bed.

Back at the Kirimaya resort we decided to spend our last morning at the outdoor swimming pool. It looked deliciously inviting, an infinity pool that spilled cool and green against a backdrop of verdant hills, but the children had concerns about the dense foliage that tumbled over the edges. 'Do you think there are snakes in there?' they asked. 'Could be, but don't worry,' I reassured them, 'snakes don't usually like swimming pools much. They don't like the chlorine.' I did vaguely remember a housing compound in Saudi Arabia where a snake lived harmlessly for weeks in the filter vent, only venturing out after dark when everyone had gone inside, but I decided that must have been an exception. Five minutes later there were squeals of terror and our girls froze mid-pool, silently pointing. A small, slender water snake was wriggling its way across the surface from one side of the water to the next. Probably harmless, but we were no experts and somehow the allure of the pool had evaporated; as soon as the snake reached the other side the girls splashed noisily out of the water and we all abandoned the pool in a hurry.

Days later and thousands of miles away in their school playground, it was not the bats, the leeches, the hornbills or the porcupines by moonlight that our children remembered most vividly, it was the ultimate horror of a-snake-in-the-swimming-pool. Khao Yai National Park may not exactly have been demanding travelling, but for Melissa and Sasha this was an introduction to jungle wildlife they would never forget.

'Apasara', Khmer dancing figure

19

Washington

Inside Counter-Terror Central

BACK AT WORK AT THE BBC IN LONDON AFTER AN ABSENCE of ten months, I experienced a brief flutter of celebrity status. People who barely knew me stopped me in the corridor and silently shook my hand, unsure of what to say; I could almost see them thinking, 'This guy has come back from the dead, we all thought he'd had it.' Others who had known me well before the Riyadh attack glanced from me to the wheelchair and back again, sometimes saying 'This is just temporary, right?' It wasn't and I was quite matter-of-fact about telling them so, but what really mattered to me right now was getting back to being a journalist and doing my job as Security Correspondent. This was, I suppose, a form of therapy in itself.

I decided to get the business of describing my ordeal to all the various radio and TV programmes over and done with in one swoop, with a blitz of on-air appearances. Within three days I was done with talking about Riyadh.

Although privately I and many others were still grieving for Simon, publicly at least it was time to move on. From then on, I expected presenters to ask me about the world of international security and counter-terrorism, not about me.

But while I was perfectly capable of getting on a plane once more, I had no desire to go back and report from places like Baghdad or Basra, which is just as well since neither place exactly topped the list of Wheelchair-Accessible Destinations of the World. The idea of having to race for cover during an incoming mortar alert at some flyblown base was, well, ludicrous when there were plenty of other people only too happy to do that sort of reporting. 'I wouldn't worry about missing out on that,' said Mark Thompson, the BBC Director-General, at a lunch to welcome me back. 'What we need is your analysis and your contacts.' So did this mean I was destined to be chained to a desk in London, poring over computer screens and endlessly ringing people up for information? True, that was an essential part of the job, but it was not the kind of journalism I wanted to be doing day in, day out, and to the BBC's credit, they made it as easy as possible for me to report live from our Jerusalem bureau during the Lebanon war in 2006. But back in London there was a whole under-reported world of secret committees, of intelligence assessments, of decisions taken behind closed doors that would affect what Britain did in the Middle East and Afghanistan. The only way to even peer in at the window of this world was through contacts who trusted you to distinguish between what was 'on the record' and could therefore be reported and attributed, and what was for 'deep background only', which meant it could not.

In September 2006, I received an unusual invitation to dinner at the Cabinet Office, along with a handful of other journalists who specialized in defence and security. America's Director of National Intelligence, 'the DNI', was in town on a flying visit, so would I like to meet him? A career diplomat, John Negroponte had recently been US Ambassador in Baghdad, so he had been right at the centre of Washington's biggest foreign venture since the Vietnam War. Now, as President Bush's 'Intelligence Tsar', his job was to oversee all nineteen US intelligence agencies – including the CIA and the FBI – with a combined annual budget of over US$40 billion. This was a man who would surely have some interesting things to say about what America called 'the War on Terror'.

We filed into the small dining room just off Whitehall and Sir Richard Mottram, the British Government's Intelligence and Security Coordinator, did the introductions. 'Dame Eliza Manningham-Buller I'm sure you all know,' he said, nodding at the redoubtable head of MI5, whose pale-blue eyes briefly swept the room. 'This is so-and-so from the Secret Intelligence Service, Michael here is on the Parliamentary committee that oversees Intelligence and Security, and so-and-so here is from the CIA in Langley.' It was like a page from a Tom Clancy novel. 'Oh, and here comes Ambassador Negroponte now.' Short, balding and stocky, the DNI entered the room flanked by his bag-carriers from Washington, nervous-looking young men who hovered near him as if on permanent standby to whisper momentous news into his ear over dessert. 'Shall we start?' said Sir Richard.

As we tinkered with our starters, the DNI spoke in broad terms about his job. 'I start work at six,' he said, causing us British journalists to exchange glances. What was it about officials on the other side of the pond that they insisted on working such horrendous hours? 'Then every morning at eight,' he continued, 'I'm the guy that has to go in to give the President his daily intelligence brief.' But if we journalists had expected to learn anything new from John Negroponte, we were disappointed. He was right on top of budget allocations, congressional hearings and structural reform in the US intelligence community – in short, all the things that our readers and audiences couldn't care less about – but he did let slip something that gave me an idea for a BBC news film. 'Of course, we now have NCTC and that's making an impact,' he told the room. NCTC was America's newly formed National Counter Terrorism Center, a clearing centre somewhere near Washington for all intelligence coming in globally on the terrorist threat to America and its allies. It was supposed to be highly secretive – so secretive, in fact, that it had no listed address and no British film crew had ever been allowed near it – but I decided to chance my luck anyway. As the chairs scraped back around the dinner table in Whitehall that evening I approached the DNI. 'Is there any chance we could come and film inside the NCTC?' I asked. There was a muffled scoff from one of the print journalists and the head of MI5 shook her head and smiled, as if to say 'You TV people have quite a nerve.' It was something of an Oliver Twist moment, but to everyone's surprise Negroponte never even hesitated. 'Why, sure,' he replied, 'I'll have my people fix it up. Call this number.'

* * *

Two months later my producer Natalie Morton and I were on the pavement outside the BBC's Washington bureau while our cameraman Ron Skeans stowed his kit in the car with practised ease. A veteran of countless US elections, he had developed a cunning system of bungy cords stretched round a porter's trolley to allow him to drag along an ungainly two-person load by himself. For late autumn it was a surprisingly mild day and as we crossed the broad sweep of the Potomac River into Virginia many of the trees around us still held their colour. The pretty suburb of Georgetown flickered into view on our right, then vanished behind the trees as we sped north. We passed a large highway sign indicating the turn-off to the George Bush Center for Intelligence – in other words, CIA head-quarters, buried in the Virginia woods at Langley. (President George Bush senior ran the CIA from 1976–77.) As a native of Washington, Ron knew this area well and we arrived at NCTC with time to spare. I have to say that America's National Counter Terrorism Center is not going to win any prizes for architectural beauty or originality: picture a giant Rubik's cube without the colours and you just about have it. Beyond the main security post where they checked our IDs, mechanical diggers were still moving earth around; it looked like a work in progress.

'So you folks are from the BBC?' boomed a voice across the car park. 'Welcome to Counter Terror Central!' It was a former vice admiral, a man known only as 'T', who ran the centre's public relations and who now guided us through more security checks as blank-faced men in suits reached for their electronic IDs on neck chains and nodded to the uniformed guards. The camera crew were shown where they could set up their kit while I was escorted upstairs. 'The boss wants to see you.'

The NCTC's Director General, Vice Admiral Scott Redd, was another US Navy man, and now he catapulted himself out of his chair like a jet launching from an aircraft carrier, greeting me with a bone-crushing handshake. I had expected an uncompromising, you're-either-with-us-or-against-us mindset, the sort of perspective that sees the world – and the Middle East in particular – in black and white, which I believe has led to all too many mistakes and misunderstandings in the Arab world. But Redd was a thinker, and, perhaps because he had commanded the US Navy's 5th fleet based in Bahrain in the 1990s, he displayed a refreshing awareness and sensitivity about events in the Gulf.

Downstairs they were waiting for us in the 'Situation Room'. At the unseen press of a button, a row of screens slid silently up from the edges of a conference table. 'This is where we hold the twice-daily conference call,' said T. 'We patch in the CIA, Homeland Security, NSA, the White House, the Joint Chiefs if we need to, and everyone else in the CT [counter-terrorism] community. That way we try to keep everyone in the loop on CT.'

This was all very well, but a windowless room in Virginia and a sit-down interview with the Admiral was hardly going to make watchable television. Our rescue came in the form of a visit to the Operations Room, a cavernous hall dominated by a huge plasma screen that stretched right across one wall, displaying tiny digital images of aircraft. 'After 9/11,' explained T, 'we don't ever want to be attacked again, so this is where we track every incoming aircraft across the eastern seaboard of the continental United States.'

I looked around the Operations Room with its ranks of computer consoles and display screens and had a sudden sense of déjà vu; somehow this place looked familiar. Yes, it reminded me of our newsroom back in London, but I was sure I had seen it somewhere else, somewhere dramatized and glamorous. T read my thoughts. 'This place remind you of the TV series *24*?' he asked. 'It should do. People call it "the real CTU", the Counter Terrorism Unit where Special Agent Jack Bauer's character is played by Kiefer Sutherland. It's not a fair comparison because we don't do operations here, we just monitor what's going on and make sure the information is passed to the people who need to know. But that said, we have invited Kiefer here and we did bring in the imaginators from Disney.' 'The imaginators?' I queried. This was a new word to me. 'Yup. These are the design people. We figured we needed to go to the experts when it came to the most effective way of sharing information with people, so we went to Disney and they came up with what you see now.' 'But this place is almost empty,' I said. 'I thought it would be a hive of activity.' T coughed and looked almost embarrassed. 'That's because we've had to sanitize it for your visit,' he said. 'All the CIA and FBI folks have had to close down their workstations and move across to the back-up ops room over there – and please don't even think of going in there.' 'So who's this guy sitting behind a desk just here?' I asked. 'Him? He's one of the cleaners.' Great. I now realized we had filmed an entire interview with the Duty Watch Officer with a very elderly cleaner plainly visible behind him, nodding off in front of a computer screen. It hardly looked like the cutting edge of counter-terrorism.

To be frank, that was the least of our problems. As we collected our confiscated mobile phones and handed in our passes at Security, I concluded that we had been shown just a tiny fraction of what went on here. What we had was going to be tough to translate into good television. But still, we had got into the nerve centre of US counter-terrorism, and with some clever post-production by Natalie in an edit suite back in London we ended up with a surprisingly fast-paced film that told people about a place they never knew existed. It was time to move on to the next assignment.

20

The Sinai

Disabled Diving

EVERY SO OFTEN IN TV NEWS A REALLY PLUM JOB COMES along. And more often than not, someone else gets it. The corridors of Television Centre still reverberate to jealous tales of the correspondent and crew who got sent to some paradise island in the South Pacific to report on the first day of the new millennium – and then couldn't get back for days. Our hearts went out to them.

In truth, such episodes are far outnumbered by all the exhausting extra shifts when big news breaks, the interrupted holidays, the apologies to families and friends, the occasional threats of violence in difficult and dangerous places. But in 2006 it was my turn for a cushy assignment. 'Have you ever made a programme for *Fast Track*?' asked the veteran cameraman/reporter John Macintyre. I had not. *Fast Track* was the low-budget, high-production travel programme shown on the BBC's international satellite channel, BBC World. Presented as a 'magazine programme', this 27-minute slot usually featured three different reports on destinations around the world, all filmed on a shoestring on a digital camera. But John had a rare specialization: like me, he had worked both behind the lens and in front of it, but now he was carving out a successful career as an underwater cameraman, producing and filming his own DVDs on diving with sharks and co-writing a book about underwater life in the Red Sea. He was already something of a legend and I jumped at the chance to work with him.

As soon as I said yes John moved into fifth gear, securing the necessary funding, promotion, training and permission, all so we could film an entire 27-minute special featuring me scuba-diving in the Red Sea – without the use of my legs. Earlier that year I had managed to get myself back on ski slopes, balancing in a sitski, a sort of bucket mounted on a monoski, but paraplegic scuba-diving? This was to be the furthest horizon for me since I recovered from my shooting.

It had been seven years since I had last gone scuba-diving and even if I had been completely able-bodied I would have been very rusty. Now I had the added challenge of not being able to propel myself underwater by kicking my legs like a normal diver would. Instead, said John Macintyre, I would have to rely on my arms, swimming breaststroke underwater. But not to worry, he added, I would be provided with a pair of webbed rubber gloves to give me added purchase.

Apparently I was not alone in being a wheelchair user who wanted to dive. When I arrived at an indoor swimming pool in Hampshire for my first legless 'try dive',

I found the place buzzing with activity. Run by the Scuba Trust, a charity that helps paralysed people get back in the water, the facility was full of divers with varying degrees of disability being helped into the pool, or in some cases doing it all themselves. I was introduced to Geoff, a particularly independent paraplegic in a wheelchair who seemed to need no help at all. Geoff had been an Army Staff Sergeant in Northern Ireland in the 1970s when he and other off-duty NCOs were lured into a honey trap. They had met some local girls in a pub who invited them back for a party at their place, but it was a set-up: as soon as they were inside the signal was given and a team of IRA gunmen burst in and shot all the British soldiers, leaving Geoff for dead. He survived, but with terrible injuries. Geoff's situation was definitely one I could relate to.

Was I nervous? Strangely, no. The hardest part for me that day was struggling into my wetsuit. For an able-bodied person, putting on a wetsuit is not much harder than pulling on a pair of trousers: the tight-fitting rubber can sometimes stick to the skin, but you soon roll it on. But if your legs are partly paralysed like mine, well, it's quite a business and it involves lying flat on a bench and rolling from side to side while inching the neoprene wetsuit up the calves and over the hips. My wetsuit might well have shrunk in the seven years it had been in storage but you would not have known it. One of the many side-effects of paraplegia is a loss of muscle mass, and while I had never been exactly stout I now had room to spare inside the wetsuit. It was like waving an arm around inside a pair of trousers.

The next step was to transfer from sitting on my

wheelchair to sitting on the edge of the pool; this was achieved in about 2.5 seconds with a couple of lads from the Scuba Trust picking me up bodily under the arms and plonking me down at the water's edge. I shrugged on the harness attached to the oxygen tank and checked the various bits of kit that dangled off it, pulled on my face-mask, put the breathing apparatus in my mouth and rolled forward into the pool. Immediately a warm, familiar feeling swept over me – who knows, perhaps subconsciously my body felt it was going back to the womb. Instinctively, I uncurled my body like a plant reaching for the sun and revelled in the freedom of being able to move about and breathe without having to keep going up to the surface.

The instructors took me through the basic drills, such as removing the facemask underwater and putting it back on, clearing it of water by breathing out through the nose and letting the rising air bubbles drive the water up and out of the mask, then practising what to do if your oxygen supply fails and you have to share your buddy's tank by breathing from his spare tube. It all seemed pretty straightforward, as of course this was a tranquil swimming pool with just ten feet of water. The instructors were happy: I was ready for the Red Sea.

As soon as we landed in Sharm El Sheikh my 'bullshit antennae' started to twitch. Years of living in Egypt – first as a student, then later as a journalist – had given me plenty of experience when it came to spotting certain mercantile types, a vociferous minority of the population, who are experts at pretending they are doing vital work on your behalf, when in reality they are inventing most of the jobs in the hope of a hefty tip. We were now being hailed by just such a conman from the car park. 'Hello, yes!' he shouted from the open door of his minivan. 'Over here!' 'Just ignore him,' I said, 'and he'll give up.' 'I'm afraid we can't,' said John Macintyre, suddenly busying himself with his camera kit. 'We've already hired him. The Cairo office said we needed a fixer and apparently he's worked with film crews before so they chose him,' he said sheepishly. A frightful crashing of gears announced the arrival of Hamdi (not his real name or he'd probably never get another job). 'You see?' he leered. 'I make special parking space for you.' Katie Pearson, the producer, muttered, 'Nice one, John,' and we piled in for the short ride to the resort.

Even in the dark I could see that Sharm El Sheikh had changed immeasurably since I had first pitched up here on a winter's night after hitchhiking down from Cairo in 1982. Back then there was little but abandoned Israeli trenches, a lone bakery, a contingent of bored US peace-keeping paratroopers and a handful of Bedouin fishermen. Now there was continual street lighting all the way from the airport to the resort. Sharm was a ten-mile-long strip of five-star hotels, beach bars, markets, cafés and clubs, and it was on the international map: the place was awash with mostly young tourists from Russia, Britain, Italy and Scandinavia. There had, of course, been a major blow to the tourist industry in 2005 when terrorists drove truck bombs right up to the hotels and blew up several dozen people, killing mainly Egyptian shopkeepers and taxi-drivers, but the place seemed to have picked itself up, dusted itself down and carried on.

'Now we have special security precautions,' said

Hamdi. 'No vehicles allowed inside police cordon.' He said this without any trace of irony as he drove us, without being searched, straight through the cordon to our hotel. 'Now,' he continued as we wearily hefted our bags into the lobby, 'you must give me your exact programme and I will make permissions.' 'We don't have an exact programme,' I replied. 'We're making a film about me trying to scuba-dive without the use of my legs and we're going to include a bit about Sharm as a tourist destination.' Hamdi's face clouded over and he made that ubiquitous Egyptian gesture of gently karate chopping one hand down at right angles on his other wrist. It meant 'We need an official piece of paper, preferably stamped several times by a chain-smoking bureaucrat in a safari suit, swivelling around behind his desk in a windowless office back in Cairo.' To be fair to Hamdi, we did need permission to film just about anything in Egypt, it just wasn't nearly as complicated as he liked to make out. 'Lose him,' advised John's Egyptian friends at the hotel. 'He'll only make trouble for you.' But shaking off Hamdi was to prove every bit as challenging as legless diving.

The Camel Dive Resort was a dedicated diving hotel with a party atmosphere, so much so that each time the air-conditioning in my room switched itself off at night I could hear the thump of dance music coming from the bar upstairs. It reminded me of when we used to live in the heart of Covent Garden in the 1990s: at whatever time we would tip back into the flat after a night out, we could still hear an unsuppressible beat coming from some late-night bar or other.

But come morning in Sharm, it was easy to shake off

tiredness. You just had to look up at the great expanse of
Sinai sky, devoid of dust or pollution and heralding
another cloudless autumn day on the Red Sea. 'Let's get
you started in the pool, then,' said Luke, my dive
instructor, a blond and tanned old Etonian who formed
part of the eclectic mix of expatriates who had made their
home in Sharm. To be honest, I'd had enough of these
seemingly endless checks and tests in swimming pools; I
did not want to be wrapped in cotton wool, I just wanted
to get out into the open water and dive the coral reefs. But
although I had done OK in that pool back in Hampshire,
nobody was really sure how I was going to perform at
depth in the open sea. Would I panic on realizing that I
could not kick my legs to propel myself where I wanted
and suddenly start grabbing other people's kit underwater? I hoped not, but you could never be sure how you
would behave if a problem arose far below the surface.

We did discover that since my paralysed legs weighed so
little my feet kept rising up to the surface, bobbing around
opposite my face and curving my body into the shape of a
banana. There was nothing I could do about this, it was
nature making its own adjustments, so Luke produced a
pair of ankle weights to weigh me down like a Kashmiri
dancer. I then hauled myself up and out of the water as I
always did and sat sunning myself on the edge. Luke
stared at me open-mouthed. 'I have never,' he said, 'ever
seen a paraplegic get themselves out of this pool unaided
and I must have taught over forty of them.' If this was his
way of building up my confidence for the open sea it was
working. When only just over half your body works
normally, things like this can make a big difference.

That evening we relaxed with mint tea and hubble-bubble pipes as the Red Sea evening in-crowd built up and I found myself slowly unwinding – despite the fact that this place had been truck-bombed only the year before – and relishing being back in the Middle East.

The next morning, bright and early, we all trooped down to the harbour with our 'jetty passes' that allowed us to go out to sea. There was a good deal of posturing from the plain-clothes security man with a pistol strapped to his jeans, Baghdad-style, then abruptly he lost interest and waved us through. I wheeled myself along the wooden jetty to the stern of the boat, where a couple of burly Egyptian boatmen hefted me neatly onboard and off we went, chugging northwards into the wind, with the stark Sinai mountains to our left, the Saudi coast to our right, and the morning sun dancing on the waves alongside. 'I'm surprised Hamdi the fixer didn't come along for the ride,' said someone. 'Yes please! Hamdi here!' said a voice from the cabin and suddenly there he was, emerging resplendent in his nautical attire, a bogus captain's hat set at a jaunty angle on his shiny bald head. Hamdi was making a stab at charging the BBC a cool US$300 a day for his 'services' on land – about twice the going rate for fixers in Egypt – and as far as John was concerned, his job did not include free-loading on our scuba excursions. As we moored up for the morning on an offshore coral reef, there was nothing for Hamdi to do except help himself prematurely to the lunch buffet, a task he took on with alacrity. Simon, the second cameraman, began to hum quietly 'Who ate all the pies?'

It was time for my first open-water dive since sustaining my paralysing injuries two years earlier. Luke, the dive instructor, gave us our pre-dive briefing using a white-board and marker pens to show us the layout of the reef beneath us, known as the Middle Garden. I wheeled myself over to the flat wooden stern of the boat, got the boatmen to pick me up under the armpits and deposit me on the edge, and Luke brought up my dive kit, which I now strapped on. I spat in my facemask to clear it, sloshed some water around it and squinted up to deliver a final piece to camera. Then I rolled forward overboard, John having pre-positioned himself and his underwater camera in the depths below me to catch my noisy and undignified entry into the Red Sea.

Instantly I found myself in a different world, a place of deep, dappled blue shadows and shoals of glinting silver fish, of sunbeams lancing downwards towards the seabed and great underwater gardens of purple and yellow coral. In the last few years Sharm El Sheikh has become famously 'over-dived', with stories abounding of dive parties having to queue underwater and wait their turn to explore the wrecks and reefs, the air bubbles from dozens of aqualungs streaming in a solid white column up to the surface. But the Red Sea is still a magical place underwater, with an incredible variety of exotic fish, some found nowhere else in the world, and while I have been lucky enough to dive in other scuba Shangri-Las like Australia's Great Barrier Reef and the Pacific coast of Costa Rica, for me, the Red Sea is hard to beat.

But now I was having problems. The partial paralysis in my legs meant that, despite the ankle weights, my feet kept floating up to the level of my shoulders; I had managed to get suncream in my eye, which is no fun when you're several fathoms below the surface and can't wipe it away; and I had bad earache from being unable to equalize the pressure by the usual method of pinching your nostrils shut and snorting out. Luke could see I was in difficulty, but he knew how much I wanted to try and do everything for myself, so instead of grabbing me and manoeuvring me back up to the surface, he thoughtfully came up with a wonderful underwater gesture of invitation, the sort of languid, open-handed movement that seventeenth-century flunkies might have used at the court of King Louis XIV. I was finding it pretty frustrating not being able to uncurl myself into the classic dive posture, where you stretch your body out flat, angled slightly downwards, and let your fins propel you effortlessly along while your arms rest at your side. I seemed to be destined either to swim in the shape of a banana or else to stand vertically in the water. Each time I did try to stretch out I kept banging the back of my head on the metal nozzle at the top of my oxygen tank.

Then, magically, after about twenty minutes, the problems started to evaporate; I sorted myself out and found my 'neutral buoyancy' – the right amount of air to keep in your inflatable jacket so that you are neither rising to the surface nor sinking to the bottom. Slowly, methodically, I propelled myself through the translucent water by doing breaststroke with my arms, my webbed gloves driving me forward. This was heaven. At last I was using my own body, not a machine, to move from one place to the next. I was thrilled by my independence in such magical surroundings. True, my legs dangled uselessly beneath me and more than once my bare feet were grazed on the coral, something I only became aware of when I looked down and saw the scraped flesh. But a kaleidoscope of fish shimmered all around: on the shallow, sandy seabed we found a Blue-spotted Stingray, a shy and beautiful creature. This one was missing the venomous barb in its tail but we still stayed well clear of it, knowing that only that month the hugely popular TV presenter and naturalist Steve Irwin had swum over a stingray while filming a documentary in Australia and it had lashed out and stung him fatally in the heart. Here in the Red Sea, in amongst the soft, waving fronds of the anemones, we watched a predatory silver Jackfish hunting smaller prey, we got right up close to the familiar orange and white stripes of little Clownfish, like the star of *Finding Nemo*, and everywhere there darted Parrotfish, Angel Fish, and a dozen other species I could not name. I was entranced, surfacing after a full fifty minutes with a huge sense of liberation and achievement. I was once more enjoying a sport that I had so enjoyed before my spine got hit. I even felt a bristle of pride when Luke and John both complained that I had swum too fast for them.

Up on deck it seemed that lunch – or what Hamdi had left for us – was barely over before the shadows were lengthening and it was time to haul anchor. It was easy to see how the Red Sea had got its name as the setting sun lit up the russet rocks of Tiran Island, which guarded the narrow entrance to the Gulf of Aqaba. To the west the jagged mountains of the Sinai became a succession of blurred blue ridges, each a fraction darker than the one before it, turning the barren, waterless ravines into a place of mystery and intrigue.

Back on land, we set up in the souk to film our interview

with the all-powerful local governor, who, like most governors in Egypt, was a presidential appointee plucked from the senior ranks of the Presidential Guard. Hamdi, needless to say, was in overdrive. First he had told us it would take him many days to arrange the interview, and then he was full of dire omens when we said thanks, but our other Egyptian friends had already fixed it up. 'He will not come! It does not work this way!' But it did and Governor Mutawali seemed genuinely pleased to be interviewed by the BBC. The resort bombings here were a thing of the past, he said, an aberration blamed on the north Sinai Bedu in league with Palestinian extremists. '*Khalaas*,' he said, wiping imaginary dust briskly from his hands. 'It is finished.'

To give our film a bit of variety, we decided to alternate the next few days' diving with a day spent filming in the starkly beautiful deserts of south Sinai, an area I came to love when I was a student based in Cairo in the 1980s. As we drove north from Sharm El Sheikh then turned westwards towards the mountains, I wondered what we would find. Whole new model towns, perhaps, with fast-food joints and internet cafés? Or would the place be deserted, with the once nomadic Bani M'Zeina Bedu tribespeople giving up on their notoriously hard lifestyle and transplanting themselves to Sharm in search of work?

The day began, as it so often does when filming in Egypt, with a huge amount of fuss and commotion. Hamdi had decided that now would be a good time to present his bill, all three thousand dollars of it, for 'preparation work' he had supposedly undertaken on our behalf in Cairo. It was an outrageous amount with little to show for it, and when John spotted that Hamdi had billed us for the day at sea when he had only stopped eating lunch to take a long siesta, our fixer appeared full of indignation, much of it, I suspect, put on. Our other Egyptian friends maintained it was all a rip-off and said they would calm him down, but Hamdi was now malevolently brooding. We managed to give him the slip by driving off in a hurry, but to our amazement we found out later that he promptly called the police and tried to get them to set up roadblocks to prevent us from getting into the desert. If we were not going to play his game, it seemed, Hamdi was bent on wrecking ours.

But all that day we were blissfully unaware of our fixer's absurd machinations. In a sunlit desert valley we drew up at a tiny cluster of ramshackle huts, where the Bedu welcomed us warmly and plied us with glasses of scalding-hot, sweet, sticky tea. '*Itfaddal! Itfaddal!*' they chorused. 'Welcome!' I had no intention of sitting this one out in an air-conditioned minibus. In fact, before we left for Egypt I had even bought myself an expensive pair of thick, off-road tyres for my wheelchair. I eased myself down from the minibus and on to the wheelchair, which Katie now tipped backwards and pushed forward so it rolled easily through the hot, fine sand that was sprinkled with fresh goat dung.

In the shade of a solitary thorn tree, I sat down on a mat and began to interview a Bedu girl in Arabic. Salwa was seventeen and bursting to talk: she was engaged, she said proudly, to a man she had yet to meet and the wedding was soon, maybe next month, she could not recall. Would we all like to come? In all her years, said Salwa, she had never been further afield than Dahab, a tiny coastal town seven miles away, but life here in the desert was good, there was no one to interfere with their way of life. I thought of Hamdi and the small army of Cairene officials who had set up shop in nearby Sharm El Sheikh and I knew exactly what she meant. A pure-white camel, tethered to the thorn tree, nodded slowly as if in pensive agreement. Life here was good.

Salwa then suddenly remembered something and fished into her dress. 'Look!' she cried. 'I have a mobile phone. Do you have one too? I know,' she said innocently, 'let's swap numbers and we can call each other.' I could only imagine how well that would go down with Bedu hubby-to-be – and I did not suppose Mrs G would be overly thrilled either – so I gently lied that my phone was broken. Yet this, I realized, was incredible: squatting on the sand in a secluded valley in the Sinai Peninsula, being offered to trade mobile-phone numbers with a Bedu girl.

Late that afternoon, we paused on the edge of the desert as hundreds of storks flew low above us, wheeling and circling over the sand, before settling on a rocky outcrop for the night. Tomorrow they would be on their way south to Africa, migrating to warmer climes for the winter, but we had our own journey to make: a date with a submerged shipwreck.

Oh, happy day. Last night Hamdi had finally conceded defeat, and after presenting another bill that included a lunch he had treated himself to yesterday at one of Sharm's most expensive restaurants, he announced with great solemnity that he was returning to Cairo 'to attend to important business'. A figure was finally settled on and I was almost sorry to see him go. With his raffish white boating hat (he neither sailed, swam nor dived), his hennaed moustache and his perpetual insistence that we needed his help to film wherever we went, he had come to provide a slice of light entertainment. 'Please,' he whispered to me as we said goodbye with an awkward embrace, having singled me out as if I alone could recognize his true talent, 'you must recommend me to your friends in England. Tell them I make everything possible for you here.'

But with Hamdi gone the air seemed to clear. Our Egyptian diving friends breathed an audible sigh of relief, and we headed for the boat with a renewed spring in our step, or in my case, a renewed whisk to my wheels. As the first rays of the dawn sun slanted over the Saudi mountains to the east, we passed the tiny mosque where a kindly imam had once invited Peregrine and me to sleep in the garden, after hitch-hiking down from Cairo in our student days in 1982. My delight at seeing that it was still standing was somewhat tempered by the fact that it was now out of bounds, swallowed up by a large police compound.

Today, for our final dive, we were to chug westwards for three hours around the south tip of the Sinai Peninsula and up into the Gulf of Suez, to reach the wreck of the SS *Thistlegorm*. This merchant vessel and her crew had to be one of the most unlucky casualties of the Second World War. She had set out in 1941 from a Scottish port, picked up her cargo of urgent supplies for the beleaguered British Eighth Army garrison in Tobruk, and then, to avoid the Luftwaffe's bombers that were criss-crossing the

Mediterranean, she sailed south all the way down the African coast, round the Cape of Good Hope and back up the other side. She stopped just short of entering the Suez Canal, waiting for orders to pass through then swing hard to port and make the final dash for Libya; she had completed over 95 per cent of her epic journey. But that night, as she lay moored up with her lights dimmed, a pair of marauding German Heinkel bombers were out scouring the seas for the *Queen Mary*, which was carrying Australian reinforcements. Frustrated, they spotted the SS *Thistlegorm* instead and made a low, lethally accurate pass. Their two bombs hit the ammunition hold, instantly killing those crew members who had been sleeping on deck in tarpaulins in the hot summer night. When the ammunition went up the explosion was so powerful it sent locomotive train engines high into the air, landing thirty metres away in the sea. The SS *Thistlegorm*, which means 'Blue Thistle' in Gaelic, has been designated a war graveyard.

Unlike the Gulf of Aqaba, the deepwater channel on the other side of the Sinai where the ocean bed drops away steeply to over a thousand metres, the Gulf of Suez is surprisingly shallow. So despite its grisly origins, the wreck of the SS *Thistlegorm* has become one of the top scuba-diving sites in the Red Sea, a fact which became all too obvious as we moored up alongside over half a dozen other dive boats a few kilometres offshore. 'Sometimes,' said Luke, 'we have to wait for nearly an hour for the crowds to thin out underwater. They're mostly Italian package tours. I'll just pop down and take a look.' Minutes later he was back, yanking off his mask, wiping the saliva from his face and hauling himself nimbly back onboard. 'There's a strong current,' he warned, 'so I'm going to need you to hold on to me for much of this dive.' The shipwreck lay at an angle, he explained, with the bow pointing up at 14 metres below the surface and the stern at 28 metres.

The rest of the crew had dropped the anchor in such a way that we were right above the wreck and now we were descending slowly into the gloom, passing our hands one over the other down along the anchor line, pausing to pinch our noses and equalize the pressure in our sinuses. The visibility was poor, which gave the wreck a sinister, ghostly feel as it loomed closer through the opaque depths. We were in the hold now, where the bowhead protected us from the current that rippled across the deck in unseen waves, and all around me were the remains of the ship's submerged cargo: motorbikes, sidecars, jeeps, whole boxes of wartime Lee Enfield rifles, a stack of Wellington boots, curiously intact after all these years. In the distance an entire steam engine lay on its side. At that moment I felt an immense sadness that the men who had sailed halfway round the world to bring this cargo to where it was desperately needed had got so far, only to lose their lives here on that night in 1941. I shivered briefly in my wetsuit; this was, after all, a graveyard. But it was hard to ignore the vibrant marine life: large Batfish with bold black stripes, hunting Jackfish, bright-blue Fusiliers, green Parrotfish and a single Lionfish fluttering its venomous white spines.

Luke grabbed my arm and pointed below, and there, perfectly camouflaged as it lay on the deck, was a

Crocodile Fish, nearly a metre long, silently waiting to ambush the smaller fish. My legs were, as usual, trailing beneath me, but now, without warning, a strange thing happened: I felt my feet bump against something solid. I suppose if I analyse it medically, my paralysed feet did not feel anything, it was the reverberation through my leg bones that I felt; but anyway, I was now standing on the steel plates of the deck, my arms touching a metal spar, my body buoyed up by the salty brine, small fish swerving in and out between my ankles. Wait a minute, I thought. I'm actually standing unsupported. This is something I have not done in nearly three years. I had already forgotten how it felt, and it felt, well, fantastic. And in that moment, floundering around down there in the warm waters of the Red Sea, I realized how far I had come.

But the best was yet to come. When we got back onboard, changed out of our wetsuits, pulled on our T-shirts and sat squinting in the afternoon sun as we chugged back to Sharm El Sheikh, Luke came up to me with a barely suppressed smile. 'Give me your diving log book,' he said, coming over all formal, which was unlike him. With his waterproof pen he wrote something small and neat beside that day's entry, then handed it back to me. 'Needs no further instruction,' read the inscription. 'Is independent underwater.'

21

Bahrain

Legless in the Desert

ONCE ARRESTED UNDER SUSPICION OF SPYING AT BAHRAIN airport, I saw a certain irony about my coming back here, ten years on, to a red-carpet welcome. In 1997 the BBC sent me, as their Gulf stringer, to Bahrain to interview the UN weapons inspectors that Saddam Hussein had effectively thrown out of Iraq. Standing beside the runway perimeter with my mobile phone clamped to my ear, commenting live for BBC World TV as the white-painted UN plane taxied to a halt, I suppose I did look suspicious. Bahrain was going through a turbulent time as Shi'ite protesters had turned violent, chafing at their Sunni-dominated government and demanding a return to parliamentary democracy. That afternoon a roving Bahraini police patrol swooped in and promptly arrested me, and I was carted off to the nearest police station to explain myself.

But ten years later, I had been invited back to Bahrain

under very different circumstances. The country was now a constitutional monarchy with a quasi democracy, and it had a young, dynamic Crown Prince who had become the driving force behind Bahrain's more grandiose economic ambitions. Sheikh Salman Al-Khalifa had been educated in Britain and the US, and to his critics he was perhaps too Westernized, too remote from the realities of the poor, rural villages where many Bahrainis still lived. But for a journalist, Sheikh Salman was good news. In a part of the world where Gulf leaders rarely gave interviews – and when they did they spoke in long, meandering platitudes, praising their 'brotherly neighbours' and avoiding almost anything controversial – here was a man who spoke in plain English. Bahrain's Crown Prince had recently delivered a powerful conference speech in which he had spoken about Iran, Iraq, terrorism and the threats facing the Gulf.

I applied to interview him, but when he came to London his office manager was evasive. 'His Highness would like to meet you first. Can you come to tea at the such-and-such hotel?' Over a pot of Earl Grey and some slightly stale biscuits we talked of Bahrain, my book *Blood and Sand* and my injuries. The Crown Prince seemed to be taking a personal interest in my story, and was keen that the horrendous attack on me in Saudi Arabia should not put me off coming back to the Gulf. 'You lived with us once in Bahrain,' he said, referring to my time there as a banker in the early 1990s, 'and we want you to think of Bahrain as your second home. Why don't you come and pay us a visit?'

Perhaps if that fateful trip to Riyadh in 2004 had been

my first foray into the Gulf Arab States I would never have returned, my view of the region poisoned by those murderous outcasts who had attacked us in cold blood in such a cowardly way. But the truth was that I liked the Gulf, and although the region did admittedly have some unsavoury undertones of profligate squandering and religious hypocrisy, I had usually found its people to be polite and kind. I suppose, if I am honest, I was also flattered that someone as busy and important as a country's Crown Prince should take the trouble to concern himself about whether I felt at home there or not. So it was agreed: the interview could wait, I would come to Bahrain on a private visit.

It was not just me who had changed, coming back in a wheelchair to the island I had once lived on as a banker, bachelor and all-round free spirit. Bahrain had changed visibly too. Being chauffeured into the capital, Manama, I could see that a majestic new causeway now linked the city to the airport, spanning a shallow lagoon where I used to water ski in my lunch breaks, in the hallowed days before mobile phones allowed Head Office to keep tabs on everyone. Now there were numerous futuristic plate-glass skyscrapers shooting up into the sky, dwarfing the low-rise potting shed of a British embassy that still sat amidst its verdant acres of prime real estate, its Union Jack wilting in the heat. A waterfront stock exchange was half-built, and down in the desert I knew there was an international Formula 1 racetrack and an entire town for sixty thousand people being built offshore on reclaimed land.

But scratch beneath the surface, as I did over the coming

days, and Bahrain, I found, had not fundamentally changed. British expatriates I knew from nearly two decades before were still here, having bought property and settled. My Bahraini friends had all done their stints working in London, Dubai and Montreal and had mostly now come back to do business here. They grumbled about soaring property prices, traffic jams and rising crime, and whinged that MPs in Parliament were wasting their time arguing over whether or not men should be allowed to work in women's lingerie shops. When I had lived here, I thought, Bahrain did not even have a parliament. So what did they think about the situation up the coast in Iraq? I asked them. For so many years Saddam's shadow had loomed over this region, as well as the smoke from Kuwait's oil fires that his troops set ablaze and which blotted out the sun for seven months, leaving dirty smudges on my washing every time it rained. Saddam's name still brought a frown, but for different reasons. 'His execution was a disaster,' said a visiting Saudi banker, toying with his half-filled glass of Cabernet Sauvignon. 'It made everyone here very angry,' he went on. 'Even some of the Shi'ites mourned him and he was no friend of theirs. Executing him publicly like that turned Saddam into a hero for people in this region. They should have just left him in prison to be a nonentity.' And what of Iran, I asked them, a country that used to claim Bahrain as its own? Were people worried that the US or Israel would attack Iran's nuclear plants? 'Oh, the Western expatriates talk about it the whole time,' said my friends. 'But look around you, business is booming, there is so much money pouring in here from around the Gulf, everyone's investing and they wouldn't be doing that if they thought there was a war coming.' Suhail, a young Bahraini businessman, leant over to me and said, 'We have a joke about Iran's President Ahmedinejad here. You know how some young guys here and in Saudi like to drag race their cars at night, they drive flat out at over a hundred miles an hour and then try and spin the car round as many times as they can without flipping it? Well, we call this *taf-hees*, and we say it sums up Ahmedinejad's foreign policy!' Another friend chipped in, saying, 'Dealing with this guy in Tehran is like playing a game of chess. You think you've got him in check . . . but then he just tips up the board and walks away!'

I had still not been summoned for my audience with the Crown Prince, so the next day I went to look at one of the country's showpiece projects, Durrat Al-Bahrain – the Pearl of Bahrain. Right down on the southern tip of the island, in an area that used to be cordoned off by the military when I lived here, this was going to be new territory for me. First we passed the ageing machinery and rusting brown pipelines of the country's dwindling oil industry. There were peeling signs from the 1950s that read 'Well Manifold No. 3' and notices outside workers' camps saying 'Never Give Safety a Day Off'. Bahrain was the first Gulf State to produce oil commercially, pumping it out from the 1930s, but its reserves were running out, which is why, like Dubai, it was now pressing ahead with diversification. We passed the Tree of Life, an ancient and solitary bush that was one of the last places you used to be able to visit before you ran up against the military boundary; I once brought a Gulf Air flight attendant here in my growling five-litre Mustang convertible to try to impress her, but then broke down in the sand and had to be rescued by a troop of amused Bahraini soldiers on exercise. Then came Sheikh Isa Airbase, once so secret that it never featured on any official map of Bahrain. During the Desert Storm campaign to evict Saddam from Kuwait in 1991, this base had reverberated to the roar of US Airforce Stealth fighters, but now it appeared all but deserted, the tranquil blue expanse of the Gulf stretching out beyond its perimeter towards the distant coast of Iran.

Just up from the southern tip of the island, the Durrat Al-Bahrain housing complex was only half-built but I could see clearly what it would look like: a collection of luxury, sun-baked villas planted on one of the most unspoilt stretches of coastline the island had left, and connected to Manama by a fast, newly tarmacked road. I could see the designers' vision, but why, I wondered, did they have to overshadow this place with a towering building that was over seventy storeys high? Perhaps the idea was to be seen from neighbouring Qatar, a country with which Bahrain had had prickly relations in the past; or was it an attempt to rival Dubai down the coast? Either way, it seemed completely OTT to me, but perhaps I was turning into another Wilfred Thesiger, the veteran Arabian explorer who had first inspired me to travel to the Middle East, with his entrenched suspicion of modern progress and pathological dislike of the motor car. I hoped not.

At midday I received the royal summons. 'The Sheikhs will see you now,' I was told on the phone. 'A driver will collect you from your hotel.' 'The Sheikhs' plural? Was there to be more than one? This sounded intriguing. Each Gulf State, I had learnt, had subtly different forms of honorific address. In Saudi Arabia all members of the ruling Al-Sa'ud family were princes and princesses; most were HH – His Highness – but the senior ones directly descended from the country's founder, King Abdulaziz, were HRH – His Royal Highness. Prominent non-royal businessmen and Saudi religious scholars were given the title Sheikh. But in Bahrain, Qatar, Kuwait and the UAE the ruling family members were called not Prince but Sheikh. Oh, except for the absolute ruler himself, who was called the Emir. Oman had a Sultan (Qaboos), Saudi had a King (Abdullah) and Bahrain, which used to have an Emir, now had a King (Hamad). It was all very confusing.

Cocooned in an air-conditioned limo, we coasted past white-walled villages, their roofs crenellated with satellite dishes and the black religious flags of Shi'ite Islam. Here were so many familiar landmarks from my former life: the dusty groves of date palms, the sandy lane that led to the old Portuguese Fort, the tiny Indian corner shops known as 'cool stores', the open patches of desert and scrub where Baluchi herdsmen tended the sheikhs' camels, the road signs to villages with names more Persian than Arab, like Karbabad, Dumistan and Karzakan. I closed my eyes and for a moment I was back in 1994, a besuited banker commuting home to my villa, my head full of deals in the pipeline and the girl of my dreams I was yet to marry, wondering what we would do tonight: would it be dinner beneath the stars or a foray into the desert, an evening of indoor ice skating or a night with our friends in the bars of the souk with their Filipino girl bands in skimpy dresses?

When I opened my eyes I was brought back to 2007

with a jolt: a North African man with an M16 assault rifle was walking over to our car. We were at the gates of the Crown Prince's palace and the imported guards were checking IDs. A quick conversation into a walkie-talkie, snapped salutes and we were through, gliding past acres of well-watered lawns where hoopoes and bulbuls flitted between the trees. This, I thought, must be Bahrain's answer to Camp David, a place where visiting VIPs could stroll in peace and privacy, discussing matters of state. The palace may have had the longest driveway I have ever driven down, but it was a surprisingly discreet and modest building, built in the traditional Bahraini style with white walls and flat roofs.

'Welcome, welcome!' beamed the Crown Prince, striding across his Persian carpet. 'Please excuse me for being late.' There was quite a gathering here, I noticed, as people rose from their seats in a ripple of white *dishdasha* robes and I wheeled myself round the room shaking hands. I was in a room with the Foreign Minister, Interior Minister, Defence Minister and various other ministers, a sort of kitchen cabinet but all very relaxed. To my surprise, there was also a tall, solitary Briton. The Crown Prince read my mind. 'Oh, that's your British Ambassador, Jamie Bowden.' The Foreign Minister, Sheikh Khaled, was not a small man, a fact he made light of as he toyed with a pistachio nut. With a twinkle in his eye he described how when he went to Tehran recently to meet President Ahmedinejad they embraced in front of the cameras, the Bahraini enveloping the diminutive Iranian leader. 'This,' teased Bahrain's king later, 'is the only time Bahrain has ever been bigger than Iran!'

We filed through for lunch and the Crown Prince gestured at the starters now being deposited before us. 'I'm not quite sure what this is,' he said. 'I think it's a sort of deconstructed vol-au-vent!' The ice broken, the conversation ranged like a spy satellite up and down the Gulf. Did Iran have a nuclear weapons programme? What were the US Navy's plans if it did? Was Iraq in danger of splitting into three regions? Had the US-led invasion made the region less secure? I learnt little new, in fact I was flattered to find these ruling sheikhs asking for my opinion on several occasions, yet it was a brief and fascinating glimpse into the world of royal decision-making.

I could see through the window that the midday glare was already gone from the day; the sinking sun was now making dancing, glittering patterns on the shallow waters that separated Bahrain's west coast from the Saudi mainland. The Crown Prince cleared his throat. 'Come on. It's time.'

The day before, his adviser had asked me if there was anything I would like to do on the island. A dozen thoughts flashed through my mind: speedboating out to the reefs, perhaps, or a scuba dive, or a spot of gentle bird-watching with my old friend Howard King from the Natural History Society around the Jebel – the tiny hill that passed for a mountain in the centre of the island. 'Quad biking,' I had replied, without really thinking. I had tried this, post-injuries, in the Sinai desert the previous year and had really enjoyed it, although bumping across the hardened ridges of the sand had left me with a very sore backside.

Now I was being assigned to the tender care of officials

from F1, Bahrain's showpiece Formula 1 racetrack, and I feared they were going to expect me to be some sort of adrenaline-junkie speed merchant rather than the cautious, risk-averse individual I had become since being made half-paralysed. While cars and drivers were summoned to the Crown Prince's palace I lingered on the steps to chat to the British Ambassador, Jamie Bowden. A former Army officer in the Royal Green Jackets, he turned out to know a friend of mine. Bowden had accompanied Captain Charles Blackmore on his Jordan desert crossing in 1985, retracing Lawrence of Arabia's route to see if the journey had been possible in the length of time he had said. (It wasn't.) I now told the Ambassador how the Jordanian Bedu I had stayed with had laughed about how much they had overcharged the British officers for the use of their camels. 'But that was me,' said the Ambassador, looking slightly peeved. 'I was the one who rented the camels!'

In the warm glow of late afternoon we drove south to the F1 racetrack. A giant poster of Jensen Button beamed down at us and a sign proclaimed this to be 'The home of motor sports in the Middle East'. Where once I had bird-watched across empty desert a large stadium now rose up and men in racing overalls scurried across spotless new tarmac. A trio of gleaming blue quad bikes stood waiting beside my two guides. Whatever instructions they had been given by the Crown Prince's office, they were obviously taking no chances with my safety. Salman, a young Sheikh from the ruling family, would ride in front; Ali would ride behind me; and there was even a Brit in an escort vehicle, a customized Humvee, to follow up behind.

Heavens, I thought, it's not as if I was trying to set a new record for crossing the Sahara here.

Ali and Salman watched with barely concealed nervousness as I transferred myself out of my wheelchair and on to the seat of the quad bike. In fact I can't stand being watched at times like this as it turns it into a bit of a spectacle, and I prefer to do everything myself. But they were only looking out for me and I accepted their offer of lifting my paralysed feet over the handlebars and down on to the foot rests like pieces of furniture on removal day. Unlike some quad bikes, these ones had no foot pedals; the brakes, accelerator and on-off button were all on the handlebars, which worked for me. There was no back support as on a wheelchair, so to keep my balance I had to rely on my abdominal muscles, which I had worked hard on in the gym, and on gripping the handlebars. Salman handed me a white gauze head-cover, of the sort worn by real racing drivers, then a helmet and my dark glasses. With a nod of the head and a mutual thumbs-up we were off.

When your legs no longer work and you cannot walk more than a few tottering steps with the aid of callipers and a frame, there is something totally liberating about riding a quad bike. I simply cannot describe the thrill of being able to move fast over the ground, fully in control of the machine beneath you, yet open to the elements, with no one but you to decide where and how fast you go. We started out on tarmac, with me nudging the accelerator up to the giddy heights of 30mph and Salman beckoning me to come and cruise alongside him. It was thrilling to feel the heat of the engine on the inside of my knees as they gripped the machine like the flanks of a horse; even my lifeless feet tingled from the hot metal.

Was I ready to head off-road? Most definitely. From the dead-straight road we swerved abruptly off-piste, as it were. At first the sand was packed and smooth, except for where it had built up in drifts, but soon we were lurching over rough ground until we came to some shallow dunes. We passed the gleaming white skeleton of a camel, picked dry by animals and blasted by wind and sand. I recognized this place as somewhere we had once tried to camp out in, one hot summer night thirteen years earlier. Back then, no sooner had we laid out our sleeping bags than a Bahraini police patrol had appeared out of nowhere, waving torches and asking for our ID before ordering us to move on; apparently we were too close to someone's palace.

'I love this place,' said Salman, taking off his helmet to admire the desert all around. 'Sometimes we come here to go falconing. Yes! Look!' he said, pointing. 'See those feathers over there, and there. Those are dead pigeons, the ones the falcons caught.'

Falconing is an ancient sport in Arabia; it pre-dates today's national boundaries yet it has survived the onslaught of oil-boom modernity. It is, traditionally, the sport of sheikhs and princes, as it is not cheap to rear and train falcons to go after Houbara Bustard and other game. The Houbara became almost extinct on the Arabian Peninsula in the last century, since instead of hunting them on camel or horseback people would chase them down in jeeps and even shoot at them with automatic weapons. Wealthy Gulf Arabs have since had to travel to Morocco, Pakistan and Afghanistan to indulge their passion for the sport. In fact, the former CIA officer Robert Baer has claimed that covert operatives sent to spy on Osama Bin Laden spotted him near Kandahar in the late nineties, but could do nothing about it because he was with a hunting party of sheikhs from the United Arab Emirates.

'OK,' said Salman, evidently relieved that I had not yet toppled off my quad bike and he had thus been spared an awkward phone call to the Crown Prince, 'you seem to be getting the hang of this. Let's see if you're ready to try this dune.' Squaring his shoulders, the young Bahraini gunned his engine and accelerated towards what looked like an impossibly steep sand dune. I watched in horror as his vehicle reared up 45 degrees and seemed to be on the verge of tipping over backwards. I had visions of him lying sprawled and trapped beneath the revving machine, with me helpless to rescue him. But at the last minute he threw his weight forward and the bike reared up and disappeared safely over the ridge of the dune.

Playing for time, I asked him to go round one more time while I made up my mind, and then, to my great surprise, I bottled out. I had two voices in my head, one saying, 'Go on, give it a go, where's your spirit?', the other saying, 'Whoa, hang on, this is not something you have to do and it's definitely not a risk worth taking.' I thought back to those terrible thirty minutes, three years earlier, when I had lain screaming and bleeding from bullet wounds in Riyadh. The prospect of Amanda being summoned to yet another hospital bed decided it; I swerved away from the dune and chose the safer path.

By now it was dusk, the sweetest time of day in the Middle East. The sun was a fast-sinking orb of deep crimson and the warm breeze was brushing our faces as we coasted home across the sand. Sitting upright in the saddle and gripping the handlebars, I found myself smiling uncontrollably. Salman caught my expression and grinned back; he too was loving this, but he could not know how much it meant to me. To be back in Bahrain was good enough, but to be doing this – quad biking across the desert at sunset without a care in the world – was pure magic. I felt more alive than at almost any time since I lost the use of my legs.

That evening the Crown Prince had a final surprise in store for me. Beneath a crescent moon the chauffeured car deposited me in a familiar white-walled village, a place of waving date-palm fronds, carved wooden doorways and crumbling, flaking walls. It was Jasra, the quiet, secluded village where I had lived for four years, and in the doorway of my old villa stood the Crown Prince, puffing on a cigar. 'I took the liberty,' he said, 'as the couple who live here happen to be friends of mine.' In a more sinister country like Saddam's Iraq this would have been alarming, with the couple in question perhaps disappearing for ever, but this was Bahrain and the couple turned out to be an Italian architect and his Bahraini wife, who welcomed me warmly. I was thrilled. The Jasra villa had been a legend at Flemings, the bank where I worked. For over a decade the company had rented it from a Bahraini sheikh, and a succession of us had lived, loved and partied in it throughout the eighties and nineties. Eventually corporate politics intervened: Flemings was bought up by the US investment bank Chase, and the lease on the villa was allowed to expire. It had been thirteen years since I had shut the villa's little wooden door for the last time, closing a chapter on my life, and I had not expected ever to see it again. Now here we were, just four of us, sipping drinks in the courtyard beneath the stars, admiring the rose bushes that my mother had planted all those years ago and sniffing the sweet scent of jasmine on the night breeze. Unburdened by minders, scribes or secretaries, we talked late into the night, our conversation ranging ever wider, interrupted only by the muffled snort of a horse from the nearby stables. True, it felt somehow wrong that Amanda, who had loved this place too, was not here, but I still felt a deep sense of contentment that night; this had to be one of the happiest evenings since my injuries.

22

Exmoor

Outward-Bound in a Wheelchair

THE FIRST SHOTS RANG OUT JUST AS I TURNED OFF THE A322. Three distinct gunshots, one after the other, there was no mistaking them. I turned down the music, wound down the window and smiled. These bullets were not for me. I was approaching Bisley in Surrey, home of British target-rifle shooting, where I was about to compete in the annual Old Marlburian Rifle Club Veterans' match. It was the first time I had heard live shooting since being on the receiving end of it in Riyadh and it did not bother me unduly.

It had been twenty-eight years since I had last fired a target rifle here, captaining our school team in my final year at school, yet it felt like yesterday. There they all were, my old team mates from school, still dressed in those curious beige padded jackets to absorb the recoil of the rifle into the shoulder, and all strung out on the long grassy mound at the 500-metre firing point, one person taking aim at the distant target, the other 'spotting' for him with a telescope and notebook, while squatting on a folding camp chair. There were dozens of school veterans competing here and as far as I could see absolutely nothing had changed since 1979. There were the intermittent puffs of smoke from the long-barrelled rifles, the blackboards with scores chalked up by hand, the thermos flasks of hot chocolate, and people perched precariously on folding shooting sticks, where you felt that just one discreet push would send them toppling over sideways.

But of course the one thing that had changed was me. I was allowed to drive over the heather and up to the firing point, but now I needed my friends' help to get down off my wheelchair to a prone firing position. When my turn came to shoot I was surprised at how heavy the rifle felt as I lifted it up off the grass, but soon my fingers were curling around the trigger guard and I felt the familiar cool kiss of the wooden butt against my cheek.

'Take your time, control your breathing, there's no rush,' said my coach. I paused and smiled, because just then I spotted John Hayward, who as a senior pupil had coached me at the school's indoor shooting range back when I was a new boy at Marlborough College in 1974. There was a sense of coming full circle that had nothing to do with my injuries. My left arm was braced tightly inside the canvas sling, my left eye was squinted shut, while through my right eye I lined up the round black bull's-eye in the precision sights and squeezed off a bullet at the target half a kilometre away. Instantly I felt the mechanical punch of the recoil drive hard into my shoulder. 'Not bad, just slightly left,' said my coach, leaning over to make a minuscule adjustment to the sights.

The rules were straightforward: you were allowed two shots to zero in, then ten shots to count. When I fired off the last one and rolled off the firing point I don't know who was more surprised, the coach or me. 'I think you're bluffing,' he said. 'I don't believe you haven't picked up a target rifle in twenty-eight years. You've just scored forty-six out of fifty.' There were certainly higher scores than this by some of the dedicated enthusiasts, but I was a tourist here today, not a regular, and when the Club presented me with a commemorative plaque to mark my return to the ranges I felt strangely elated. To be honest, over the years I had rather forgotten about the sport and never imagined I would do it again, with or without my injuries. But now this was another small milestone passed. Disabled shooting: I could do this.

Shooting at Bisley was all very well, but by now I was curious to see what other sports I could still do. I drew the line at Disabled Karate, but when the spinal injuries charity BackUp Trust asked if I would like to join them on Exmoor for a long weekend of outward-bound activities for people in wheelchairs I thought, why not? I had already relearnt how to drive, using easily adapted controls that let you brake or accelerate with a hand lever instead of by foot. But now I was driving down to Devon, not entirely sure what to expect.

In a grey stone hostel on the edge of Exmoor we gathered in the fading light, a dozen paraplegics and tetraplegics, together with our able-bodied 'buddies', the young volunteers who were going to shepherd us wheelchair-users through four days of outward-bound activities in the rain. I was not at all sure why I was doing this. I had a busy job and a loving family at home; yes, Exmoor was beautiful in all weathers, but it did not exactly fit my idea of a far horizon, and I had already done most of the activities – like abseiling and kayaking – long before my crippling injuries. Was this going to be one of these California-style, touchy-feely get-to-know-your-inner-self exercises, I wondered?

At first my fears were confirmed. 'Right,' said Sean, the team leader and himself a paraplegic after a snowboarding accident in Scotland, 'now we're all here, let's get to know each other. It's time for the ice-breaker. I want you all to turn to the person on your right and find out three things about them.' I turned to the girl next to me. 'Who annoys you most on television?' I asked. 'What?' she replied, flustered. 'Can't you give me an easier one?' The poor girl, I had no idea at the time that it was her first night out of Stoke Mandeville hospital since being paralysed in a car crash a year earlier and she was secretly terrified. When it came to my turn to speak up I was in a mischievous mood. 'Robyn's favourite colour is green, she took five hours to get here, and she fancies a bloke called Darren . . . OK, I made that last one up.' It broke the ice, but I noticed one of the carers, a good-looking Ben Affleck type, shifting uneasily as he stood against the wall. Well how was I to have guessed his name was Darren? From then on, things warmed up. 'This is Barry,' said his carer, indicating a jolly giant of a man, motionless in his electric wheelchair and completely paralysed from the neck down. 'And he's got a cock below his knee.' There was a stunned silence. 'It's true,' said Barry. 'I've got a tattoo of a cockerel just below my knee. I had it done years ago for a laugh after playing football.'

There followed a slideshow of what we could expect in the coming days – spectacular coastal scenery and, it seemed to me, an awful lot of hard work. Then it was up in the lift to the bar, where in my experience wheelchair people spend a large proportion of their waking hours. Gradually, as the bottles of Tuborg and Somerset cider slid down and everyone unwound, the stories came out. One by one, we quizzed each other on all the things paraplegics like to know about each other. What level is your injury? (How far up or down your spine the break is largely determines how much use you retain in your limbs.) How long have you had it? How did it happen? The stories were both heartbreaking and humbling, yet I detected not one hint of bitterness or self-pity. These were young men and women in their twenties and thirties who had come to terms with the catastrophic blow of spinal-cord injury and were now trying to get on with their lives. Chris had been a black-belt martial-arts instructor, but one day he and a friend had been messing about, running at each other in great padded Sumo suits, and the impact had broken his neck. 'That's terrible,' I said lamely. 'Did he apologize?' 'Oh yes,' said Chris. 'It was Darren over there, he's my brother-in-law.' Rhys had been dirt-biking seven years before when he took off into mid-air. 'I should have thrown aside the bike,' he told me in his melodic Welsh accent, 'but I landed on it and look what happened. I've got a C6 injury in my neck.' I watched as his partly paralysed hands grappled with a pouch of tobacco, preparing a roll-up with a skill born of years of practice. 'I love me roll-ups, me. Never without them.' And with a parting wink he wheeled himself out into the night for his first smoke of the evening. 'I thought I had just broken my wrist,' said Sean, describing the day he became paraplegic, 'but in fact I had somersaulted over my snowboard and snapped my neck.' Sean was lucky: the Scottish medics quickly arrived on the scene and stabilized his neck immediately, taking him straight to a spinal-injuries unit, with the result that he can now stand unsupported for short periods, a luxury denied to most paraplegics. 'Heard the joke about the stairs?' chipped in Big Barry. Barry had broken his neck in a car crash eleven years ago, swerving to avoid a badger on the road and hitting a tree side on. The police had searched the scene for clues as to what had happened and found the badger's corpse beside the skid marks. 'So go on, what's the joke then?' said someone. 'Well, you know how we all have difficulty going to the loo when we want?' said Barry. 'So you should try going down a flight of stairs in your wheelchair. It'll frighten the crap out of you.' Barry grinned; he had plenty more where that one came from.

The morning greeted us with a lowering grey sky, threatening rain. 'It's bound to cheer up,' said Rhys, ever the optimist. 'In Wales this would count as a fine day.' Straight after breakfast it was into the gym for 'wheelchair skills', starting with a ludicrous game of wheelchair tag. Each time you were tagged you had to sit there with your arms out until someone wheeled past beneath them and 'released' you. I half-closed my eyes and took in the scene:

the big room was like a teeming ants' nest, with people wheeling around at random, swerving, braking, crashing into each other. The clear winner was Barry. He may have been the most disabled person in the room, but he had the strongest spirit and in his hi-tech motorized wheelchair he overtook everyone else to huge applause. Rhys then showed us how to do 'back-wheel balances': rocking back on our rear wheels so as to lift the front ones clear off the ground. I have known wheelchair-users turn this into something of an art, but it is not one of my favourite activities, having never quite shaken off the sneaking feeling that I am about to tip backwards and smash my cranium on the concrete.

It was time to head off for the four-mile coastal push. We piled out of the white community-care bus on to a rainswept hilltop where we seemed to be in the middle of a cloud. 'It's a great view normally,' said Olly the organizer, as everyone fussed with cagoules, capes and anoraks. Down a road, through a gate and along a muddy, sodden track. This was not fun. Suddenly a cry went up from somewhere behind me, followed by a round of applause: Chris the Sumo-suit casualty had fallen out of his chair, inadvertently tipped out by his brother-in-law.

Gradually the rain eased, the cloud lifted and there, far below us, was the Atlantic – well, the Bristol Channel to be precise. Clumps of heather and yellow broom spilt over the path and the purple hills of north Devon stretched far into the distance. A shadow passed over our group as a pair of ravens glided past, dark and croaking. 'We've seen porpoises just offshore from up here,' said Olly. 'And whales?' asked someone. 'Yeah, you can just make it out in the distance,' quipped Barry.

As we made our way along the track, the BackUp Trust volunteers got it just right: if you didn't want to be pushed they left you alone; if you wanted a shove over the stony, uneven ground they tipped your chair back and propelled you forward on the big rear wheels. Tradition dictated that the coastal push ended with a drink around trestle tables at the local pub.

That night a diabolical device was brought out in the bar. Someone with a perverse sense of humour had brought an electric-shock game with them: each player had to grip a metal handle while the current built up, the last one to let go being the winner. Personally, I'm done with pain, having had more than my fair share of it just before, during and after my seven months in hospital, so I couldn't see the attraction of electrocuting oneself for fun. But almost everyone joined in, even tetraplegic Barry, who got someone to hold the metal handle next to his nose, so that he could feel the full joy of the electric shock.

'You see?' said Rhys. 'I told you it would turn out nice, like.' As the morning sun broke through the mist and the temperature struggled to break into double figures, we filed outside to be issued our lifejackets for sailing. 'There are three types,' announced Olly, 'according to how much mobility you've got. I know what you're all thinking – Am I going to capsize? Well don't worry, the dinghies have all got long keels so we've never lost anyone overboard yet.'

There followed a brief lesson on the subtle art of tacking – zigzagging across the water to catch the maximum amount of wind in the sails – then we wheeled down to the jetty and manoeuvred ourselves into the deckchair-style seats in the boats. Barry had no intention of missing out on this and he was winched across in a hoist and lowered into his boat like bonded goods. I teamed up with Jacques, a former South African soldier who had broken his back falling out of a jeep on operations in Angola and whose good-natured stoicism I found immediately appealing. Neither of us really knew what we were doing, and having set out in a squall and rapidly found ourselves tipping over at a 45-degree angle we soon found ourselves becalmed in the doldrums. 'Well, this is fun,' said Jacques as we sat there, completely motionless, two paraplegics in a boat, marooned on a lake that was as still as a millpond. To our shame, we had to be rescued by the control boat and towed back towards the jetty, before turning in a respectable second out of three in the sailing race. Then came kayaking, where the two-person crew is supposed to work in perfect harmony, the blades of our paddles striking the water at exactly the same moment, but in our case we managed to mistime it to perfection so we were effectively working against each other. With nothing to brace my legs against I found myself continually sliding down into the bottom of the kayak, so I had to raise the paddle above my head to propel myself, getting showered with lake water in the process. I am not a natural sailor.

When we had arrived for that first touchy-feely ice-breaker session we were asked to write down our hopes and fears. Answers ranged from 'Making new friends' to 'Not falling out of the chair'; I wrote 'To ride horseback again.' During all my months in hospital my abdominal muscles had atrophied, but I had since built them up again, partly thanks to an excellent physiotherapist, Leigh Forsyth, and partly by forcing myself to sit up straight in my wheelchair and not slump against the backrest. Now I wanted to find out if I had regained enough balance and stability to sit up straight in the saddle, and not topple sideways and fall to the ground in a heap.

Jacques and I wheeled ourselves into the stables to be hit by the familiar stench of hay and manure. 'Right. Two helmets for you lads. Let's see . . .' said the girl from the Riding for the Disabled Association. 'We'll put you on Bee and Honey.' I replied that Dobbin would do just fine for me, something very docile and unexcitable, but she gave me an understanding look. 'Don't worry, we'll take good care of you.' And they did. The first challenge was to get up on to the horse; this involved wheeling ourselves up a steep slope on to a raised platform on the same level as the saddle, while the horse stood waiting patiently. Jacques managed this easily since his spinal fracture is incomplete so he can stand upright for short periods, but I needed a fair bit of help to haul myself into the saddle. My lifeless feet were never going to be able to transmit any commands to the animal, but these horses had been trained to respond to voice commands. To my delight and relief it felt fine to be back on horseback, at least at a walking pace, and before long I stopped gripping the leather front of the saddle for stability. It was a far cry from galloping full tilt across the sands of Giza, which I used to do in Cairo, but still, it was progress and soon we were trotting.

It was the final day of the course and there was one last barrier to break down: abseiling. In a wheelchair. At first I thought the organizers were joking. I mean why on earth would anyone want to descend a rockface in a wheelchair?

But apparently this was to prevent us paraplegics from scraping our knees, since we could not kick away from the rockface.

Once again, Jacques went first, going over the edge with a soldier's smile, and I followed. It worked like this: you sat on a harness which itself sat on the wheelchair; the harness was attached through various carabiner clips to a frame at the top of the small cliff, while another rope held the wheelchair. You then controlled your descent, just as you would for a normal abseil, letting yourself slide slowly down the cliff at 90 degrees to the surface.

'Weren't you scared?' asked Amanda later. In fact I wasn't, because the whole thing seemed so absurd I could not take it seriously. But all in all, the course was a brilliant way of bonding everyone together, of showing people who think, 'Well I'll never be able to do that again' that in fact, with some adaptations and adjustments, life does go on after spinal-cord injury.

23

The Cascade Mountains

Survival School in the Snow

I HAVE ALWAYS BEEN CURIOUS ABOUT WHAT GOES ON AT
SERE School. It stands for Survival, Escape, Resistance
and Evasion, and it is where the US military trains its
pilots, aircrew and other 'prone-to-capture' servicemen
and women, teaching them how to survive in the wilderness after being shot down, how to evade capture, and
how to resist interrogation and attempt escape if caught.
As one seasoned Special Forces officer put it to me, 'It is
always preferable to be an observer at SERE School than
a participant.'

So much of the course is classified secret that I was
hardly surprised when my first request to film at SERE
School was met with silence. And the second. The US
military did not actually refuse me access, they just rather
hoped that if they ignored my emails I would eventually
lose interest and give up. But I had seen pictures and
descriptions of the place and thought it would make great

television: shaven-headed servicemen hiding away in forests in the foothills of the Rockies, surviving on mealy worms and swimming up to their necks across ice-cold rivers. So I persevered, and after three months the permission – or rather, the 'authorization' – finally came through.

The US Navy had their own SERE School and so did the US Army's Special Forces at Fort Bragg, North Carolina, but I had opted for the oldest, biggest and most established survival school, the one set up by the US Airforce after the Korean War. All right, said Airforce Public Affairs, the BBC can film survival training and parachute training, but we are not showing you the resistance or the evasion phases. I decided to take whatever they were offering and see how far I could push things once we got there.

I looked at the map: the school was based at Fairchild Airforce Base outside Spokane in Washington State, right up in the far north-west corner of America, just south of the Canadian border. We would have to fly all the way over to Seattle, nearly a ten-hour flight, then catch a domestic connection, and here lay my dilemma. Since my gunshot injuries, sitting in an economy-class airline seat for much more than a couple of hours had become quite painful, since I could not relieve the pressure by lying flat. BBC News had thoughtfully declared that I could always fly at least Economy-Plus class, but to lie down on a long-haul flight like this would mean upgrading to business class, which would cost a cool £4,000. At that price this filming trip would simply become unaffordable for the cash-strapped news division, but I really wanted us to do it, so I decided I would just have to grin and bear it.

British Airways managed to deftly ignore all my hints about an upgrade to business class, but they did excel themselves on the inflight entertainment. Watching Matt Damon's character battle his way through jaw-dropping fight sequences in *The Bourne Ultimatum* helped take my mind off my own discomfort. By the time we began the descent my buttocks were numb with pain and there were uncomfortable nerve tingles in my legs. Above all, I worried that this prolonged pressure on my skin would leave me with a pressure sore, something which I had so far avoided but which could potentially result in weeks or even months of enforced bedrest on my side.

We had taken off from London on a wet winter afternoon, flown westwards over Greenland for ten hours and it had never once got dark. Now we were landing on another wet winter afternoon in Seattle. I looked for famous landmarks but saw only rain-washed bungalows and a weak, watery sun setting over the Pacific. A change of planes, a short hop on the alluringly named Alaska Airlines, and we touched down in Spokane, Washington, not to be confused with America's capital, Washington DC, which lies nearly three thousand miles eastwards. A damp, chill fog enveloped the airport as we wheeled our kit out to the car park; it had snowed, then turned mild again, as if winter had changed its mind and called the whole project off. A sign read 'Welcome to the Inland North-west', but then we drove for miles with almost no sign of habitation until we crossed into Spokane's grid-square suburbs. It was not an inspiring sight. Wet snow lay banked up on the kerbs in blackened, dirty drifts and a kaleidoscope of blinking neon beckoned, but it was all deserted fast-food restaurants and empty video stores. This was Saturday night in Spokane and hardly a soul was about; perhaps they were all at home watching Hillary Clinton and Barack Obama battle it out in the US election primaries. At our hotel, the Doubletree, we struck gold: it turned out to have one of the best-stocked wine cellars in Washington State. Rob, the cameraman, and I ordered glasses of Cloudy Bay from New Zealand – well, we were on the Pacific – and a plate of Alaskan King Crab legs. 'Do you realize,' he said, holding his glass up in a toast, 'that it's five a.m. London time? I'm off to bed after this.'

That night I had one of those escaping-from-trouble dreams. I was running full-tilt through a forest – in most of my dreams, my legs still worked as normal. I suppose that if you spend the first forty-three years of your life with all your limbs functioning normally, and if you have only been in a wheelchair for the next four, then when you are fast asleep and dreaming your mind has still not caught up with reality. So there I was, zigzagging through a forest, running away from God knows what, when this electronic bell started sounding, getting louder and louder. Of course. My alarm clock. It showed 05:30, the time I had set it to, so as to be up and ready in time to meet our US Airforce escort who was to chaperone us around the training.

Captain Harley, needless to say, was bang on time and we were not; he had one of those tanned but weather-beaten faces with crows' feet around the eyes that spoke of long months exposed to the elements. But he loved the outdoors, and for him being an instructor at SERE School was a dream job.

'Resistance to Interrogation' may have been classified, but we were at least to be shown 'Stress Inoculation'. 'This is how we train the aircrews to survive a crash into the sea, in a storm,' announced the Master Sergeant instructor, a tall, rangy man who looked fit enough to jump out of a helicopter at a hundred feet. We were in an indoor-swimming-pool complex on Fairchild Airforce Base, a warm and cosy place where replica sharks hung on the walls to amuse the base families' children. But there were no families here today, only twenty or so nervous-looking trainee aircrew sitting buckled into a metal compartment that now dangled over the water on the end of a hoist. It was made to look like a helicopter fuselage and this test was to see if they had what it took to get out alive if their craft ditched them underwater at night. They did not know it yet, but they were about to go through a dramatic and terrifying experience.

'Run sequence,' said the instructor quietly. Suddenly the lights went out and from speakers all around came the sound of helicopter rotors. A recorded soundtrack drawled, 'This is Tango Three Nine. We are currently experiencing adverse weather conditions south of point Crimson. Stand by.' Thunder crashed through the speakers and the indoor pool was lit by flashes of simulated lightning. The mock-up helicopter, I noticed, had started to sway as the hoist began to swing it out over the pool. I could only imagine what the recruits onboard would be thinking. It was now mandatory in the US Airforce for all aircrew to go through this test. Without it, said the Master Sergeant, 'They're gonna be flipping burgers or driving the camp bus.'

'Attention all crew, this is your pilot,' came the tannoy once more. 'We have an emergency! You have just sixty seconds to don your survival suits. We are ditching! I say again, we are ditching!' Caught in the half-second lightning flashes were the silhouettes of the aircrew frantically pulling on their rubberized survival suits. The hoist operator dangled them cruelly over the water, lowered them, raised them, lowered them, stopped, then finally dunked them with a splash below the surface of the pool.

After a few seconds they began to emerge, swimming out from beneath the submerged fuselage, making for the twenty-man life raft that had inflated near by. But by now the overhead sprinklers were full on, spraying cold water down on them from thirty feet up, while the instructors aimed pressure hoses at the recruits, knocking them back into the water to simulate a storm at sea. The thunder-and-lightning soundtrack continued relentlessly and there were so many shouts and screams it was hard to tell which were real and which were recorded. Once in the life raft they had to bail out with buckets, dive over to rescue an injured comrade and pull the tarpaulin over them before sending out a distress signal.

I noticed a girl being pulled out of the pool and sat down on a bench. 'She kinda freaked out,' said an instructor, 'so we had to take her out of the exercise.' I wheeled over to find the staff consoling her as she sat there quivering, still in her helmet and survival suit. 'I just felt everyone pushing me down as I tried to get on the raft,' she gasped. 'I thought I was going to drown.' Stacey, as she was called, had set her heart on flying, but she would have to pass this course if her career in the Airforce was to take off, so she steeled herself to join the next batch as they went through the sequence all over again. I was willing her to make it, but when the lights came back on there was Stacey dressed, unlike the others, in her combat fatigues, her hair neatly combed and parted. 'I flunked,' she admitted. 'I thought I could do this swimming part, but I guess there's something in my childhood I can't get over.' The instructors eyed her sympathetically, but they were not going to make any exceptions for her. 'We let her on a flight and she could endanger not only herself but the whole crew.' 'So what happens to her now?' I asked. 'Well, we'll send her for psycho evaluation and try to find out what her problem is. But I guess if she can't get over it then it's the front gate for her.' I am pleased to say that a few months later we heard that Stacey passed.

In the dark and fog we drove north out of Spokane in Captain Harley's Chevy pickup, my wheelchair quickly acquiring a veneer of wet snow as it lay on its side in the back. The temperature gauge read minus 4 degrees. We passed the frozen, mist-shrouded River Oreille, where a pair of Bald Eagles stood watch from a treetop, and on past isolated log cabins, where only a thin wisp of woodsmoke betrayed any evidence of habitation. It was, we agreed, overwhelmingly bleak, a perfect place to learn wilderness survival and E&E (Escape and Evasion).

A pale-brown animal dashed across the empty road ahead of us and vanished into the forest. 'Bobcat,' pronounced the Captain. 'I think you folks call it lynx.' We passed a yellow metal sign nailed to a tree that read: 'Caution. USAF Survival Training in Progress' and suddenly, as if it were all part of the programme, the tall, pointed firs changed from being black and bare to being frosted with snow. This seemingly impenetrable forest hid bears, wolves, coyotes and even the occasional mountain lion. It was very different from the tame forests of the Alps, which harboured nothing bigger than a chamois. 'We had a bit of a problem with a cougar, a mountain lion, a few months back,' said the Captain. 'We figured she was stalking two of the students up here while they were doing their navigation. She'll attack anything if she's hungry so the instructors had to change the route. But don't worry, we ain't seen her for a while now.' Great. A mountain lion, a forest and me in a wheelchair. It sounded suspiciously like lunch on wheels to me.

The Captain switched off the engine and parked up in the snow. We had come as far as we could by truck, now we would have to make the rest of the journey on a snow-mobile. When I had originally applied for us to film the SERE training it had been summer; I'd thought that with a bit of bureaucratic delay we might make it up here in the autumn. I had never envisaged us coming in mid-January like this, with about a metre of snow on the ground, and this was clearly going to present logistical challenges for me. Transferring on to the snowmobile was no problem – in fact later I got to drive one by myself, following fresh moose tracks in the snow – but I had to grip the sides hard as another instructor gunned the engine up over treacher-ous humps, swerving to avoid fallen boughs and accelerating to get through troughs of deep snow.

We reached a makeshift camp where the instructors were boiling a can of hot Gatoraid (a high-energy drink) over a log fire, but there was no time to stop. To get to where the recruits were, through deep, uneven snow, I had to stretch both arms round the shoulders of two of the instructors while they carried me, staggering unsteadily through the deep drifts. My shoulders were soon burning with the effort of holding on. After fifty metres or so we reached a clearing where the recruits were practising building survival shelters, and the instructors went back for my wheelchair so I could sit down; this was starting to get embarrassing. Absurdly, perhaps, I had decided to wear my callipers and bring my standing frame – or Zimmer frame – so that I could do a standing piece-to-camera for this TV report, since all the recruits would be standing behind me. If it could possibly be done, I wanted to do it, but now a new problem presented itself: it was one thing to plonk down my Zimmer frame on the flat floor of the TV studios back in London, but it was quite another to find a level platform of snow out here in the wilds. The rubberized legs quickly sank deep into the snow, so that if I had tried to stand up I would have found that the top of the frame was about level with my knees, and would have lost my balance and crashed forwards against a tree-trunk.

Stuart Hughes, my resourceful producer, stepped in with a solution. He himself was missing half his leg from having stepped on a mine in northern Iraq in 2003, but he always made light of it, wearing his prosthetic lower limb beneath his trousers so no one could even tell, then occasionally removing it and using it as a pillow when we all went for summer lunches al fresco on the grass in White City. 'You realize,' he quipped, 'that this team of three of us from

London have only got three good legs between us?' Stuart used a shovel to beat down a flattened bed of snow for the Zimmer frame to stand on, then he crouched down and hollowed out a scrape for my wheelchair so that I was now at last on the right level to stand up. Days later, when I told Amanda about this, she said, 'Why didn't you just stay in your wheelchair and save everyone the trouble?' She was right, but for me, being based in a wheelchair, day in, day out, I find it so liberating to occasionally stand eye-to-eye with my peers. The US Airforce seemed to revel in the challenge; they had Googled me on the internet before we came out, and seemed to be rather enjoying making a fuss of someone who had survived extreme adversity in real life.

It was time for the recruits to make their first kill. All day a trio of plump pet rabbits had been hopping tamely around the campfire, nibbling at pine branches and generally being cuddly and adorable. Nobody wanted to see them go, but this was, after all, Survival School, and learning how to skin and cook one could one day save their lives. 'We do not have enough time in the few minutes of remaining daylight,' said the instructor, 'to show you how to set snares, which we would normally do, but rabbits are plentiful in the wild and once you have caught one you have to kill it humanely, as quickly and as painlessly as possible.' He held the animal upside-down by its hind legs, smoothing down its back to calm it, and then with no warning delivered a sharp karate chop to the back of its head. Immediately blood started to drain out of its mouth, 'Which is a sure sign it is dead.' The instructor removed the pelt, sliced open the carcass and removed the gall bladder, but kept most of the other innards for a stew. 'With a small animal like a rabbit there is not much flesh on the head, so we will discard that, although some people do like eating the eyeballs.' Really? Who were these weirdos?

By now it was getting late, the snow was falling thick and hard, and to my mild regret we were returning to Spokane for the night. The recruits had slowed down visibly, having struggled through deep snow all day on comparatively few calories. 'Back on base,' said Captain Harley, 'they would normally get around 2,800–3,000 calories a day. But out here in the woods we deliberately restrict them to around 800–900 calories, just so they can start to experience hunger and learn what it is like to hunt for their own food. We searched them this morning to take away any candy bars or cookies they thought they might bring along with them. Out here we call that "contraband".'

The next morning the temperature had plummeted by ten degrees and we arrived in the forest to find the recruits stamping their feet and blowing on their hands as the instructor launched into his lecture on Escape and Evasion. 'OK, listen up,' he said, looking at that moment rather like the British survival-programme presenter Ray Mears in his thick, hairy, woollen shirt. 'You've just crash-landed over there. The enemy has seen your 'chute come down. What are you gonna do?' 'Er . . . get away?' offered the recruits. 'Damn right you are!' For the sake of training, the recruits wore snowshoes to get them across the deeper drifts, but as the instructor took off at a sprint through the trees they still stumbled and fell, crashing into snow-laden pine boughs or falling head-first into snow-holes. 'Do not all set off in the same direction!' shouted the instructor. 'Why? Because your pursuers will figure out where you're headed and cut you off. Use your imagination. Pick a different route, change your direction.'

It was a strange feeling, watching all this from a wheelchair, knowing that I could never conceivably be expected to do anything like this, Wheelchair Escape and Evasion not being a course option. These recruits would have several more days of navigation, escape and 'vectoring' in the forest – signalling to rescue choppers overhead – before being brought back to camp and put through isolation, sleep deprivation and interrogation – none of which the US Airforce was, understandably, prepared to show us, the media. But we had got what we came for, having witnessed and filmed a glimpse of survival training in some of the most beautiful wilderness in the world. True, I was disappointed not to have seen a moose ('Aw, you shoulda been here last week'), but I had pushed myself further and harder than at any other time in the last four years in terms of personal mobility while making a TV report in the field. I felt I had crossed a new boundary, but I still had one more thing to do. Beneath a pale, crescent moon, just faintly visible through the still falling snow, I mounted a snowmobile and revved the engine. Then with a clear, empty track ahead I pointed the front ski down the hill and set off with a roar. Before my injuries I might have frowned on such a noisy, mechanical form of transport in this pristine, snowbound wilderness, no doubt preferring to trek quietly around on snowshoes like everyone else. But having been piggy-backed around the place like a small child, I was craving independence. So, with a wave to the others, I set off, losing count of how long I spent careering along that snowy road in the dark, the wet kisses of a thousand snowflakes tingling against my frozen cheeks, the snow piled up in drifts on either side of me, whooping like a drunken coyote in the sub-zero night of the Pacific north-west.

24

Afghanistan

Korans and KitKats

O N RETURNING FROM THE SNOWBOUND FORESTS OF Washington State, I found that a plan was being hatched to get me out to Afghanistan, of all places, to report on an unusual and previously untold aspect of the conflict there. Project Bravo, as it became known, was not the BBC's idea, but the brainchild of Alex Gardiner, a big, bearded, ex-SAS warrior-adventurer who looked as if he had escaped from the film set of *Pirates of the Caribbean*. Born in the United Arab Emirates, Alex had joined the British Army's Royal Green Jackets before going on to serve in the SAS, leaving to join the Sultan of Oman's army at exactly the wrong time for a career soldier – just before Britain sent 45,000 troops to fight in Desert Storm, the campaign to evict Saddam's troops from Kuwait. Alex sat out the war in sleepy Salalah, where his wife Beatrice discovered there was a lively international export market for Omani clothing. In a cunning twist on the SAS regimental motto they started a fashion label called Who Wears Wins. Since then Alex had discovered there was a tidy niche for someone with his skills mentoring Abu Dhabi TV teams in the field, first during the Iraq invasion of 2003 and latterly in Afghanistan's Helmand province. In between, he had managed to get himself over to Riyadh to help the BBC sort out my evacuation back to the UK after I was shot.

Now that I had recovered my health up to a point, Alex had a proposal, which he broached one morning in the BBC canteen. 'Did you know,' he said, a steely gleam in his pale-blue eyes, 'that the UAE military is operating discreetly in Afghanistan?' Indeed I did know this. A couple of months earlier I had flown down to Abu Dhabi at the invitation of one of the ruling family members, Sheikh Mohammed Bin Zayed, to address his Ramadan *majlis*, an annual gathering of three hundred prominent Emirati sheikhs and sheikhas, all packed into a huge tent on a warm November night in the Gulf. At the Sheikh's instigation, I spoke for forty minutes in Arabic on what had happened to me during that attack in Riyadh. That evening the Sheikh handed out medals, some posthumously, to eight journalists, including me and my late cameraman Simon Cumbers, who was killed in Riyadh. The Zayed Medal for Journalism was an extraordinary piece of craftsmanship: as heavy as a stone, it was a large round disc, fashioned, incredibly, from a meteorite using a laser, and hence was the first of its kind. A small leaflet came with mine telling me that it had been cut from the Qambar meteorite that had landed in Argentina in September 2007, so now I had a small piece of Outer Space to keep as a trophy. Later that night, over a banquet of flavoured rice and baby camel, Sheikh Mohammed leant over and told me with some pride that, unknown to most of the world, his country's soldiers had been deployed for some time with the Coalition in Afghanistan, delivering humanitarian aid and reconstruction to some of the country's most dangerous areas.

'They're performing outstandingly,' said Alex Gardiner as he brought me a cup of frothy cappuccino in the BBC canteen, 'and I say that as a former SAS officer. They've come on in leaps and bounds since they started and they're really making a difference in the areas where they're operating. Because they're Muslim soldiers they're welcomed in places where the Coalition isn't. We should get you out there to take a look.' I laughed into my coffee cup. 'Yeah, right! Me in Afghanistan in a wheelchair, I can see that.' 'No, really,' persisted Alex, who had a commendably can-do attitude to life. 'We'll get you on to a C130 transport plane and fly you direct from Abu Dhabi into Bagram Airbase. It's safe there and the UAE team will be happy to host you.' 'You're serious about this, aren't you?' 'I am. Let's call it Project Bravo, as in B for Bagram.'

Often in journalism people suggest stories, offer ideas, come up with plans, that never actually materialize. You nod politely and file them away in your head, knowing they'll never come to fruition. But Alex was true to his word, and when he started pinging me emails showing he had actually started planning this thing I thought I had better get round to proposing it to my BBC bosses. The World News Editor was Jon Williams, who had flown out to Riyadh as soon as he heard I had been shot, where he had met Alex when they all stayed at the embassy. Jon did not mess around agonizing over decisions, he took them swiftly and accepted the consequences. 'Do it,' he said, before I had even finished my spiel. 'Just make sure you clear it with the high-risk team.'

After years of deploying news crews to difficult places like Bosnia, Baghdad and Afghanistan, BBC News now had a finely honed procedure for assessing the risk on assignments. It was decided that it was fine for me to go, provided I did not venture off Bagram Airbase, a vast, sprawling US-dominated camp considered largely safe these days. I knew this was going to be immensely frustrating from a journalistic point of view, watching my crew drive out of the gate to get the pictures, but I could fully appreciate that we could not have a situation where if the convoy was struck by a mine, or worse, someone would have to risk their own skin to carry me to safety. Besides, adventure was one thing, but I was never keen on danger, even before my injuries. At least this beat doing the story from London. But Alex had another cunning plan up his tailored sleeve: because I could not get out of camp to interview the various Afghan figures who were involved with the UAE humanitarian-aid programme, they would bring them to me to interview on base. By happy chance, I managed to secure two of the best people in the business: producer Dominic Hurst, who had worked with me in Afghanistan before my injuries in 2003, and cameraman Eddie Stephens.

Four years earlier, when I lay sick and weak in hospital, reminiscing with Dominic about our adventures in Afghanistan, the idea of my ever returning to that distant country had seemed like a pipe dream. Yet now here we both were, out on the tarmac at Abu Dhabi's Bateen Airbase, watching the sun rise in the sky and feeling the spring heat of the Gulf slowly building. Dominic opened his mouth to shout something but I could not catch a word above the roar of engines. A few feet away stood a UAE Airforce C130 Hercules in gunmetal grey, our transport to Bagram. All right, I thought, so where is the ramp at the back I'm supposed to wheel myself up? 'No ramp!' shouted a crewman. 'All full with cargo!' Great. I was looking at a small hatch in the fuselage from which dropped down a retractable set of metal steps, so narrow there was no way on earth my wheelchair could be carried up it. I looked doubtfully at Alex, but he just shrugged and picked me up like a child, carrying me bodily through the hatch into the aircraft and plonking me down on a seat.

Five minutes later we were all aboard, including my dismantled wheelchair, the Emiratis had lit up their cigarettes in the back and we were rolling down the airbase runway. The C130, the four-propellered, all-purpose workhorse of any airforce, has a remarkably short take-off and landing distance and it seemed as though the instant we reached full throttle we were lifting clear. As I glanced out of the tiny porthole window beside me at the receding villas and farms of Abu Dhabi, a crewman in a beige jumpsuit nudged my elbow to offer a tray of sandwiches. It may have been an airforce transport plane, but you could not fault the in-flight service.

We flew east, over the less prosperous emirates of Ras Al Khaimah and Fujeirah and out over the Gulf of Oman, crossing into Pakistani airspace and flying north over the parched and wrinkled valleys of Baluchistan. Four hours after take-off the first snows appeared, dusting the mountaintops and filling the north-facing ravines of Waziristan. 'Thirty minutes to landing,' shouted an Emirati crewman above the roar of the Hercules' engines.

We came in low over the foothills of the Hindu Kush, and banked over the familiar four-square mud-walled compounds that make up villages in this part of the world. Directly below us lay a string of bomb craters, all in a neat line, a memento from the years when the mujahedin fought the Russians here in the 1980s. Just then the green crops and dusty villages gave way to what looked like a purpose-built new town, a clean and tidy place where the buildings were all in neat lines along straight roads with plenty of traffic. Wow, I thought, there really is some tangible development going on here, this place looks truly modern. But then I realized I was looking down at Bagram Airbase, headquarters of the US-led Operation Enduring Freedom, and I felt rather stupid.

We banked twice over the busy runway and landed abruptly in a swirl of dust. When the steps came down I was once more carried through the doorway, manhandled from one soldier to the next like a crate of goods, then it was down on to the tarmac. After nearly five years I was back in Afghanistan.

We had come dressed for the tail-end of an Afghan winter, but I immediately regretted wearing my roll-top and fleece, for the spring sunshine had broken through the clouds and up here at over four thousand feet above sea level the sun was burning our cheeks. But there was no time to hang about chatting about the weather; a reception committee of beaming Emirati officers had driven out to greet us, led by the Taskforce Commander, Lieutenant Colonel Ali, a slight man with a quiet intelligence and a twinkle in his eye. 'Welcome back to Afghanistan, Mr Frank,' he said, extending his hand. 'It is our pleasure to have you with us.'

A short drive from the runway brought us to the UAE compound within Bagram Airbase, where a barrier lifted and we drove past a sandbagged mosque, a parade ground and rows of accommodation huts, and then dismounted beside a cluster of satellite dishes and antennae. I remembered from the Kosovo campaign of ten years earlier how good the UAE forces were at making themselves as comfortable as possible in camp. There, on the Albanian border, their well-guarded refugee camp had been known amongst journalists as the Gucci Camp. Now I could see they had done the same in Afghanistan. Every hut had air-conditioning, hot and cold running water, carpets, and

UAE Camp Mosque, Bagram, Afghanistan, March 2008

satellite television with an array of channels. After five years here, hundreds of well-tended rose bushes were flourishing, lending a curious air of serenity to what was still, essentially, a Forward Operating Base.

To my embarrassment, the Emiratis had insisted on allocating me the VIP hut, a sort of miniature villa with faux Roman columns and rows of sandbags. With typical Arab generosity and consideration they had even got their Afghan carpenters to construct a wooden ramp from the ground up to the raised doorway of my quarters, and I could see it had been freshly painted. 'Time for scoff,' said Alex when I had finished my round of thank-yous, and we filed into the mess hall, where the cooks had laid on a feast of lamb nestling on great trays of rice with cashew nuts and cardamom seeds. Alex and I followed our hosts' example, rolling up our sleeves and diving in with our right hands, massaging the rice and meat into greasy balls which we then tossed into our mouths. 'Goat grabs', as Westerners call them, are not to everyone's taste – they are a far cry from the crisp, sizzling joint of roast lamb we are used to. Instead, they resemble a beast that has failed to survive a very bad car crash: all mangled and twisted limbs, with the meat so fatty it is often indistinguishable from, well, the fat.

Back on the balcony of my VIP villa, basking in the sunlight of an early Afghan spring, I took in my surroundings. To the north, just beyond the perimeter wall, lay Bagram village, a typical low-rise huddle of mud-brick houses where colourful washing flapped in the breeze. Beyond that was a line of dark, jagged mountains, and beyond them, dimly visible through the haze, were the snow-covered peaks and slopes of the Hindu Kush.

A deafening roar split the air, swiftly followed by another. It was a pair of US Airforce F15s taking off on a 'presence patrol', the orange flames from the afterburn boosters on their twin engines streaking across the mountainside like a lit match. When Dominic and I had last been here in 2003 we could hardly wait to get out of Bagram Airbase, with its tightly controlled media access, its tedious routine of official briefings and commutes to the mess hall; the delays seemed interminable before we were finally allowed to go on a chopper to somewhere more interesting. But this time was different. We were here to report on a very different aspect of the Afghan conflict: how an Arab Muslim army was using its Islamic credentials to win the trust of the Afghan population and better their lives by building mosques, schools and housing projects. This was the tenth UAE taskforce to serve out here, with each one lasting six months, and they were not just operating around Kabul and the north-east of the country.

They certainly looked a confident bunch, dressed in desert camouflage with sand-coloured headdresses, or sometimes black woollen caps. They came from all over the UAE, I found, although most were from rural desert farms rather than the pampered comfort of downtown Dubai. Military service is not always a popular career in some of the oil-rich Gulf States, but these men seemed highly motivated and in high spirits.

It was time for a tour of the wider Bagram base, which seemed to have grown even larger and more permanent since my last visit; there were now over eleven thousand troops here, mainly American, and the place resembled a small town in the US. Driven by a UAE officer in his desert uniform and headdress, we cruised slowly down the main boulevard, called Disney Drive. It seemed as if half the US Army was here, dressed in a variety of uniforms, from matching jogging outfits to dusty camouflage fatigues. Everyone was carrying an assault rifle or machine gun, even though no insurgents had ever attacked inside the base; the weapons looked remarkably clean and unused. 'Yeah, it looks good, doesn't it?' said a grizzled Australian officer I met. 'But apart from the 82nd Airborne, who've just arrived, most of the troops here are really just eaters and crappers, they don't do any fighting.'

Suddenly there was a loud rap on the window of our van and a female US Army sergeant with Korean features was shouting at us to stop. 'Hey! You were filming! You're not allowed to do that on the FOB.' The FOB? Ah yes, that would be the Forward Operating Base. It was true, Eddie had been idly filming nothing in particular out of the back window, more out of a desire to do something than anything else, but now this looked as if it could turn ugly. 'Show me your ID!' she demanded, eyeing our driver's Arab headdress with deep suspicion. This was awkward, as we had not yet been given our local ID cards, and to avoid months of bureaucratic delays it had been decided not to inform the rest of Bagram base that we were coming. For an instant, Dominic and I could see the whole filming trip going up in smoke, cameras being confiscated, raps on knuckles for our hosts, our whole team confined to quarters. Then, quite unexpectedly, the US sergeant lost interest and she waved us on.

That evening the Emiratis gave us a formal PowerPoint presentation on all the humanitarian or 'Civil Affairs' projects they were carrying out around Afghanistan: a mosque here, a school there, wells dug in this village, a clinic set up in that one. It did not seem vastly different from what other countries, including Britain, were doing in this impoverished, war-torn country, but knowing how important Islam was to most Afghan villagers, the Emiratis would address their religious needs first, either by building them a small mosque, sometimes for as little as £7,000, or just by distributing freshly printed Korans packed into cardboard boxes. Our crew were to see first-hand the effect this had, with grey-bearded Afghan sheikhs kissing the green-bound Korans and rubbing them all over their faces. Only then, said the Emiratis, could they discuss other more secular projects like building a school or a hospital.

Of course, in an ideal world I needed to get out and see all this with my own eyes, but since I was under strict instructions from the BBC's safety man, Julian Clover, not to venture offbase, the Emiratis now presented me with a long list of various Afghan officials they planned to bring in for me to interview. I bit my lip: there were eighteen people on the list, far too many for us to squeeze into a five-minute film. I knew what a sweat it was going to be, both for them and for the Emirati troops, to get these people through US security on the gate and into the base. There were Governors on the list, well-educated, besuited men who wielded great power and influence in their own fiefdoms, and for them it would be humiliating to be held in a queue outside the gate, shouted at to move forward, then frisked by some nervous soldier from the Midwest who suspected every candidate could be a terrorist. I decided we needed to pare down the list to the minimum, preferring that wherever possible our crew should go out and film these people in situ, so I drew up a list of what the crew would film each day and what I would film onbase; in these days of multi-skilling it came in handy that all three of us knew how to film.

It had been a long day, but no sooner had I withdrawn to my absurdly comfortable sandbagged villa than the base tannoy went off and I nearly jumped out of my skin. 'Attention all personnel!' commanded a metallic American voice, and I thought, Oh hell, this had better not be 'incoming' because I'm not sure I can get myself down off this wheelchair and under the bed in a hurry. But Bagram was Safesville and the tannoy continued, 'The aerial gunnery range is now hot! I say again, the aerial gunnery range is now hot!' Seconds later there was a curious distant buzzing noise, the sound of an A10 Warthog attack jet firing its rotating Gatling cannon into the empty mountainside at a withering 6,000 rounds per minute. There followed the boom of a practice bomb being dropped. There was no mistaking that Bagram was an operational airbase, but the novelty swiftly wore off when at four a.m. I was woken by a deafening roar as first one then another F15 jet took off into the night. I drifted back to sleep, only to be awoken minutes later by the dawn call to prayer from the UAE camp mosque. This was all very strange: the combination of these noisy night-time bombing runs and the familiar sound of the mosque muezzin; I woke up with absolutely no idea where I was.

In the morning there was bad news. Alex was pacing the pitted tarmac of the base, looking unusually ruffled: it turned out that the promised patrol to the Tagab Valley had been cancelled. This was indeed a bit of a blow. Before setting out from London we had put out clear signals that in order for this film to work we needed to see the Emirati soldiers going about their normal business – patrolling, meeting and greeting Afghans, handing out whatever goodies they hand out – and all of it as if we were the proverbial 'fly on the wall'. We did not want them doing anything for our benefit that they would not be undertaking anyway as a part of normal operations. These planned interviews were all very well, but if we had no scenic patrol into the villages then we would have no good pictures to hang the rest of the film on. Last night it had been agreed that our camera crew, Dominic and Eddie, would accompany a UAE patrol into the remote Tagab Valley, but apparently there had been a couple of incidents there in the last few days and the latest intelligence warned it was 'hot'. Any mission there would need on-call support from a helicopter gunship or those fearsomely armed Warthog attack jets, but the Americans were understandably unwilling to provide it for a non-essential patrol like this. They had an operation of their own going on and were apparently short of planes.

The UAE Taskforce Commander took me to one side to explain his situation. 'If we go to somewhere like the Tagab Valley and run into problems . . .' 'What kind of problems?' I interrupted. 'Well, if we get hit by an IED [Improvised Explosive Device] and then ambushed by the Taliban we need to call up air support to cover us while we withdraw. If we can't be sure we'll get that air support then I cannot take the risk of sending a patrol to that place.' This seemed logical enough to me – the last thing I wanted was anyone taking any unnecessary risks on our behalf – so I suggested a compromise. 'All right, how about somewhere closer to base? Some village you would go to anyway, even if we were not here?'

The Commander looked up at the sun and squinted, as if much depended on where it was in the sky. Actually the weather did have a part to play, since in the winter months the insurgents tended to back off, go home, regroup and re-supply themselves, ready for the spring and summer fighting seasons. It was now late March and there were reports that the Taliban were building up their forces here in the north-east. 'It is possible,' said Lieutenant Colonel Ali at last, 'we will go to a village we know.'

The Emirati troops were impressive: they planned their patrol down to the last detail and we were allowed to sit in on their briefing. The patrol commander delivered his orders by PowerPoint, with schematic diagrams for the order of march, showing the formations they would adopt if attacked and listing the radio frequencies they would switch to. There would be US-made Humvees mounted with powerful .50-calibre machine guns, French Panhard armoured cars and heavily armoured South African RG31 patrol vehicles, but there was one wild card: the Afghan National Police. The Emiratis were keen to 'show an Afghan face' to their patrols, so the plan was to put the Afghan police out front, but they were notoriously unreliable and no one could be certain if they would turn up.

It felt very odd for me to be sitting there in the shadow of the sentry post beside the gate of the base, waving off the patrol with my two colleagues aboard, and staying behind 'in the rear, with the gear, where there is no fear'. This was not something that came naturally to me. But Dominic and I had equipped ourselves with Thuraya satellite phones, so he was able to send me regular updates and text messages, and the patrol ended up providing us with a perfect example on camera of the sort of problems the Arab troops here were facing.

At first, all went well when they arrived in the village of Qalat Baland, north of Bagram. The Emiratis were welcomed, both as bearers of gifts and as fellow Muslims – one young Afghan told our crew that at first he had thought these soldiers were American and he wanted them to leave, but when he realized they were Muslim he was happy; others were less picky, saying they did not mind where the troops came from as long as they helped the village improve its standard of living. Boxes of sweet, sticky dates from the Gulf were unloaded from the back of the truck and handed out to the grey-bearded village elders, the children were given KitKats, satchels and school notebooks, then Major Ghanem, the officer in charge, took the time to sit cross-legged in a courtyard and listen to a young boy chant verses from the Koran by memory. Unlike most Coalition officers, who served a six- or nine-month tour of duty in Afghanistan, he had spent two and a half years here running the UAE military's Civil Affairs projects, devoting his time to this humanitarian cause while his young family grew up without him back home in the Emirates.

The scene in the village looked a picture of harmony, almost a blueprint for winning hearts and minds, but then things started to go wrong. As word spread that the Emiratis were in town handing out gifts, a crowd built up outside the gates of the village hall, then a rumour started that there was not enough to go round and suddenly the crowd surged, pushing and elbowing their way past the uniformed troops to get at the plastic-wrapped goodies. The Afghan police, who had now turned up, weighed in with unrestrained brutality, breaking off branches from nearby trees and using them to lash the villagers as well as shoving them hard, a task they appeared to take to with great enthusiasm. More than once Major Ghanem could be seen restraining an arm as it was about to strike some hungry, hapless villager, and you could hear him appealing for calm. 'Brothers!' he shouted in Arabic, which was then translated into Dari. 'If you act like this then we will not return to this village. Is that what you want? Please, we must have order!' And eventually order was restored, without a shot being fired.

The days passed with similar excursions for my crew – to an orphanage, a mosque, and by Blackhawk helicopter to a UAE-funded university in volatile Khost – with Dominic sending back text messages of varying degrees of optimism. 'Great pictures,' he would write, 'lots of colour, some wonderful faces,' or the next day, 'endless formal speeches, very dull, ready to come back for lunch now . . . zzz.'

On the UAE base in Bagram I duly greeted and interviewed a succession of prominent Afghans, all of whom were wearing smart business suits and ties, which looked out of place here in this dusty, sandbagged camp. There was the Chancellor of Khost University, who had reluctantly come back home, he said, after twenty-seven years of working in Germany as a chemical engineer, and there was a junior minister for Orphans, Widows and the Disabled, who told me his country had one million disabled people to support and a further two million widows and orphans. There was also an elderly but energetic member of Karzai's government, Meraj Uddin Patan, who spoke perfect English and had some outspoken views about his fellow governors. 'They are drug runners,' he said flatly as he reeled off a list of provincial governors he claimed were all up to their necks in the opium trade. 'How can we expect people to respect the Afghan government when you have people like these in charge?' There were clearly some problems with unity inside this Government. 'Listen,' he continued, swatting away a fly, 'when I was Governor of Khost we had thirty-six agents across the border in Waziristan and they would phone in with tip-offs each time a suicide bomber was heading our way, giving us a description of the man and his vehicle. We caught nineteen bombers that way. When I took over as Governor in 2004 all the shops shut at two p.m. and no one dared go out after that. Boys were kidnapped for ransom and only 2 per cent of women were in education. I changed all that. I started a campaign against the sort of thugs who intimidated the population. Do you know how?' No, I didn't, I said. 'When we caught a Taliban insurgent we would shave his head and put him on a donkey facing backwards and parade him round the city.

But now . . .' he paused and I caught a look of genuine sadness on his face, 'now it has gone back to being a very bad situation. In the past few months many girls' schools have been burned down.' I suspected there was an element of personal rivalry going on here, but I was keen to put all this into some kind of national context so I asked Governor Meraj the 64-million dollar question: 'To what do you attribute the Taliban's success in making a come-back since they were defeated here in 2001?' 'That is easy to answer,' he said. 'There are three reasons: weak govern-ment; no unity among the police, national army and the Coalition allies; and the Taliban has unrestricted freedom of movement in their rear area in Waziristan. Now you must excuse me, I must attend a meeting in Kabul.'

At this point I caught sight of Alex Gardiner pacing contentedly around the camp rose bushes, trying on his new waistcoat which he had got me to bring out from his tailors in London's Savile Row. He may have spent much of his adult life in dark and dangerous places but you had to hand it to him, he had style. Alex, who had set up this whole trip for us and acted as a go-between with the UAE military, was looking decidedly more relaxed now we had the footage of the humanitarian patrol filmed. 'I must admit things looked a bit wobbly on that first day,' he confided. 'When they cancelled the patrol to the Tagab Valley I began to worry I'd brought you guys out here on a wild-goose chase. But you seem to be getting what you came for. How about we celebrate with a game of table tennis?'

Table tennis was something I still enjoyed from my wheelchair, although I usually had to get my opponent to gather up the dropped balls, but Alex was not playing a straight game. 'Of course I've hardly ever played,' he lied, with a twinkle in his eye, and then proceeded to demolish me with a series of Chinese spins, slicing his bat horizontally beneath the ball so it spun way beyond my reach. In fact I did not mind at all – I would much rather lose decisively than score a dubious victory over someone playing down to me.

It was the final morning before we headed back from Afghanistan to the Gulf, returning the way we had come, on a C130 Airforce transport plane. The F15 jets were still roaring off into the pale-blue sky, circling once against the pristine white snow of the Hindu Kush before departing on some unpublished mission. A pair of Blackhawk helicopters took off in a hurry, one after the other, with red cross markings beneath their fuselage, no doubt to rescue some troops caught up in a firefight somewhere in this country. And a Spectre gunship flew low overhead, its huge artillery just visible as it poked out of a window on the side. As the roar of its engines faded I could just make out the sound of a football game in the mud-walled village of Bagram on the other side of the perimeter. It was, all in all, a typical day on Bagram Airbase.

'I think they want to give you something,' whispered Alex, and sure enough a small crowd of Emirati officers had gathered with their pocket digital cameras. The Taskforce Commander, Lieutenant Colonel Ali, stepped forward to shake my hand and said some very nice words about it being an honour to receive our team on their base. I reciprocated in Arabic and then, to my embarrassment, the Emiratis presented me with a massive gilt-framed ceremonial sword and inlaid scabbard, mounted on a red velvet backcloth with a metal plaque, inscribed with the words 'With compliments from UAE Operations Command Taskforce 10'. I was flattered and pleased. We should have been thanking them for their hospitality, but it was typical of our hosts that they should see it the other way round. I had spent a happy week here, in unexpected comfort, with people who were quietly courteous and polite. Above all, this trip had enabled me to pass another milestone in my long-term rehabilitation from my injuries. Flying out in an Airforce cargo plane to report from Afghanistan would have been inconceivable to me during those long, painful months in hospital, yet we had accomplished this with remarkable ease. We had our story, we had our film. Now I just had to make sure that if we ever came again I thrashed Alex Gardiner at table tennis.

25

Colombia Revisited

Kidnappers and Cloud Forest

R EMOTE, MOUNTAINOUS AND WITH A REPUTATION FOR drugs, girls and guns, Colombia had been well off the beaten track when we went there in the 1990s. No one had threatened us then, but there had been a palpable edginess even to the capital Bogotá, while upcountry the sight of soldiers festooned with machine-gun belts emerging from the jungle on to a rural backroad was not unusual. But by 2008 this country was starting to recover from its violent excesses. Kidnapping, once the scourge of Colombian society, was down 90 per cent since 2002 when President Alvaro Uribe came to office. So when a producer for a BBC Radio 4 documentary entitled *The Cult of Kidnapping* asked me if I would like to present the programme and also pick a country to visit, it did not take me long to choose Colombia. There were certainly other countries in Latin America, like Mexico, where kidnapping was on the up, but how much more interesting, I thought, to examine first-hand a place where the tide was turning against hostage-taking. Was it all down to police action? Was the population behind it? Was success being achieved at the expense of terrible human-rights abuses?

My reporting stint in Afghanistan in the spring of 2008 had ratcheted up my confidence once more; if I had been able to get myself and my wheelchair out there without too much difficulty, I reasoned, then there should, theoretically, be no limit to my horizons. Journalistically, Colombia was the best of both worlds: perhaps unfairly, it retained a dreadful reputation as 'the kidnap capital of the world', which warranted our going there for the programme, even though the government had made such dramatic improvements in security that Bogotá was now considered by risk-assessment analysts to be no more hazardous than Sicily or Corsica. Also, Ingrid Betancourt, the glamorous one-time presidential candidate, was that May still being held in the jungle. I had kept track of her story and had a feeling that there would be developments by the summer: if we were going, I said, we needed to go now, and the BBC agreed. But quite apart from these professional reasons for wanting to go to Colombia, I had really liked the place and its people and this seemed a perfect excuse to return. Secretly, I suppose, I was also attracted by the idea of reporting from two distant and relatively inaccessible countries like Afghanistan and Colombia in the same year, proving to myself as much as anyone that my wheelchair should not be a barrier to getting back out into 'the field'.

Still, the statistics for Colombia were daunting: 188 people kidnapped so far in 2008 and we were not yet halfway through the year. That may have been well down from the peak of 3,500 a year in 2002, but it still meant that on average one person a day was getting snatched in the country we were going to. In addition to the radio producer, David Coomes, a veteran of Radio 4 but a novice to Latin America, I had chosen the Spanish-speaking Keith Morris as our cameraman. Keith and I had filmed together in Morocco years earlier and I had long since forgiven him for telling me my voice was too posh to report for national bulletins (in fact we had gone to the same school, Marlborough, so it was said without malice).

So there we all were, one May afternoon, Keith, David and me, sitting in the transit lounge of Madrid airport peering at the laptop presentation of a British brewery executive who was on our flight out to Colombia. His employers had given him an extensive briefing on the risks of crime and kidnap in Bogotá and now he was sharing some of the highlights with us. 'Don't walk around at night,' the computer screen instructed. 'Don't take taxis from the street because thugs will get in and mug you . . . Don't open your car windows or robbers will spray in an incapacitant gas.' Great.

One glance at our fellow passengers queueing up to board and it was obvious we were leaving Europe for somewhere very different. The queue was dominated by very sun-tanned men with crew cuts or shaven heads, sunglasses and bulging muscles. They had flat, pockmarked, Indian faces and they wore sombreros, leather jackets and stonewashed denim. They all looked like hired hitmen. 'Who *are* these guys?' I said to Keith somewhat nervously. 'Colombian Army,' said the all-knowing one. 'They're just

back from a tour of peacekeeping duty in the Sinai desert.'
Ah. So that would explain the tans and the bulging
muscles then. So not hitmen, after all. I was glad to have
Keith around: a natural journalist as well as a fine cameraman, he had an uncanny ability to absorb information; he
had only to stand in the vicinity of a group of South
Americans and he could tell you what was going on.

Nine hours across the Atlantic and the inflight rolling map
showed we were crossing the Venezuelan–Colombian
border near a town called Bucaramanga. The two
countries had appeared to be almost on a war footing in
March 2008 after Colombian troops carried out a cross-
border raid on a rebel base just inside Ecuador. The
left-leaning governments of Ecuador and Venezuela
howled in protest and moved troops up to their borders
with Colombia. Tensions had gradually subsided, but
Colombia remained deeply suspicious that Venezuela was
arming and funding its arch-enemy, the FARC guerrillas,
Latin America's longest-running Marxist revolutionary
movement, which still held sway over large tracts of jungle
in the south and east, financed by both the drugs trade and
hostage ransoms.

Coming in to land that afternoon at Bogotá's El Dorado
airport, I watched the lush green valley rise up to meet us
and the clouds roll in from the Andes like an advancing
army. At 2,600 metres above sea level, this was the third-
highest capital in South America, after La Paz in Bolivia
and Quito in Ecuador; we had even been warned about
nosebleeds.

Into the terminal building, past two unsmiling soldiers

in green fatigues and jungle hats, through Passport Control and off to the money exchange to pick up a bundle of pesos, with a thumbprint for a signature. Keith, who appeared to have taken up half the plane's cargo hold with his TV equipment, was mystified at how I could come all the way to South America with only hand luggage. Curiously, I have often found that the further I am going and the longer I am going to be away, the less I take with me. For a weekend visit to somewhere in Britain or Europe I would probably take a bulky suit-carrier, balanced across my lap in the wheelchair, but for a week in Colombia? A couple of T-shirts, one smart shirt for interviewing any VIPs, a waterproof and a baseball cap, a washbag the size of a clenched fist and a daily change of underwear just about does it for me. Before my injuries I always preferred to travel light enough that I could carry whatever I had on my shoulders; since being in a wheelchair it has become an important facet of my independence that I still carry everything myself on my lap.

'I have bad news for you,' said a voice outside the terminal with an American twang. 'Everybody cancelled on me, one by one. This morning is a total disaster!' It was Maria Ines, our locally hired Colombian fixer, and she was literally wringing her hands in despair. I glanced at Keith, who had hired her, but he was wrestling manfully with his small mule train of equipment. I looked at David and his face said it all: brilliant, we've flown halfway around the world to record a bunch of interviews that don't exist. Now what?

But on the drive into town, Maria Ines recovered herself. As we entered the well-to-do northern suburbs of

Bogotá we were down to 'OK, some people have cancelled.' By the time we pulled up at our hotel we had established that actually it was just a couple of fellow journos who had asked to reschedule; all our main interviewees were in place, we were back in business. On Keith's advice we were booked into a discreet, mid-budget hotel on a quiet street. 'The big international ones are watched,' he said. 'Robbers sometimes keep an eye on who's coming and going and they can always tell a local from a gringo.'

That night I slept with the windows open, catching the breeze coming off the mountains in the hope that it might dispel the smell of old cigarette smoke embedded in the furniture. There were sirens at night, birdsong at dawn, dogs barking, salsa on the radio, the distant rumble and hum of traffic seven floors down and the intermittent shrill of a traffic policeman's whistle. I was back in South America.

We breakfasted on hot, fresh Colombian coffee, the country's other famous export, then drove off to meet one of the most powerful men in the capital. Colonel Humberto Guatibonza was the head of the Police Anti-Kidnapping Unit, GAULA, that had been partly responsible for the dramatic fall in abductions. A broad, square-jawed man with the body of a wrestler, he greeted us at the door of his high-rise office, from where he surveyed the city like an eagle in its eyrie. A large emblem on the wall read: NATIONAL POLICE – ANTI-TERRORIST AND EXTORTION DIVISION. Of course, extortion. In all the reading-up I had done on political kidnappings, I had almost forgotten that most kidnap victims in Colombia are simply held for ransom by criminal gangs.

Within minutes of our meeting, the Colonel was warming to his subject, waving over junior officers with pages of statistics, maps and diagrams. 'The way the kidnappers work here,' he told me, 'is they have three teams. The first is for surveillance – they watch the target's family and try to work out how much money they've got. Then there is the "lift" team who set up the false roadblock or lead the victim into a trap. Finally, there are the carers.' 'Carers?' I asked. The last time I had heard this expression was in a hospital spinal-injuries unit, where men and women of infinite patience wheeled paralysed patients round a ward or spoon-fed them dinner while sneaking sideways glances at their watches. 'Yes, carers,' continued the Colonel. 'These are the people who look after the hostages once they have been seized. They feed them, move them around and provide proof of life. In hostage negotiations, the first twenty-four hours are vital. The key is to keep the hostage alive, so we open negotiations while trying to eavesdrop electronically on the gang's conversations. We only go in when we think we have a 90 per cent chance of success. Sometimes we launch rescue operations by helicopter, sometimes stealthily on foot, it depends on the terrain.'

'Excuse me,' I interrupted, sensing the call of nature, 'do you have a *baño* on this floor?' 'Yes, of course,' obliged the Colonel and he directed me to his own private suite next door. I could not decide whether the fact that this man had his own private bedroom and bathroom right next to his office meant he was incredibly busy solving kidnappings, or if they were just the local trappings of power. When I noticed that his towels were personally monogrammed I decided it was probably the latter.

This is incredible, I thought, as I emerged from the Colonel's bathroom. He is actually showing me plans for a live operation they are planning to launch any day now. On his lap was a printed file labelled 'Antioquia', a province to the north, and inside were aerial photos taken by spotter planes through gaps in the clouds.

'We know exactly where they are holding the hostages, how many are guarding them, where they slept last night, everything,' said the Colonel. 'For us, human intelligence is the key. We have lots of informants these days.' So how, I asked, did they actually effect a hostage rescue operation? The Colonel began reeling off figures: three to four weeks to plan, twenty-strong attack platoons backed up by a hundred-strong screen force. Then he stopped, said, 'Why don't we show you?' and summoned an aide, reeling off a list of instructions.

The following morning we drove south, with a police escort, to the GAULA training base at Sibaté, a few miles outside the capital in lush, rolling farmland. It seemed a strangely pastoral place for such a lethal profession: sheep were grazing contentedly beneath fruit trees, swallows flitted between groves of tall eucalyptus and roosters crowed from an adjacent village. But once the striped barriers had been lifted and we were waved inside, there was no mistaking what went on here. A fusillade of shots rang out, followed by shouting, then more shots, before thirty soldiers emerged from a building in helmets and visors. This was 'the killing house', the purpose-built breeze-block shed where Colombia's own version of America's SWAT teams trained intensively to blast their way into a building, kill or capture the kidnappers and release the hostages unharmed. Of course, it did not always work out quite that way. I subsequently learnt from more than one critic of the government that on one operation GAULA had ended up shooting the hostage by mistake, and rather than own up to it they had reported him as an armed terrorist instead of a civilian. I could not help thinking of our own parallel in Britain, when in 2005 the innocent Brazilian electrician Jean Charles de Menezes had been shot dead by police marksmen who mistook him for a suicide bomber, and it was only much later that the full story emerged.

Getting me into the GAULA's killing house at Sibaté so I could watch what was going on from a safe distance presented a serious logistical challenge. On the first floor there was a viewing gallery that ran all the way round the building so that observers could watch every phase of the training, from the initial entry charge that blew down the door, to the clearing of rooms by pairs of men, firing as they went, to the dragging out of a plastic dummy hostage. The problem was that the metal stairs and railings that ran up to the gallery were built like a fire escape and were too narrow for my wheelchair to fit between. So a tall Colombian police captain in reflective sunglasses grabbed one part of the chair while his juniors grabbed the rest and somehow we staggered up to the first floor. Now, though, the railings turned upwards, forcing the police to lift me up even higher. They couldn't do it, since everyone was out of breath at this altitude. I felt the man behind me lose his balance and my wheelchair lurched backwards. I was now at right angles to the ground, facing the ceiling, poised to fall out, my lifeless lower legs threatening to topple crazily on top of me. I contemplated the possibility that as the Colombians lost their grip I could be tipped right out of the chair and fall several metres to the ground below. This was not what I had in mind for rehab, I thought. At that moment I spotted an American trainer – sorry, 'mentor', our hosts were very specific about this term – and shouted for him to give a hand. He lent some muscle just in time and my wheels touched safely down on the gallery floor.

After that near freefall experience I was strangely unfazed by all the live rounds going off below, as the twelve-man entry team burst in wearing balaclavas and fired at their dummy targets in quick succession, the frangible bullets disintegrating on contact. All this time Keith and David were recording like mad. It was only weeks later, back in Britain when the radio documentary went out, that I realized how uncomfortable it must have been for people close to me at home, especially my parents, to listen to all that shooting and shouting, which must have brought back painful memories of Riyadh for them. Yet, strangely, it did not do so for me.

Over the rest of that week in Bogotá we met people whose stories would melt the stoniest of hearts, like the congresswoman Consuelo Gonzalez de Perdomo, released a few months earlier after being held by FARC guerrillas for six years. During all those stolen years stuck in the jungle her husband had died, her daughter had given birth, and her family had tried to go on living a normal life without her. So when halfway through our planned interview the sound of her granddaughter playing in the next-door room with her daughter became so loud that we had to stop, I really could not blame her for saying, 'Excuse me, I need to be with my family now.'

There was a woman we met on the steps of a chapel in the cobbled main plaza, whose last sight of her kidnapped brother was a grainy video sent by his captors nine years before; since then, there had been nothing.

And there was Juan Carlos LeCompte, the husband of the country's most famous hostage, the French-Colombian politician Ingrid Betancourt, kidnapped at a FARC checkpoint in the south in 2002. Within minutes of meeting him in their flat high above the capital I realized he was chain-smoking. 'I took it up five years ago, after Ingrid was taken,' he explained, gazing out across the twinkling lights of this Andean capital. 'I did not smoke before, but now I do, and smoking is unpopular here so I feel like an outcast.' Juan Carlos had just come back from scattering 100,000 photos of Ingrid's children over the jungle where she was thought to be held. He had hired a Cessna and flown from one Amazon airstrip to another, hurling some photos out of the window above the tree canopy, giving out bundles of others to the native Indians when he landed in the hope that they might come across the people holding his wife. Juan Carlos, I realized, represented the other side of the coin: people like him, with relatives already kidnapped and held for years, were the losers from the government's tough, no-compromise stance towards the guerrillas. The FARC were prepared to negotiate, but they wanted a temporary 'demilitarized zone', a swathe of southern Colombia the size of Manhattan where they could sit down with mediators without fear of capture. But the government was taking the view that this was just a ruse for the guerrillas to re-arm and regroup and was holding out, much to Juan Carlos's despair. Unknown to both of us that week, the Colombian military was in fact hatching a bold, imaginative and highly risky plan to rescue Ingrid and several others, but this was still six weeks away from fruition.

To cover both angles of kidnapping in Colombia, we needed to meet both victim and perpetrator. In Bogotá it was not hard to find victims, but thanks to the resourcefulness of Maria Ines, our fixer, her earlier pessimism turned out to be unfounded. 'I have found you a guerrilla who has been involved in kidnapping,' she announced triumphantly. 'He will come to your hotel at two p.m.' Was she serious? In a country still struggling with its reputation as the kidnap capital of the world, this was like a red rag to me. 'Don't worry,' said Maria Ines, 'he's a reformed kidnapper.' 'I don't care,' I replied rather rudely, 'I'm not having someone like that check out where we're staying. How do we know he hasn't got accomplices – or people following him? We have to meet him on neutral ground.' A suitable venue was then found: a high-rise hotel in a safe part of town, owned by the military and guarded daily by an armed soldier in full battle dress. This sounded reassuring, although I realized as we got out of the cars that the soldier was really more interested in chatting to his girlfriend, who was buying him ice cream from a street vendor.

'Jairo', which was the assumed name our ex-guerrilla

wanted to be known by, was exactly how I had imagined he would be: short, stocky and leather-jacketed with a wide, pockmarked face, narrow eyes and a nasal twang to his Spanish. Jairo looked younger than me, yet he had, he said, spent twenty-two years with illegal armed groups, first as a drug-smuggler, then as a guerrilla with the FARC, then switching sides to join the right-wing paramilitaries. He had deserted with only his radio and his uniform and was now in a government rehab programme. In fact, Jairo appeared to have undergone some sort of epiphany: he felt terrible, he told us, for the bad things his people had done and now he wanted to return to the mountains to warn others not to follow his path.

'How did you treat your hostages?' I asked him. Jairo looked uncomfortable. 'I didn't handle them myself, of course,' he replied, 'but sometimes my comrades would cut off a finger and send it to the victim's family, together with their identity card, as proof of life, and to put pressure on them to pay the ransom. We would film the hostage chained to a tree and tell them to look as miserable as possible, then we would send the DVD to the family. I found it very sad because sometimes by the time they got it their relative had already been killed.' 'Why?' I said. 'Why did you have to kill them?' Again, Jairo looked uncomfortable, but he took a deep breath and continued. 'The forced marches were very tough, sometimes eight hours non-stop over very difficult terrain. Some of the hostages from the city just could not cope. Eventually they would drop to their knees and cry out, saying they could not move another step and that we might as well shoot them now. So we did, just like that, on the spot.'

Sitting here in this hired hotel room in comfortable north Bogotá, it was hard to believe he was talking about the same country. I looked past Jairo at the tranquil scene outside the window. A woman was selling some trinkets in the shade of a big tree; a column of schoolchildren filed past a colonial, whitewashed building in their neat, freshly laundered uniforms. We had lunched that day in a central district known as La Candelaria, a pretty quarter where cobbled backstreets climbed up the hill past blue-painted cafés towards the mist-shrouded hills and forests. There was no question about it, Bogotá felt safer, less threatening, less edgy than it had in 1996.

But the south of the city was very different. Late one afternoon we drove down to the rough suburb of San Carlos to interview an elderly couple with a missing son and even our driver blanched. 'This is not a good place,' he remarked with commendable frankness. The potholed streets were full of muddy pools and there were a lot of young men hanging around on street corners, watching every car that went past. Our cars were not expensive ones, but still, we must have stood out as strangers in a quarter where everyone knew everyone and I felt distinctly uneasy about being there. When we pulled up outside the door of the family to be interviewed I made a decision. 'If you guys really, really want this interview,' I said to Keith and David, who were starting to unload their recording equipment, 'you go inside. But I'm not getting out of the car. In fact, I'm not even staying here, I'm going to ask the driver to keep moving. Call me on my mobile when you're done and we'll come back and collect you.' They nodded without argument. Left unspoken in the air was what had happened in Riyadh four years earlier, when my cameraman and I had stayed too long in an area that turned out to be unsafe, costing him his life and me my legs. Bogotá did not have a problem with Al-Qaeda-related terrorism, but life on the breadline in these impoverished South American neighbourhoods could be cheap, and crime was common. Sure enough, when we returned to pick up my colleagues the other driver came over to tell us of a near disaster. 'Your friend, the Englishman, he came out of the house to make a call on his mobile phone and he has all this expensive radio equipment on his shoulder. Just then I see two robbers, they are coming past with a car stereo they have just stolen. They are discussing how much they will get for it. But, *gracias a Dios*, they do not see your friend. I think today he is lucky.'

Our reporting had gone well, but I was adamant that I did not want this week in Colombia to be solely about kidnappers, hostages and dodgy, potholed *barrios*. If I squeezed my eyes half-shut then north Bogotá was not so dissimilar to a dozen other cities I could think of, but I knew from my last visit in '96 that there was a whole other world out there, no more than an hour's drive away, a world of whitewashed villages where salsa music spilled out of the shadows into the sunlit village square. Before we headed home, I was determined to see something of the country beyond the confines of the capital.

Maria Ines expressed surprise. 'You don't want to spend your last day shopping in town?' No, I didn't. 'But surely,' she protested, 'Colombia is so hard for you in a wheelchair?' She was right about that; Bogotá, like most places in South America, did not seem to have heard of wheel-chair access; in fact it was probably the least wheelchair-friendly city I had visited so far, apart from Cairo. Any enquiries we made about the whereabouts of a loo were usually met by 'Yes, we have one downstairs in the basement,' or 'Sure, there's one upstairs on the second floor, but it has a very narrow door.' So to get through the day with minimum discomfort I had to half-starve myself from breakfast onwards. And yet here I was, arranging to be up at dawn on our last day, so as to squeeze in a bit of rural birdwatching while Keith and David went sight-seeing and shopping. Maria Ines had arranged for me to keep our driver, a redoubtable man called Liebermann who, having once chauffeured the chief executive of a multinational company, now confided that he had under-gone a defensive-driving course. I found this both reassuring and alarming: reassuring that I was in the hands of someone who knew how to do a rapid handbrake reverse out of a threatening situation, alarming that he needed this training at all. '*Tranquilo*,' he reassured me. 'We go only where it is safe.'

South once more through Bogotá's grim, rain-sodden suburbs, where red-brick tenements crowded above end-less rows of motor-repair shops, oil-blackened garages and quick-change exhaust-pipe retailers. I have often thought, when passing through these Latin American suburbs, that it is as if one has entered a strange cult where the internal combustion engine is king; light relief comes only every few hundred yards in the form of a neon-lit café announcing the magic word '*Hamburguesos*'. 'It is not beautiful,' said Liebermann, reading my mind, 'but soon we will leave the city behind.'

Within minutes of passing a police checkpoint, where bored and blank-faced patrolmen in waterproof capes waved the traffic past, we were jolting down a country road between stands of tall eucalyptus. Cattle and sheep grazed in the fields on either side; to be honest, it felt more like New Zealand than South America. But something was different from last time I had ventured this way and it took me a while to realize what it was. 'These motorcyclists that go past,' I said to Liebermann, 'they've all got big numbers on their jackets and helmets. What's that about?' He smiled and swerved to avoid a pothole. 'It's the law now,' he replied, 'because we used to have a big problem with motorbike assassins, "*los sicarios*" we called them. If the drug lords wanted somebody bumped off they just hired hitmen to follow him on a bike and shoot him. They got away with it because nobody could identify them in their helmets and they used to drive off so fast. But now every single motorcyclist must wear an identification number so it is much safer.'

We drove on in amiable silence, scanning the road ahead not for motorbike assassins but for signs to the Chicaque Cloud Forest, an elusive wilderness I had found on the internet but which almost no one had heard of. Maria Ines had done her best to fix me up with a guide, an elderly Colombian who professed to be an expert on birds, but when we had driven round to his place early that morning as arranged, he stank of whisky and could not even identify the birds in his back garden, so I paid him off and dumped him back on his doorstep within half an hour.

The Chicaque Cloud Forest, when we found it, was

everything I had hoped for. At close to 3,000 metres above sea level the air was cool and moist and it carried with it the scent of dark and impenetrable forests. We drew up in the empty car park and headed for the solitary café, painted in the traditional creamy yellow and blue. A squat woman in a wide dress was frying up maize patties for her breakfast, while the rhythmic beat of *cumbia* music crackled from a radio on the table. Silently she served us up two tiny cups of strong espresso coffee, or *café tinto* as it is called here. Liebermann downed his in one swig, like a shot of tequila, and announced, 'Let's go.'

Somehow the two of us got me down a hundred stone steps (I counted), which led like a secret pathway into the cloud forest, where he left me alone and content.

After the rush and bustle of Bogotá this was heaven, sitting silently in my wheelchair halfway up the Andes, watching a dazzling green hummingbird hover and whir barely more than an arm's length away, then dart away amidst the lush foliage still dripping with freshly fallen raindrops. The cloud forest was exactly that: every few minutes the cloud would roll in and envelop everything, reducing visibility to a few yards, and then suddenly it would clear to reveal a plunging, jungle-covered valley that fell away on either side. From somewhere deep within the jungle a monkey cried out, to be answered by another, and when I glanced up I saw a pair of vultures gliding past on upturned wings, their scrawny heads swivelling left and right, before they vanished once more into the clouds.

Something started tickling me on the outside of my thigh and for an instant my mind raced to thoughts of a hairy, bird-eating spider crawling up my leg (thanks to my paralysis I would not have noticed until it had reached my knee). But the reality was rather more mundane – it was my mobile phone on vibrate.

'Yes, Keith, what's up?' I answered. 'You need to come back to Bogotá at once,' he said. 'There's a rumour going round that the commander of the FARC has been killed.' This was big news. Manuel Marulanda, or Tirofijo (Sureshot) as he was known, had been running Colombia's most infamous guerrilla group since the 1960s. Only two months previously the FARC had lost its second in command when Colombia staged that controversial cross-border raid into Ecuador, so now, if this was true, the rebel group could be in serious trouble. 'So is it a rumour or is it true?' I asked. 'Don't know,' said Keith, who was once the BBC's man on the spot in South America. 'It may take a few hours to check out.' I looked at my watch: less than four hours to go before I was due to fly home. I would have to pass on this one.

There was something undoubtedly prophetic about that day. When we came down from the high cloud forest and stopped in a village near El Dorado airport, the car began to shake. I looked at Liebermann in consternation, because the engine was switched off. 'Earthquake,' he explained, and we waited to see how bad it would get. Compared to the devastation wreaked that year on China's Sichuan Province this was but a tremor, just 5.8 on the Richter scale, but it was the only time I had ever experienced one and it was a weird, unsettling experience. For a few seconds I had the sensation of being in the grip of some huge, powerful force as the car rocked gently from side to side, and then it was over.

I did not know it that afternoon as I rolled through Customs and took off eastwards towards the Atlantic, but big things were afoot in Colombia. Six weeks later, Ingrid Betancourt, the French-Colombian hostage whose name had been on the lips of so many during our trip, burst once more on to the world's television screens. In a bold and brilliant ruse the Colombian military had tricked her captors into loading her and fourteen other hostages, including three Americans, on to helicopters, believing they were all going to be flown across the jungle to meet the FARC commander. Instead, as soon as they took off, the disguised soldiers overpowered the rebels and pinned them to the floor of the chopper, shouting to the hostages, 'We are the Colombian Army! You are free!'

Covering the story in London that week, I felt a surge of relief that I had made the journey to Colombia and was

back in time for this momentous news. Although I had never met Ingrid Betancourt, I felt a distinct connection with this oft-maligned South American country, which was fighting hard to shake off its reputation for drugs, kidnap and extortion. Yes, it still had a very long way to go and yes, there were still some dark and shameful practices going on in the name of national security, but thanks to this trip I felt that somehow I was a witness to its rebirth. I had seen lying on the glass-topped coffee table in the Vice President's office in Bogotá a big, glossy book on the national parks of Colombia. Waiting to interview him, I had leafed through tantalizing photos of azure lagoons, snow-covered mountain passes, verdant jungles and picturesque villages. Were they all beyond my reach, I wondered? Perhaps they did not have to be, and so I made a decision. If Colombia could make the effort to rid itself of its excessive violence then I would surely make the effort one day to come back in my wheelchair and explore this country properly. Colombia, I believed, deserved it.

26

Cambodia

Back to Packpacking

DEAFENING. THAT IS THE ONLY WAY TO DESCRIBE THE constant electric screech from the cicadas, strumming their insect bodies in manic chorus as they clung to the thorn bushes beside the road. Ahead of us, a sandbag and barbed wire barricade, flanked by blast bunkers and machine-gun posts. Fluttering in the limp breeze, a Thai flag, torn and frayed at the edges, its reds and blues leaching colour into the saturated air. Next to that, a large skull-and-crossbones notice: a minefield. Beyond that a sign announcing the 'Democratic Republic of Kampuchea'. Cambodia in 1981 was definitely not welcoming visitors.

'Should we press on?' asked George, a half-smoked roll-up clamped between his finger and thumb. We were in the final days of our two-month unplanned wander around South-east Asia in the university summer holidays. We had already had our dramas on the volcano in Sumatra and the incident with the rabid dog was still playing on our minds, but we felt we couldn't leave the region without having a stab at getting into Cambodia. We had grown up hearing of the horrors of the Khmer Rouge's takeover of the country in 1975 while we were at school and just starting to take an interest in world affairs. Over the next four years the murderous cadres led by Pol Pot, the Khmer Rouge leader who liked to be called 'Brother Number One', had emptied the cities, driving millions into the countryside, persecuted to death anyone suspected of being a 'bourgeois intellectual' and eventually caused the deaths of two million people. On a per capita basis that would be the equivalent of killing off over fifteen million people in today's Britain.

Two years before George and I pitched up in South-east Asia the Vietnamese army had invaded Cambodia from the east, putting an end to the Khmer Rouge's reign of terror, and driving their fugitive leaders into the jungle. Now we were sitting on the Thai–Cambodian border, tantalizingly close to the overgrown ruins of Angkor Wat, having chugged up by train for six hours from Bangkok.

'Probably not,' I said, in answer to George's question about pressing on; it did not look very promising up ahead. 'How about we ask the Thai border guards?'

Half an hour later, the sun now directly overhead, we walked slowly out of Ban Nong Ean, the last village on the Thai side before the road gave out into the bush. We had an escort: two Thai soldiers, teenagers no older than us, armed with M16s and what looked like more ammunition than they could carry. As long as they were happy, we reasoned, we were safe; after all, we had just seen a herd of cattle come down this road.

Boom! We froze in mid step. The explosion was quite some way away but we both knew what it was. One of the cattle must have strayed off the road and trodden on a mine. The soldiers gave a theatrical impression of a cow being blown to pieces – in fact they seemed to have it down to a suspiciously fine art. They crouched low, pretending to aim their weapons, shook their heads and pointed down the road, repeating, 'Vietnam! Vietnam!' Not a good idea to carry on, then.

If we could not get into Cambodia safely, we decided, then the next best thing would be go and meet the Cambodians. We had discovered that there were no fewer than 42,000 refugees living in a nearby camp called Khao-i-Dang. We needed official permission to visit them, so we hitched a lift with a Thai Red Cross truck and presented ourselves at the headquarters of an outfit called 'Taskforce 80'. There the official squinted at us over his thick-rimmed glasses, blew out a stream of coarse cigarette smoke and shook his head. 'You get permission Bangkok,' he said. 'No here.' 'But I'm doing a degree in Oriental Studies,' I protested. This was a slight embellishment, given that I was studying Arabic, but it did the trick. 'OK, you read rules here,' said the official, handing us a list of don'ts: no taking photos, no giving anything to the refugees and no staying beyond five p.m. We were in.

While I had been arguing our case, George had been casually reading a letter lying face-up on the official's desk. The letter gave some idea of the danger still posed by Khmer Rouge fighters in this border area. It reported that a number of captured Khmer Rouge guerrillas who had been interned in the camp prison had reported sick, been taken to the lightly guarded clinic, then escaped into the bush. The police guard in the hospital, said the letter, should be doubled immediately. Having been driven out of most of Cambodia, Pol Pot and his murderous clique of black-pyjama-wearing followers had fled westwards to the jungles of Siem Reap province, where they were attempting to establish a government in exile. Now fighters were regularly crossing over this stretch of the border into Thailand, disguised as refugees.

Khao-i-Dang refugee camp was vast, a temporary town of over forty thousand. Right on the Cambodian border, this was a huge complex of neat, clean bamboo- and thatch-huts with water distribution points, craft centres, schools and surgeries.

'Monsieur! Monsieur!' We had only been inside the camp two minutes when giggling girls ran up to sell us their now worthless Cambodian banknotes, engraved with tranquil scenes of water buffalo and rice paddies that spoke nothing of the horrors their country had just emerged from. '*S'il vous plaît*,' said a young man, introducing himself in the language of Cambodia's former colonial rulers. 'My name is Man Marann, and you must come to tea.' It seemed an absurdly polite and formal invitation, but Man Marann had a story to tell. In his early twenties and the eldest of nine, he had managed to get his family out of Khmer Rouge Cambodia, but it had taken two months to smuggle them from the capital, Phnom Penh, to the Thai border. 'We made the journey in three stages,' he told us. 'Three of us at a time rode on a motorbike, then I went back to fetch the others. Here, please have a *jang-jurong*, it's a peanut cake from our country.'

'So did you have to leave everything behind?' I asked. 'Were you bribing everyone as you went?' At nineteen years old I was already displaying worrying journalist symptoms. 'We converted our savings into gold dust,' answered Man Marann. 'We didn't have much but we sewed it into the hems of our sarongs. But on the last leg of the journey, as we were coming through the forests near the border, we got caught by the soldiers of the Khmer Serai, the "Free Khmer". They attacked us and ripped our clothes and stole all the gold dust. I was the last to arrive here. I got here a few months ago riding the last few miles on a water buffalo. We have nothing left.'

For a while we sat there in silence, which was broken only by a peal of thunder. As the rain fell in sheets we shared our lunch of 'luxury cream cookies, coffee flavour' with our Cambodian hosts. The thunder grew more insistent, until we eventually realized it wasn't thunder after all. From the jungle-clad hills a mile or so beyond the camp came bangs, explosions and bursts of machine-gun fire. Pol Pot's men skirmishing with the Thais? We had no idea. Jeep loads of Thai troops in combat gear raced up and down the waterlogged road, dodging the rice supply lorries. 'I feel like we're in the middle of a film set,' remarked George, inhaling another of his interminable roll-ups.

Another thatch hut, more Cambodian hospitality and a glimpse into the nightmare of the past few years. The men gathered round to greet us, the women sat quietly and listened as the stories spilt out through a young interpreter. 'We were all herded out to the hills and fields under armed guard,' began another young man, his eyes watching ours for reaction as his words were translated. 'We were made to work from three a.m. till eleven p.m. in those fields – a twenty-hour day! Can you imagine what that's like? Men who had been city-dwellers and who wore glasses were often made to work the hardest. Many people died from snakebite. Families who had owned a buffalo were also singled out for special treatment; often the buffalo was shot. No one was allowed to wear coloured garments. We all had to wear black pyjama trousers, black workers' shirts and Chairman Mao caps. It was also compulsory for everyone to wear Pol Pot sandals.' 'Pol Pot sandals?' 'Yes. Made from tyres. Here, we will show you one.' Somebody produced one for us to examine and it was a monstrous thing, with a great sole several centimetres thick which must have weighed over a kilo.

'And the children,' he continued. 'The children were all separated from their parents and taken away to special camps. Most never saw their parents again.' He paused and I suspected that there was something he would rather not talk about here, so I changed the subject quickly. 'What about food? How did you survive?' 'Our diet never changed,' he replied. 'Every day the same. Just a tiny amount of rice and some brackish water. We got used to seeing hundreds drop dead all around us, from exhaustion, from hunger, from disease. The Khmer Rouge piled up the corpses in mass graves.'

At this point it came as something of a relief when Man Marann tapped my elbow gently. 'Time to go. You have to leave the camp by five o'clock.' As we broke into a gentle run to beat the curfew, he told us what we had been half expecting. 'That young man you were talking to just now? He was not so lucky as me. He did not get his family out and he lost everyone except for his sister. He is very sad now.'

Pochentong airport, Phnom Penh, August 2008. The chrome-ball camera swivelled to capture my image and seconds later the squirly entry visa was stamped by an immaculately dressed 'Colonel Tho Sreng'. 'Welcome to Cambodia, Mr Gardner.'

Thanks, it had only taken me another twenty-seven years to get here.

Outside the terminal, the warm night air carried the scent of jasmine and open drains; from somewhere beyond the trees came the sound of traditional Khmer music, rhythmic and exotic. James Maughan and I mentally adjusted ourselves to our new surroundings. We were back travelling together after a gap of twelve years, an interval that had seen us both get married, then him divorced and me shot. We were travelling light: a small rucksack each, mine slung over the extendable handles at the back of my wheelchair.

As we were waiting for a taxi, a man approached us, holding out his fingerless hands, asking for money. Of course, a landmine victim, it seemed callous to refuse him. Cambodia had rather a lot of them, we were soon to learn, a legacy of the Vietnam War and the large number of unexploded mines and bomblets that had littered the fields. The taxi whisked us through darkened streets unlit by street lamps, past rickshaws and whole families riding a single motorbike, swerving expertly to avoid last-minute collisions. In a previous life, we would have pitched up at some dollar-a-night fleapit, unfurled our sleeping bags beneath a slowly rotating fan and passed a sleepless night slapping at mosquitoes. Instead, we pulled up at the almost embarrassingly grand Raffles Hotel Le Royal, a palatial relic of the French colonial era, now lovingly restored. Where war correspondents once tapped out their dispatches, now white-tunicked waiters scurried discreetly across its polished teak floors; in the Elephant Bar, still famed for its happy hour, we ordered Singapore Slings over a game of pool. This was rather stretching the definition of backpacking.

Early morning in Indo-China. In the dappled shade of a hibiscus tree, where sunbirds flitted between the crimson blooms, we chewed our croissants and spread out a map.

There is something rather exhilarating about arriving in a new city with no fixed agenda and all day to follow it. Phnom Penh, we could see, was a peaceful, low-rise city with wide, tree-lined boulevards, where people's smiles were natural and infectious; this was very different from the dash and din of Bangkok. *Lonely Planet* recommended a visit to the uninspiringly named 'Central Market' but this proved to be a treasure trove of hidden delights. Here we found the Spider Woman, a lady selling six bowls of assorted creepy-crawlies. There were giant spiders, clones of tarantulas, all glazed black and shiny, their bristly legs protruding over the sides of the bowl; there were smooth green beetles; mustard-coloured crickets; and a pile of something I am fairly certain was fried cockroaches. A man bought a bag of them, which crunched and crinkled as he packed it away. 'If this is Cambodian cuisine,' said James, 'I'm sticking to the croissants.'

But we were in for a pleasant surprise: at the Romdeng

restaurant, an enterprise staffed entirely by trainee student cooks, Jamie Oliver-style, we feasted on Khmer-beef-and-peanut curry, grilled beef brochettes marinated in lemon grass, then rice-flour-and-turmeric crêpes filled with caramelized banana topped with coconut ice cream, all for just £7 a head. We certainly needed fortifying for what lay ahead the next day.

Off a nondescript sidestreet called Monivong Boulevard stood what had once been a three-storey schoolhouse. It looked exactly like any other high school in Asia: bare concrete walls mottled with mould, flat roofs and palm trees in the courtyard. But for four years in the 1970s this became the Khmer Rouge's most secretive detention centre known as S-21, the Special Security Prison, which seventeen thousand Cambodians passed through on their way to the Killing Fields.

Rather than bulldoze it to the ground, the government has preserved it intact, rebranding it as the National Genocide Museum. While Pol Pot's fanatical cadres were busy expelling entire urban populations into the countryside, those deemed 'enemies of the revolution' were brought here for imprisonment, interrogation and execution. Much of the paraphernalia has been left intact: the shackles, the buckets, the barbed wire. In silence, James and I sat on the iron bed frames where 'VIP' inmates were held during interrogation, stung repeatedly with scorpions and centipedes or taken outside and hung upside-down in jars full of sewage until they 'confessed' to crimes they had never committed. A sign preserved from the time forbade prisoners from crying out during electrocution.

What was so shocking was the massive scale: the prisoners held here were ordinary men, women and children – normal members of society in any other country, but damned here by their brush with education and culture. Their guards were mostly young teenage boys, some as young as twelve, but fanatical in their work, having been indoctrinated and brainwashed in camps for years. In bare, whitewashed rooms I lost count of the thousands of black-and-white photographs of inmates who stared out, confused, terrified, probably at a loss as to why they were there. Amongst all the photos there were those of the young guards, their faces staring out blankly from beneath their flat, Chairman Mao caps, with hard unfeeling eyes that spoke of an alien, dehumanizing brutality. But the picture that stays in my mind is that of the Australian tourist who sailed his yacht too close to the Cambodian shore while chugging up to Thailand to buy teak for his deck. He was captured by Khmer Rouge gunboats, taken to Phnom Penh and accused of being a spy. He too was tortured and killed.

Outside in the courtyard of the old schoolhouse, where the sun beat down through a blank white haze, a pair of singing birds, bulbuls, chased each other through the hibiscus trees, a reminder that life goes on. We would have liked so very much to leave it there, but Cambodians we met urged us to finish 'the tour'. And so, ten miles out of town, we pulled up at an unremarkable area of flat, marshy countryside peopled by fishermen and farmers. This was Cheung Ek, the infamous Killing Fields, where the doomed inmates of S-21 were deposited in trucks, murdered and dumped in mass graves. The cadres used to sprinkle DDT on the corpses in case any were still alive.

This is without doubt a pretty grisly form of tourism and it was unquestionably one of the least enjoyable afternoons I have ever spent. But for Cambodians the genocide of the recent past is a key part of their history and they clearly wanted visitors to know about it. Beside a tall stupa containing countless skulls unearthed from the mass graves, we read an inscription that said it all: 'The Khmer Rouge have the human form, but their hearts are demons' hearts.'

I blew out slowly and closed my eyes as our taxi lurched over a pothole as we nosed slowly back into Phnom Penh. Mercifully what we had seen was now history, and after that a visit to Phnom Penh's Royal Palace was like a soothing lotion. We strolled amidst immaculate lawns and well-watered flowers in the heat of the afternoon, gazing at the ornate red-tiled pagodas, with the capital's traffic a world away beyond the high walls. We hired a guide who led us to the Silver Pagoda, with its huge Italian marble staircase and its five thousand silver tiles, each weighing a kilogram. Every bit as beautiful as Bangkok's Wat Phra Keo, this was one of the few bits of Cambodia's heritage spared by the murderous Khmer Rouge.

We downed ice creams then headed for the waterfront, where the mighty Mekong oozed past, bearing clumps of driftwood and lilies. Men in conical sunhats and baggy trousers rolled up to their knees balanced poles on their backs, from which hung buckets of dried squid.

That night we ate at the famous Foreign Correspondents' Club or FCC, the one-time haunt of all the press corps covering Cambodia's descent into war from 1970–75. I thought of Jon Swain, the British journalist who nearly lost his life when he declined the last helicopter out and stayed on as the Khmer Rouge swept triumphantly into the city, frantically scribbling his dispatches, a period he described so evocatively in his book *River of Time*.

A three-storey building on the waterfront, the FCC had, predictably, no lift, which posed an interesting challenge for me in a wheelchair. But a couple of dollars bought the services of two strong Cambodians who lifted me up the steep flights of stairs with great effort and good humour. Upstairs we found a breezy bar overlooking the Mekong at dusk, a place where tiny geckos skittered up the yellow walls and the ceiling fans sliced rhythmically through the cloying air. 'Cocktails, gentlemen?' The waiter's smile was as wide as the Mekong as he brought us pomegranate cocktails. We shared a table with two young British entrepreneurs who had decamped from Dubai. 'The future's here, mate,' they confided. 'Take it from us.' From somewhere behind us came the music of Duffy, the Welsh pop sensation of 2008. It was time to head up-country.

Back at Pochentong airport, my wheelchair was causing quite a few heads to shake. The plane to Siem Reap sat there out on the tarmac, ready and waiting, its turboprop propellers poised to cough into life. But how to get this Englishman up the steps to the door if he could not walk? Managers were fetched and dismissed until eventually a solution was found. A member of the ground staff gave me a piggyback up the steps, one of the dubious joys of a country that has yet to fully submit to Health & Safety regulations. We landed that evening in the middle of a thunderstorm and I was carried back down the steps in a monsoon downpour by the co-pilot, both of us in fits of laughter at the absurdity of it all.

Siem Reap is the provincial capital of the province, home to the fabulous Khmer temples of Angkor Wat, but at night, in pouring rain, it looked an unappealing place – all neon signs for pizza, foot massage and newly opened chain hotels; mass tourism had arrived. Could this really be the place my friend George and I had hankered after visiting as students in the 1980s?

But the splurge in development had not stopped Cambodia from being refreshingly good value. For £30 a head, we decided to continue the trend and book ourselves into another indulgently comfortable hotel, this time with soft lighting and minimalist decor. We were welcomed in person by the Australian manager, who insisted on escorting us up to our room. The door was thrown theatrically open to reveal the grand double bed, with both sides turned down and a spray of orchids laid out across its covers. I think it might even have had our names entwined together on some sort of embossed welcome card, but we were already well into our explanations. 'I'm sorry,' we said (why were we apologizing?), 'we are not a couple. Could we have an extra bed, please?' Beneath his deep tan, the manager blushed. 'Of course, right away,' and he clapped his hands. Someone in Reservations was going to be pulling a string of night shifts for this little misunderstanding.

To come to Siem Reap and not see Angkor Wat would be like, well, going to Arizona and not seeing the Grand

Canyon. But, curiously, we were in no great hurry to head to the temples. This was a rural province and we wanted to experience something of Cambodian village life before launching ourselves at its archaeological treasures.

'So you want to go to Tonle Sap?' said a a small, neatly dressed man outside the hotel the next morning. Darit was a driver and he had a jeep, which seemed the best way to get us and my wheelchair off the beaten track, and Tonle Sap was South-east Asia's largest lake, a great breathing waterway that shrank and expanded with the seasons, its depths rich in fish and its inhabitants living in huts built on stilts.

We pulled up at the village of Kampong Kleung in a swirl of dust, its only road a single dirt track on a raised dyke, flanked by huts balanced precariously on the lake. In some countries people might have made a fuss about getting a man in a wheelchair on to a boat, tut-tutting and shaking their heads, but I found that Cambodians, like Thais, had a commendably can-do attitude. Within minutes of arriving I was manhandled with minimal fuss off the jeep and into a low boat with a wooden roof, and we were chugging out across the glass-flat surface of Tonle Sap.

Trailing our hands in the warm green water, we passed intricate fish traps, mangroves and whole villages balanced on stilts. Boys laughed as they launched themselves off wooden platforms into the water, their legs kicking in mid-air before they hit the surface with a crash. Women smiled and waved as they chugged past in dugout canoes. It seemed a happy place. We lunched in the hut of a fisherman's family and then stayed on with them for the rest of the afternoon, one of those wonderfully unplanned and spontaneous days that make independent travelling so worthwhile. All right, so the gnarled, dessicated fried chicken was almost inedible; we only got it down by spooning on the chilli paste, and James hid most of his beneath some rice, no doubt daydreaming about those fresh croissants in Phnom Penh. But lying back in a hammock afterwards, my head level with my paralysed feet, watching the Cambodian children take turns to push each other round the hut in my wheelchair, was a return to the sort of travelling I had enjoyed for so long before my injuries. My senses were registering a whole host of things, all of which were pleasant: the wood smoke from the fire, the giggling of the children, the glancing patterns made by the sunbeams as they picked out the drifting motes of dust, the splash of a jumping fish in the lake below. For the first time since coming out of hospital, I felt like a traveller once more.

'It is best we start with the main temple.' James and I nodded solemnly, still digesting our breakfast as Darit checked the jeep's oil. Angkor Wat, we had learned, was not just Cambodia's principal attraction, it is the world's largest religious building. In fact, Angkor is only one of a complex of massive stone temples scattered around the province and dating back as far as AD 800, remnants of a once glorious empire and a city that housed a million people. Some, like the main, lakeside temple of Angkor Wat itself, are neatly preserved, fringed by cut grass or coated in wooden scaffolding. Other more remote temples are shrouded in foliage, humming with mosquitoes, all but reclaimed by the all-powerful jungle.

By mid-morning the heat was already intense. Leaving

our rented jeep in the shade, we wound our way down an avenue of trees, insects humming and an owl calling softly from deep within the tangled foliage.

Banteay Kdei
Cambodia
2008

For the next two days we roamed over Angkor's ruins, staring in awe at the magnificent stone faces of Bayon, the carved heads that guard the gateway to Angkor Thom and the exquisite stonework of Banteay Srei, so fine it is said to have been carved by women rather than men. But we were not alone. What the postcards and guidebooks rarely tell you is that over a million tourists a year are now coming to Angkor and the famous vignette of Angkor Wat temple beside the lake was awash with tourists – and this was supposed to be low season. Still, we reasoned, it had to be a marked improvement on having the Khmer Rouge run the place.

To escape the crowds, we took the jeep to Ta Phrom, the

most mysterious, enigmatic and atmospheric of all Angkor's temples. This was a ruined temple half swallowed up by jungle, where towering silk-cotton trees arched above the ruins, their sinuous roots spilling down and intertwining themselves with the ancient masonry. In the dappled light and shade butterflies flitted and lizards basked. The effect was somewhat marred by the arrival of a Korean tour group, their leader dressed like Kim Jong-il as he barked information through a megaphone to his twenty protégés. But the group moved on and peace returned, broken only by the raucous squawk of parakeets high up in the tree canopy. Angelina Jolie's producers knew they were on to a good thing when they filmed part of *Lara Croft: Tomb Raider* here. So enveloped was this temple by the lush forest that entire trees were growing on top of the ruins, so that in places giant, serpentine roots snaked down over the lichen-covered stone, as if slowly squeezing the life out of them. As the shadows lengthened over the tumble of fallen stones, the secretive archways and passages, the crumbling walls held up by jungle roots, I half closed my eyes and tried to imagine a time eight hundred years ago when there were said to be eighty thousand people tending to this temple, including hundreds of dancers. But a whine in my ear brought me back to the present: mosquitoes, in the jungle, at dusk – never a good combination.

On the way back we lurched to a halt as a low boom came from the edge of the jungle. James and I looked at each other, both thinking the same thing: was that a landmine going off? But it was a saffron-robed monk, banging a cowhide drum in a nearby monastery, the Buddhist equivalent of a muezzin's call to prayer. It was a moment of perfect peace, watching the monks file in, light joss sticks, then press their palms together and bow their heads as they chanted. The heat of the day had subsided and behind the monastery, lit up by the slanting rays of the dying sun, lay another exquisite temple, nine centuries of crumbling history.

It was time to head back to the hotel and tonight's tasting menu, eaten stretched out on hanging couches suspended from the ceiling. Across the courtyard the moon rose, and a chorus of frogs rang out. From somewhere came the sound of Khmer music once more, and for a moment I could have sworn I could smell jasmine. Cambodia, we admitted, had entranced us, and I was finally back on the road.

Afterword

TRAVELLING AGAIN AFTER VERY SERIOUS INJURIES IS MOST definitely therapeutic. True, I still have to call up the airline in advance and explain that I cannot walk from the door of the plane to the seat, I still have to starve myself before short-haul European flights because there is no means of conveying me from my seat to the onboard toilet, and I still have to buy a business-class ticket for long-haul journeys to avoid getting pressure sores on my bum. But mentally, I have crossed a barrier: I no longer think, 'That trip is too far or too hard,' I just find myself working out the practicalities of getting over the various obstacles. It is almost as if there is a sliding scale whereby the less accessible a country is for someone in a wheelchair, the more people there are on hand to help. In Cambodia, the only way for me to get on and off the little turboprop plane to Siem Reap had been courtesy of a piggyback from two of the aircrew.

Not for one minute would I pretend that travelling is better now in a wheelchair than it was before. Quite the opposite, it is endlessly frustrating. To be unable to descend with my family into the spectacular rocky gorges of Bryce Canyon in Utah on holiday, for example, was almost unbearable for someone who would otherwise have been leading the charge. But I have found there is usually a more ready acceptance by the people whose country you are passing through, as if I could not possibly present a threat or an intrusion. And this imposed immobility has had another spin-off: years after abandoning it, I have resumed sketching, since I am now assured of a chair and a stable lap wherever I go.

But for more than four years after the injuries that put me in that wheelchair I had a nagging curiosity about one thing: I wanted to meet the man who saved my life that night in Riyadh. Dr Peter Bautz is a South African trauma surgeon, a gunshot-wound specialist whose team in Cape Town was treating an average of 114 victims a month. It was my incredible good luck that he happened to be working in a Riyadh hospital when I was shot; in fact he was in the final months of his five-year contract and was making preparations to leave. In the seventeen days when I was in his care at the King Faisal Hospital before I was airlifted back to Britain I never met him consciously; heavily sedated, I was only occasionally aware of someone in the room with a deep, Germanic-sounding voice. But Bautz and I had since exchanged text messages, with one of his earlier ones completely confusing me. 'You had an acute case of lead poisoning,' it read; only later did I learn this was medical black humour for being shot multiple times. He and his family had emigrated to Australia and while we often talked of going to see him it never quite happened. Then in December 2008, Bautz announced that he was coming to London for a conference and we arranged to meet in a hotel in Kensington.

'Frank?' said a deep voice from behind and above me, as I wheeled up to reception. It was more of a statement than a question. This was, after all, the man who had cut me open to save me and had stayed up through the night as I hovered on the cusp of life and death – he knew exactly what I looked like, inside and out. But now I saw him for the first time: tall, powerfully built, in his early fifties, with curly hair, a faint smile playing about his lips and a surgeon's air of precision about him.

We sat down at a café table and ordered cappuccinos as Bautz powered up his laptop. 'I hope you're ready to see these,' he said. 'I've brought the pictures I kept from Riyadh.' When the waitress brought our coffees she nearly dropped them on the floor and Bautz had to close the laptop quickly. The image on the screen must have looked like the final scene from a snuff movie: it was a close-up of my blood-soaked backside where a bullet had gone in, exited lower down, then gone into my thigh and come out again, four wounds from one shot. Once she had gone, Bautz continued his slideshow from hell, warming to his subject. 'Now this one's a beauty,' he said, pointing to a neat entry wound, 'but the exit wound on the other side is a shocker.' I stared at the screen, surprisingly unsqueamish for once, looking at this mangled body on the operating table and feeling strangely detached. It felt almost as if this had happened to another person, not me.

'Protoplasm,' said Bautz. 'Sorry?' 'Protoplasm. You survived because you had good protoplasm. It's the condition the body is in at the time of trauma. If you had been older, heavier and a smoker your body would not have been able to fight so hard for survival, and yours was really fighting.' I found myself silently thanking Marine Sergeant Terry Paliser for beasting me up all those Austrian mountains as a teenager. 'So why don't I remember anything about the hospital in Riyadh?' I asked. 'I can't have been in surgery the whole time, can I?' 'No, you weren't, but we gave you a drug called Medazalan intravenously. It's a memory obliterator.'

Outside the window a woman was arguing with her dog, wagging her finger and shaking her head as it ran circles round her in the park. Kensington Gardens was cosily familiar to me: my father had taken me sledging there as a child, and then in the 1990s Amanda and I used to rollerblade through it at weekends, mercifully unaware that I would one day be looking out on it from a wheelchair. But there was one final footnote to come on this whole surgical survival saga. Bautz was giving a lecture the next day on damage control in trauma surgery at the Royal London Hospital in Whitechapel. He would show his pictures, then I would appear as the 'one he prepared earlier'.

So, on a cold clear December day I drove myself to the hospital I had last left strapped to a bed in an ambulance, to be met by the smiling face of Frank Cross, the consultant surgeon who did such a brilliant job of managing my recovery there in the months after I was airlifted back from Riyadh. Inside the lecture theatre Bautz calmly discussed such grisly topics as Abdominal Compartmental Syndrome, where the intestines become so swollen during surgery that the abdomen cannot be closed up for days – a condition which, needless to say, I had. Wearing my callipers beneath my trousers, I duly stood up, gave the medics the patient's perspective on being shot and lifted my shirt up to show how the scars had healed, while Bautz and Cross smiled and nodded like a pair of genial godparents. Then, at my request, we went up to the helipad on the roof. This was hugely symbolic for me, because it was where I had been brought in four years earlier by the Helicopter Emergency Medical Services, choppered in from Luton airport in a little red helicopter after a flight from Riyadh in a Saudi air ambulance. I looked across at the London landmarks on the skyline and down at the teeming streets of Whitechapel far below, and I know it's a cliché but it felt good to be alive. When I was brought here that summer afternoon in 2004, morphined up and exhausted, incapable of surviving on normal food, I was a patient to be processed – I even had a codename, Dan Kilo. But now I was a visitor, peering in through the window at an unhappy juncture of my past life and feeling glad to have put it behind me, despite the continuing paralysis in my legs. It was a good moment.

So the horizons that once receded only to the lime-green walls of my hospital ward beneath that helipad are now rolling back once more. I still harbour ambitions to take our daughters to see orang-utans in the wild before either they all disappear or the girls grow up and become more interested in another kind of hairy primate. West and East Africa are high on my wish list for future destinations and as I write, we are saving to go on safari in Namibia. I am all too aware that there remain very real limitations imposed by my injuries, physical limitations that no amount of optimism and can-do attitude will ever get over. I have given this some thought, but just as when my ribs were broken in the karate gym all those years ago, just as when I sustained those terrible gunshot wounds in Riyadh, I have taken a deep breath and moved on. It is the only thing to do.

Picture Credits

p. 12: Portrait of the author, aged forty-four, by Grace Gardner, 2006.

Text illustrations by the author. All photos by the author unless listed below:

Photo inset one
On the Arctic Circle, near Rovaniemi, Finland, 1980: anon.
Sketching in my journal, Samosir Island, Lake Toba, Sumatra, 1981: Heimo Aga.
Posing at the rim of Gunung Merape volcano, Sumatra, 1981: George Seel.
Petra, 1989, on the 'Boys' tour' of Jordan: anon.
With James Maughan in Quito, 1990: anon.
Xavier, our Quechua Indian boatman, 1990: James Maughan.
In South America, a continent that enthralled me since childhood: anon.
White-water rafting on the Zambezi River, Zimbabwe, 1994: Saf Par.

Photo inset two
Resuming scuba-diving two years after getting shot, Red Sea, Egypt, 2006: Katie Pearson.
'Legless diving' off south Sinai, Egypt, 2006: John McIntyre.
Comparing mobile phones with a Bedu girl in the Sinai, 2006: Katie Pearson.

Acknowledgements

To the team at my publishers, Transworld, including my ever-patient editor Simon Taylor, for backing this book, and Kate Samano, for keeping a cool head, and to my well-connected agent, Julian Alexander of LAW Associates, for recognizing my renewed love of travel after all my injuries even before I did.

To Michael Palin, the traveller's traveller, for so generously sparing his time to write so eloquent a Foreword.

To the BBC's former South America stringer-turned-ace-cameraman, Keith Morris, for his corrections to my dodgy spelling of Colombian names, and to Katy Brown for her corrections to my even more suspect spelling of Hungarian.

To George Seel, Tim Yates, Carrie Hill, Peregrine Muncaster, John Donald, Guy Bonser, James Maughan, Amanda, Eduardo Zandri, Natalie Morton, John

Macintyre, Katie Pearson, Will Griffiths, Sean of BackUp Trust, Stuart Hughes, Dominic Hurst, Alex Gardiner and everyone else who's ever had to put up with me on the road: thanks.

Blood and Sand

Frank Gardner

On 6 June 2004, in a quiet suburb of Riyadh, BBC security correspondent Frank Gardner and cameraman Simon Cumbers were ambushed by Islamist gunmen. Simon was killed outright. Frank was hit in the shoulder and leg. As he lay in the dust, pleading for his life, a figure stood over him and pumped four more bullets into his body at point-blank range . . .

Against all the odds, Frank Gardner survived, and this is his remarkable account of the agonizing journey he's taken – from being shot and left for dead to where he is today, partly paralysed but alive.

It is a journey that began twenty-five years earlier, when a chance meeting with explorer Wilfred Thesiger inspired in the young Frank what would become a lifelong passion for the Arab world – an abiding interest that would take him throughout the Middle East and lead to his becoming a BBC journalist. And this same passion would, in the wake of 9/11, send Frank on another journey that came to dominate – and nearly end – his life: his coverage of Al-Qaeda.

Honest, moving and inspiring, *Blood and Sand* reveals a deep understanding of the Islamic world and offers an insider's compelling analysis of the ongoing 'War on Terror' and what it means in these uncertain times.

'Gardner tells his remarkable tale well and bravely, with an astonishing lack of anger and enduring love and respect for the Islamic world'
Sunday Times

'What makes Gardner's moving, often humorous, deeply personal story so important is the fact that he has woven into it a brilliantly dispassionate, clear-eyed account of the Islamic world'
Scotsman

9780553817713